THE GOSPEL: THE BIBLICAL MEANS TO IDENTIFY FALSE TEACHERS AND FALSE GOSPELS

Curtis Braun

New Harbor Press
Rapid City, SD

New Harbor Press
1601 Mt Rushmore Rd, Ste 3288
Rapid City, SD 57701
www.newharborpress.com

Ordering Information:
Quantity sales. Special discounts are available on quantity purchases by corporations, associations, and others. For details, contact the "Special Sales Department" at the address above.

The Gospel/Curtis Braun —1st ed.

ISBN 978-1-63357-262-1

First edition: 10 9 8 7 6 5 4 3 2 1

Contents

Preface

This book was written for these purposes:

1. To help define the gospel
2. To help define the essential components of the gospel
3. To help define a false teacher
4. To help define how to deal with a false teacher

There is a great need for gospel clarity as well as discernment to be able to deal with false teachers who carry the banner of Christianity. As you'll see, without gospel clarity, addressing false teachers would be an impossible task. Therefore, this book was written and organized with a very specific structure. This book will follow the sequential steps listed above to provide gospel clarity, which gives way to identifying false teachers who corrupt the gospel, leading to a false gospel.

Of significant importance, this book would not have been written if God had not saved me. I had church membership but no heavenly membership. I was alive to sin, but dead to God. I was baptized in a visible church, but did not belong to the invisible church. I had gone through confirmation, but there was no regeneration. In my life there was much perversion against Christ, but there was no conversion to Christ. Adultery, pornography, manipulation, lying, stealing, and cheating marked my life rather than holiness, godliness, love, goodness, and mercy. I give all thanks to God who saves the worst of sinners, of whom I could be considered foremost.

Please do not marvel at this book, but marvel at the one who saves sinners. Marvel at His gospel. Marvel over the reconciling, propitiating, expiating, redeeming, regenerating, justifying, and glorifying work of God. Marvel at how much He loves the church by protecting them against falsehood and false gospels. Marvel at how His Word is completely sufficient to show mankind how to be reconciled to God, sanctified in our walk with Him, protected against false gospels, and one day be glorified to be with Him forever. After being saved in my thirties, I still stand in awe of Jesus every day. There are two song lyrics I love to listen to which capture my awe of Jesus Christ.

Amazing Love How Can It Be
Amazing love how can it be?
That you my King would die for me
Amazing love, I know it's true
It's my joy to honor you
In all I do
I honor you

How Can I Keep from Singing
How can I keep from singing Your praise
How can I ever say enough
How amazing is Your love
How can I keep from shouting Your name
I know I am loved by the King
And it makes my heart want to sing

Acknowledgments

Jesus Christ—To the King, eternal, immortal, invisible, who caused me to be born again and who is able to keep me from stumbling and present me blameless before His presence. To Him be all glory, majesty, dominion, and authority, before all time and now and forever.

Laura—For being a faithful wife when I was an adulterous and porn-addicted husband. For having a beauty that comes from your inner life, the unfading beauty of a gentle and quiet spirit, which is of great worth in God's sight. Stand firm in the faith and be steadfast, immovable, always abounding in the work of the Lord. No one after lighting a lamp covers it with a jar or puts it under a bed, but puts it on a stand, so that those who enter may see the light.

Pax and Keryx—Be watchful, stand firm in the faith, act like men, be strong. Contend for the faith. Fight the good fight of faith. Defend the gospel. Love the Lord your God with all your heart, with all your mind, with all your soul, and with all your strength.

Pastor Randy—For faithfully shepherding the flock of God that is among you, exercising oversight, not under compulsion, but willing, as God would have you, not for shameful gain, but eagerly; not domineering over those in your charge, but being an example to the flock. For rightly handling the word of truth and being considered worthy of double honor. Our family loves you very much.

Pastor John Macarthur and Pastor Steve Lawson—For your teaching and preaching ministries which have helped build our family in the faith. Thank you for being faithful men of God.

Paul Patterson – To my friend and brother in Christ. Thank you for encouraging me to persevere and to publish this book. Thank you for your faithful companionship. For God is not unjust so as to overlook your work and the love that you have shown for His name in serving the saints, as you still do.

"Here is a wise word of warning for our wayward times. Curtis seeks to enable his readers to hear the warnings of Jesus and His Apostles as to the threat of false teachings. It is a timely and insightful word."

— Randal S. Anderson
Pastor of First Evangelical Free Church in Sioux Falls

Chapter 1: The Gospel

Romans 1:1 –Paul, a bond-servant of Christ Jesus, called as an apostle, set apart for the gospel of God.

There really is no way to deal with false teachers and false teaching outside of knowing the truth of the gospel. It is only when one can grasp and understand the gospel can one identify false teaching and false teachers. If you are wrong about the gospel, you will be wrong on many other biblical doctrines. If you are wrong about the gospel, you will be wrong on interpreting Scripture. If you are wrong about the gospel, you will be wrong about salvation. If you are wrong about the gospel, there is a good chance you'll be wrong about the objective facts of the person and work of Jesus. If you are wrong about the gospel, there is a good chance you will be wrong about the subjective response of repentance and faith to the objective facts of the person and work of Jesus. Therefore, if we are not able to properly define the gospel, we have already embarked on a meaningless task to identify false teaching and false teachers. There is no point in discussing the topic of false teachers unless the truth of the gospel is understood and defined. Another reason why we'll devote an entire chapter to understanding the gospel is because the Bible consistently characterizes false teachers as those who teach a false gospel. False teachers and false gospels are inextricably linked together. Of course, it is possible for one to teach the true gospel and have no fruit of a regenerated life, but the Bible consistently depicts false teachers as those who teach and preach a false gospel and lead people away from the truth of salvation.

Another reason why we'll spend an entire chapter understanding the gospel is because of a lack of gospel clarity in the evangelical community. If you were to ask many professing Christians what the gospel is, you would most likely get different answers from just about everyone you asked. For example, if you were to ask the question "What is the gospel?," you may get such replies as, "The gospel will help you live a Christian life," "The gospel is the Bible," "The gospel is the first four books of the New Testament," "The gospel is Jesus Christ," "The gospel is all about the love of Jesus," "The gospel is how to have your sins forgiven," "The gospel is Christianity," "The gospel is the good news," "The gospel is how to go to heaven," and so on. The purpose of the first chapter is to bring together a thorough explanation, understanding, and definition of the gospel which will help us set the course for the rest of the book. We will go through Romans 1:1–6 (1) to help us develop an understanding of the gospel.

Romans 1:1—Paul, a bond-servant of Christ Jesus, called as an apostle, set apart for the gospel of God

Paul, the *Doulos*, of Christ Jesus

As we work our way through Romans 1:1-6, perhaps the first thing that we should recognize is who is writing the book of Romans: Paul. Before Paul's conversion to Christ, he was a Pharisee. *Pharisees* were the religious teachers and leaders of Judaism. They were known to be the conservative religious leaders of their time and meticulous in preserving both the Old Testament Scripture as well as oral tradition. Paul talks about his zeal for Judaism in Philippians 3:5–6, where he describes taking pride in his circumcision (Philippians 3:5), being of the esteemed tribe of Benjamin (Philippians 3:5), being knowledgeable in the law

(Philippians 3:5), being zealous for Judaism (Philippians 3:6), and being externally blameless (Philippians 3:6).

Not only was Paul a Pharisee, but we find out in Acts 22 that Paul was educated by a Pharisee named Gamaliel (Acts 22:3). When the apostles were brought before the Sanhedrin for publicly teaching, we are shown that Gamaliel was a teacher of the law and honored by all people. Gamaliel was so respected he was able to reverse the intentions of the Sanhedrin when the apostles were brought before it (Acts 4:34–40). In Rabbinic literature, it describes Gamaliel as being given the honorary title "the Elder" like his grandfather before him (Mishnah Sotah 9:15) and was the first of only seven men in all history to have bestowed upon him the title *Rabban*, "our master," as opposed to the more common *Rabbi*, "my master" (2). Additionally, as a Pharisee, Paul believed that one became ceremonially unclean by not washing one's hands before eating (Matthew 15:1-9). Paul was well educated in all the ceremonial washings such as washing of clothes (Numbers 31:24), bathing (Leviticus 14:8-9), sprinkling with the water of purification (Numbers 19:17-19), and washing hands and feet (Exodus 30:17-21) which never justified man before God (Hebrews 9:9). Paul was aware of the burnt offering (Leviticus 1), the grain offering (Leviticus 2), the fellowship offering (Leviticus 3), the sin offering (Leviticus 4), and the guilt offering (Leviticus 5) which never justified man before God or gave him right standing before God (Hebrews 9:9). Paul knew that circumcision never gave man right standing before God (Romans 4:9-12). This was Paul, a zealous Pharisee who studied under the most honored Rabbi, and who was known for persecuting the church and trying to destroy it (Galatians 1:13). Paul was a blasphemer, a persecutor, and a violent man (1 Timothy 1:13). In all of Scripture, we have the account of only two conversions of Pharisees, which include Paul (Acts 9:1–19, 22:3–21, 26:2–23; Philippians 3:3–9) and Nicodemus (John 19:38–42). In the New Testament, there was far more denunciation of Pharisees than accounts of Pharisees being converted to Christ. In fact, Jesus had told the Pharisees during the last week of His earthly life and ministry in Matthew 21:31, "Truly I tell you, the tax collectors and the prostitutes go into the kingdom of God before you." This was Paul's preconversion life as a Pharisee.

Let's also note the title that Paul gives himself which comes to us in English as a bond servant or, rather, a slave. The word *bond servant* is translated from the word *doulos*. *Doulos* refers to someone who belongs to another without any ownership rights of their own. Paul saw himself as a slave of the Lord Jesus Christ. Paul saw himself as one who had been redeemed, ransomed, rescued, and was now under new ownership and was now a slave to Christ and a slave to righteousness (Romans 6:15–23).

Slavery was common in the ancient world, was common in the history of Israel, and was common in the ancient Middle East. Although it has extremely negative connotations today, this was not always so. In fact, there were some conditions of slavery that were so wonderful and fulfilling that the slave would choose never to be turned loose. In Exodus 21:5–6, it describes the wonderful relationship between slave and slave owner where it says, "But if the servant declares, 'I love my master and my wife and children and do not want to go free,' then his master must take him before the judges. He shall take him to the door or the doorpost and pierce his ear with an awl. Then he will be his servant for life." Although being a slave did not always yield this type of affection between the slave and slave owner, there were such relationships that occurred between the slave and slave owner that were prosperous and beneficial to both sides. Paul sees himself as this kind of *doulos*. He saw himself as a slave who claimed no rights, but only sought to do the will of his Master. In Philippians 1:21, Paul gave his perspective on who ran his life where he says, "For to me, to live is Christ, and to die is gain."

Not only did Paul consider himself a *doulos*, but in 1 Corinthians 4:1, he gives his thoughts on being a lowly servant of Christ where he says, "This is the way any person is to regard us: as servants of Christ and stewards of the mysteries of God." The word *servant* is from *hupéretés. Hupéretés* is a compound word that consists of *hypo,* which means "under," and *ēressō,* which means "to row." *Hupéretés* was used to describe an under rower who mans the oars on a lower deck. *Triremes* were ancient war galley ships with three levels of oars. The bottom group of rowers that manned the oars was known as *hupéretés,* or those who were subordinate, with low, menial tasks. In other words, Paul just considered himself as the lowest member in the lowest row of the boat who would never be seen but would just faithfully row his oar. In Acts 26:16, while Paul is giving his appeal to King Agrippa, he tells King Agrippa what the Lord had told him which was, "But get up and stand on your feet; for this purpose I have appeared to you, to appoint you as a servant and a witness not only to the things in which you have seen Me, but also to the things in which I will appear to you." When the Lord is calling Paul a "servant," the word that the Lord chooses to call Paul is a *hupéretén,* an under rower who serves his master. Another title that Paul used to describe himself in 1 Corinthians 4:1 is *steward,* which is *oikonomos. Oíkos* is a "house or household" and *nemo* is "to allot, apportion." Essentially, this word is used to describe a household manager. Paul essentially saw himself as an owner of nothing and a steward of everything. Paul would have certainly thought of himself in this manner, "Just consider me a slave of Christ. Just consider me a man who has no rights. Just consider me a man who was ransomed by Christ. Just consider me an under rower. Just consider me the lowest rower on a galley ship. Just consider me one who will faithfully row his oar as commanded by his master. Just consider me as one who has been entrusted to properly handle the great and glorious gospel which I received from Christ Jesus my Lord." Paul is a messenger of the gospel and not the author of it. He simply saw himself as the lowly messenger of the gospel.

Paul, the Apostle of Christ Jesus

Not only was Paul a slave of Christ, he was also an apostle of Christ. Although Christ is considered "the Apostle" in Hebrews 3:1, the term *apostle* was a commissioned messenger sent on an envoy and this term was used to describe Jesus' disciples. However, to be more specific in terms of what an apostle was, there have been more clearly defined attributes describing what qualified one for the title of an apostle, which includes the following:

- Considered someone who had seen the Lord and was able to testify of Him and His resurrection from personal knowledge (John 15:27, 1 Corinthians 9:1, Acts 1:21, 22:14– 15)
- One who had been called to this office by Christ (Luke 6:13, Galatians 1:1)
- One who was infallibly inspired and, thus, secured against all error and mistake in their public teaching, whether by word or by writing (John 14:26, 16:13)
- One who had the power of working miracles (Acts 2:43)

Paul had seen the resurrected Christ (Acts 9:1–19), he had been commissioned as an apostle by the Lord (Galatians 1:1), Peter acknowledged Paul's letters as wisdom that was given to him by God and considered them as Scripture (2 Peter 3:15–16), and he was given power to perform miracles (Acts 19:11–12). Paul had great humility. In fact, one could say his growth was one of downward trajectory where he would continue to grow in humility with a lower view of himself and a growing and exalted view of Christ. As an apostle of Christ, Paul would make stunning statements about himself that would almost seem to be self-deprecating. While Paul was not one to practice false humility, he certainly thought less of himself the more he knew of Christ. Around AD 55, he would claim to be "the least of the apostles, and not fit to be called an apostle, because I persecuted the church" (1 Corinthians 15:9). Around AD 60–62, he would claim to be "the very least of all saints" (Ephesians 3:8). And, around AD 62–64, he would also claim to be the chief of sinners where he said, "It is a trustworthy statement, deserving full acceptance, that Christ Jesus came into the world to save sinners, among whom I am foremost" (1 Timothy 1:15). This is all to say that Paul never got over what Christ had done for him. Paul loved the Lord Jesus Christ and considered himself a loving and willful slave to Christ who only wanted to do the will of his Master. Paul loved the Lord Jesus Christ and the gospel.

The Gospel, Owned and Authored by God

As we transition to the last half of the verse of Romans 1:1, where Paul says, "Set apart for the gospel of God," we need to pay careful attention to what this means. In Galatians 1:15, Paul says that, "He who had set me apart even from my mother's womb and called me through His grace was pleased to reveal His Son in me so that I might preach Him among the Gentiles, I did not immediately consult with flesh and blood." Here, Paul is confirming the foreordained plan of God for his life in that God had a plan to use Paul to spread the gospel. Paul didn't set himself apart to preach the gospel from his mother's womb. No, it was the foreordained and pre-determined purpose and plan of God to convert Paul from a zealous Pharisee to a slave of Christ who would preach the gospel of God. In Galatians 1:11-12, Paul says this important statement regarding the gospel he received, "For I would have you know, brothers and sisters, that the gospel which was preached by me is not of human invention. For I neither received it from man, nor was I taught it, but I received it through a revelation of Jesus Christ." What a statement by Paul! Paul is confirming the origin of the gospel. First, let's notice that God is the owner and the author of the gospel. This gospel was planned, authored, fulfilled, and executed by God. Man will get no credit for this gospel. Man will have no room for boasting with this gospel (Romans 3:27). God will receive all the glory for this gospel as Paul says in Romans 11:36, "For from Him, and through Him, and to Him are all things. To Him be the glory forever and ever. Amen." The exclusive authorship and ownership of the gospel belongs to God. Therefore, any trifling with God's gospel is a serious matter. Second, let's note the definite article of *the* gospel of God. There is but one gospel. There are not many gospels. There are not many ways to God. There is one way to God. Jesus said in John 14:6, "I am the way and the truth and the life. No one comes to the Father except through Me." There is the Author. There is the Way. There is the Truth. There is the Life. There is salvation in the Name (Acts 4:12). There is the Mediator (1 Timothy 2:5). There is the gospel for the glory of God. **Thus, an essential component of the gospel is that God is the author and owner of the gospel.**

So, what is the gospel? The word *gospel* is a compound word in the original language which is *euaggelion*. The word *eú*, means "good, well." We see this word *eú* being used at funerals where there is often a eulogy or "good word" that is spoken. The word *angellō* means to "announce, herald." Therefore, it comes to us in English as good news or glad tidings. E*uaggelion* is used seventy-six times and *euaggelizó* is used sixty-two times in the New Testament. The gospel is God's good news of salvation to men. However, before we go too far, it is essential that we know the bad news. The good news is not good news until we know the bad news. Just as we would put a diamond against a black backdrop to see the color, cut, clarity, and carat, so we must compare the good news against the bad news. For when we thoroughly explore the bad news, the good news shines vibrantly and in all its glory against the black backdrop of the bad news. For the purposes of this chapter, we will wait to give a definition of the *gospel* until we've worked through understanding Romans 1:1–6. This is not meant to cause confusion, but, rather, to fully understand what Paul is saying in these first six verses with regard to the gospel.

The Bad News—Sin and Death

If we are to understand God's good news, then we must understand God's bad news. The bad news is not that we have credit card debt, a house payment, loss of a job, no food to eat, politics, wars in the world, the education system, illness, injury, bad in-laws, a car that won't run, low self-esteem, no friends, no spouse, no children, social inequality, income inequality, or any of the like. The bad news is that man has sinned against God and God must deal with man's sin.

Therefore, we need to understand *sin* and define it. *Hamartía,* also known as "sin," carries the meaning of "missing the mark" or "loss (forfeiture) because of not hitting the target." 1 John 3:4 helps define sin which says, "Everyone who makes a practice of sinning also practices lawlessness; sin is lawlessness." *Anomia* comes to the English as "lawlessness," with *A* meaning "not" and *nomos* meaning "law." Thus, we can understand that *sin* is lawlessness or disobedience against God's law. John can help us even further define *sin* where he says in 1 John 5:17, "All unrighteousness is sin." Unrighteousness comes to us from *adikia,* with *A* meaning "not" and *díkē* meaning "justice" or, properly, "God's standards (justice)." Thus, we can understand *sin* being anything that does not conform to God's standard of righteousness and justice. In Romans 14:23, Paul gives us another definition of *sin* where he says, "For whatever does not proceed from faith is sin." Here we can see that whatever is done absent of faith is also sin. James gives us yet another definition of *sin* and says in James 4:17, "So whoever knows the right thing to do and fails to do it, for him it is sin." Here we can see that sin is not only what we do, but also what we don't do. Thus, a good definition of sin would be as follows: ***sin* is breaking God's law by either not doing what God's law demands or doing what God's law prohibits by**

any thought (Matthew 5:28), word (Matthew 5:22), deed (Matthew 5:39), or intent (Matthew 6:1). Developing a definition of *sin* is one thing, but we also need to understand God's disposition or attitude toward sin.

It's important to define sin and it is equally important to understand God's disposition toward sin through Scripture. If it were not for Scripture, we would have no idea what God's attitude toward sin would be. We will take a very small sampling of Scripture to help us grasp God's attitude and disposition toward sin. In Psalm 5:5, it says, "The boastful shall not stand before your eyes; you **hate** all evildoers." In Psalm 5:6, it says, "You destroy those who speak lies; the LORD **abhors** the bloodthirsty and deceitful man." Psalm 7:11 says, "God is a just judge, and God is **angry** with the wicked every day." In Psalm 7:12–13, it says, "If a man does not repent, God will whet his sword; he has bent and readied his bow; he has prepared for him his deadly weapons, making his arrows fiery shafts." In Psalm 11:5, it says, "The LORD tests the righteous, but his soul **hates** the wicked and the one who loves violence." In Isaiah 64:6, it says, "We have all become like one who is unclean, and all our righteous deeds are like a polluted garment." A polluted garment is in reference to a woman's menstrual cloth. In James 4:17, it says, "You adulterous people! Do you not know that friendship with the world is **enmity** with God? Therefore, whoever wishes to be a friend of the world makes himself an enemy of God." *Enmity* is translated from the word *echthra,* which can also mean "hostility, alienation" or, properly, "an enemy with irreconcilable hostility." In Psalm 21:9, it says, "You will make them as a blazing oven when you appear. The LORD will swallow them up in his **wrath**, and fire will consume them." In Proverbs 22:12, it says, "Lying lips are an **abomination** to the LORD, but those who act faithfully are his delight." In Psalm 7:9, David says, "Oh, let the **evil** of the wicked come to an end, and may you establish the righteous—you who test the minds and hearts, O Righteous God!" It doesn't take much reading through Scripture to understand God's disposition toward sin. God is not partial to sin. God is not indifferent to sin. God doesn't think sin is a trivial matter. No, the God of the Bible has made it abundantly clear how He feels about sin.

God hates sin. God hates wickedness. God is angry with the wicked every day. God abhors sin and wickedness. God sees sin as filthy and defiling like a woman's menstrual cloth. God sees sin as open hostility and warfare toward Him. God is pictured as aiming deadly weapons at the wicked, ready to destroy them. God's fierce anger toward sin and the wicked is one of swallowing them up in the fire of His wrath. God considers sin an abomination. God considers sin evil. God considers sin wicked. God simply hates sin with all His being. This is God's immutable disposition and attitude toward sin.

We've developed a definition of *sin* as well as gained an understanding of God's disposition toward sin. Now we must also understand the devastation and death that sin brings. Thus, we must understand how God has punished sin. The first sin man committed was disobeying God and eating from the tree of the knowledge of good and evil which occurred in the Garden of Eden (Genesis 3). Man was promised that the day he ate of the fruit, he would surely die (Genesis 2:17). The repercussions of one sin were astronomical, which included woman being cursed (Genesis 3:16), man being cursed (Genesis 3:17–19), the earth being cursed (Genesis 3:17), death came into the world (Romans 5:12, 1 Corinthians 15:22), sin was imputed to all mankind (Romans 5:12), man's relationship with God was broken and man died spiritually (Genesis 3:22–24), and man earned the wages of both physical and spiritual death (Romans 6:23). We can see the seriousness of sin by how God dealt with the first sin. Sin is serious. There is nothing that sin doesn't corrupt. God has given man food and man has turned it into gluttony. God has given man sex and man has turned it into pornography, homosexuality, and every type of sexual immorality. God has given man money and man has turned it into gambling. God has given man true religion and man has turned it to false religion. God has given man humor and man has turned it into crudeness. Sin hates God and who He is (Romans 1:18–32). Man's sinfulness and enmity towards God is most fully demonstrated by man's desire to kill God which was accomplished and put on display when man demanded that Jesus be crucified and put to death (Matthew 27:22-26, Luke 23:21).

Another facet of sin that must be understood is man's depravity because of or man's total corruption to know or obey God due to his sin. In Jeremiah 13:23, it says, "Can the Ethiopian change his skin or the leopard his spots? Neither can you do good who are accustomed to doing evil." Psalm 7:14 says, "Behold, the wicked man conceives evil and is pregnant with mischief and gives birth to lies." Ecclesiastes 7:20 says of man's sin, "Surely there is not a righteous man on earth who does good and never sins." Simply put, man can do nothing within himself to change his sin problem as sin has corrupted his whole being, which includes body, soul, and spirit. The only thing that man does is continually give birth to sin and wickedness. As Jesus said in John 3:6, "That which is born of the flesh is flesh, and that which is born of the Spirit is spirit." Man's depravity of flesh and sin only produces more flesh and sin and cannot produce righteousness or spiritual life.

The depravity of man's sin gives way to understanding the depth of man's sin. Therefore, we must also understand the depth of sin. In Psalm 51:5, David says this of his corrupted nature due to sin, "Behold, I was brought forth in iniquity, and in sin did my mother conceive me." In Psalm 51:5, David says, "In sin did my mother conceive me." Additionally, in Genesis 6:5, it says this regarding man's proclivity and ability to sin and man's inability to do good, "The LORD saw that the wickedness of man was great in the earth, and that every intention of the thoughts of his heart was only evil continually." Given these two verses, we learn of the depth of sin in that, once we are conceived, we are passed on a sin nature and from the time of conception, we only commit sin and evil. Therefore, the depth of sin corrupts man upon conception and perpetually keeps him in this state of open rebellion and sinfulness against God.

Now that we have a definition of *sin*, understand God's disposition toward sin, understand the death and destruction of sin, understand man's depravity because of sin, and realize the depth of sin, we must now understand how God deals with sin. God must deal with sin according to who He is which is in accordance with His attributes.

The first attribute of God that we'll discuss is that He is an infinite or eternal being (1 Timothy 1:17). Therefore, we must consider that a finite creature has sinned against an infinite God. First, let's look at an example of punishment when a man sins by murdering another man. In Genesis 9:6, God tells Noah, "Whoever sheds the blood of man, by man shall his blood be shed, for God made man in his own image." In Leviticus 24:17, God says, "Whoever takes a human life shall surely be put to death." In Exodus 21:12, God says, "Whoever strikes a man so that he dies shall be put to death." In the case of a mortal man taking the life of another mortal man, the penalty is death to the man who took away the life of another man.

Let's look at another example of punishment when a man sins against another man by stealing. In Exodus 21:1, God says, "If a man steals an ox or a sheep, and kills it or sells it, he shall repay five oxen for an ox, and four sheep for a sheep." As you can see in the punishment of stealing, the recompense to the one who stole was paying back five times as much for stealing an ox and four times as much for stealing a sheep. In Roman civilization, this was known as *lex talionis,* which is the law of retaliation. Lex talionis bears the same biblical principle where a person who has injured another person is to be penalized to a similar degree by the injured party. The question is, "What is a just punishment for a finite man who sins against an infinite God?" The undeniable answer is that the punishment must match the injustice that offended the innocent party. Since the offended party is an eternal God, the punishment must be eternal. Therefore, the penalty for man sinning against God demands an eternal punishment because God is eternal.

A second attribute of God that the sinner must deal with is that God is a loving God. Psalm 136 captures this excellently where the psalmist says, "For his steadfast love endures forever." Since God is love (1 John 4:17) and His love endures forever, God must also hate that which is evil. For example, since God loves marriage, He hates divorce. Since God loves children, God hates abortion. Therefore, since God must hate that which is evil, His love requires that He must deal with sinners who commit the very sins that He hates with an eternal punishment because He is an eternal and loving God.

A third attribute of God that the sinner must deal with is that God is just. Abraham knows of the justice of God when he asks the LORD regarding the impending destruction of Sodom in Genesis 18:25, "Far be it from you do such a thing, to put the righteous to death with the wicked, so that the righteous fare as the wicked! Far be that from you! Shall not the Judge of all the earth do what is just?" Abraham knew that God would not deal out punishment to those who were righteous and not deal out punishment to those who were wicked. Abraham knew God's just character would not allow for justice to be withheld from the wicked. Additionally, in Ezekiel 18:1–32, the Lord says to Ezekiel that He will be just and judge everyone according to their deeds. In Ezekiel 18:20, the LORD says, "The righteousness of the righteous will be upon himself, and the wickedness of the wicked will be upon himself." The LORD is essentially saying that He will treat the righteous people as righteous and will treat the unrighteous people as unrighteous. In Ezekiel 18:30–32, the LORD says, "Therefore, you Israelites, I will judge each of you according to your own ways, declares the Sovereign LORD. Repent! Turn away from all your offenses; then sin will not be your downfall. Rid yourselves of all the offenses you have committed and get a new heart and a new spirit. Why will you die people of Israel? For I take no pleasure in the death of anyone, declares the Sovereign LORD. Repent and live!" The LORD promises that He will deal justly with men according to their ways. The LORD will deal justly with sin by punishing sin.

In Deuteronomy 32:4, it says this regarding the LORD's perfect justice, "The Rock, his work is perfect, for all his ways are justice. A God of faithfulness and without iniquity, just and upright is he." In Job 34:10, Job says of God's justice, "Therefore, hear me, you men of understanding: far be it from God that he should do wickedness, and from the Almighty that he should do wrong." In Job 34:12, this of God's perfect justice, "Of a truth, God will not do wickedly, and the Almighty will not pervert justice." Lastly, in Jeremiah 17:10, the LORD says this, "I the LORD search the heart and test the mind, to give every man according to his ways, according to the fruit of his deeds." It is simply not in God's character to leave sin unpunished. God deals justly and equitably with sin. God is not a corrupt judge that will ignore sin. God is not a biased judge that will overlook sin. The God of the Bible is a God who deals justly with sinners who commit the very sins He hates. Thus, the sinner must deal with God who will see to it that every sin is eternally and justly punished because He is an eternal, loving, and just God.

A fourth attribute of God that a sinner must deal with is that God is good. Psalm 25:8 says, "Good and upright is the LORD; therefore he instructs sinners in the way." Jesus affirms God's goodness in Mark 10:18, when Jesus is talking to the rich young ruler, He says, "Why do you call me good? No one is good except God alone." This word *good* is translated from *agathós,* which means "inherently or intrinsically good," which includes good in nature of what is seen and unseen. Because God is good, He cannot be bad. To leave sin unpunished would not be good, it would be bad. Even the unregenerate man knows that it would be bad to let a serial killer go unpunished without jail time or any form of punishment. In His goodness God must punish sin because He is an eternal, loving, just, and good God.

A fifth attribute of God that a sinner must deal with is God's faithfulness. Lamentations 3:22–23 says, "The steadfast love of the LORD never ceases; his mercies never come to an end; they are new every morning; great is your faithfulness." A. W. Pink explains God's faithfulness in this way, "God is true. His Word of Promise is sure. In all His relations with His people God is faithful. He may be safely relied upon. No one ever yet really trusted Him in vain. We find this precious truth expressed almost everywhere in the Scriptures, for His people need to know that faithfulness is an essential part of the Divine character. This is the basis of our confidence in Him." Just as God has promised to be faithful to those who trust in Him, so he is faithful to condemn those who reject Him. Since God is faithful, He must also be faithful to punish sin which He hates. Therefore, God will punish sin since God is an eternal, loving, just, good, and faithful God.

A sixth attribute of God that a sinner must deal with is God's omniscience. The psalmist says of God in Psalm 147:5, "Great is our Lord, and abundant in power; his understanding is beyond measure." Because of God's omniscience, He is aware of all things past, present, and future. There is nothing in all creation that is hidden from Him (Job 38:4–7, 38:16). In fact, in Hebrews 4:13, it says, "Nothing in all creation is hidden from God's sight. Everything is uncovered and laid bare before the eyes of him to whom we must give account." Because God knows everything and knows of every sin, He must punish all sins ever committed. Therefore, since God is an eternal, loving, just, good, faithful, and omniscient God, He will punish sin.

A seventh attribute of God that a sinner must deal with is that God is immutable. James says of God in James 1:17, "Every good and perfect gift is from above, coming down from the Father of the heavenly lights, who does not change like shifting shadows.

In Numbers 23:19, it says, "God is not man, that he should lie, or a son of man, that he should change his mind. Has he said, and will he not do it? Or has he spoken, and will not fulfill it?" God doesn't change. God can't get better, for if He could get better, He would not be God. God can't get worse, because if He became worse, He would be less than God. Therefore, God's disposition toward sin will never change. God's disposition towards homosexuality as sin will not change (Romans 1:26-27). God's disposition towards adultery as a sin will not change (Matthew 5:27). God's disposition towards idolatry will not change (Matthew 6:24). God's disposition towards false teachers who pervert the gospel will not change (Galatians 1:8-9). God's disposition toward sin will always be one of abhorrence and hate. Thus, God must punish sin because He is an eternal, loving, just, good, faithful, omniscient, and immutable God.

An eighth attribute of God that a sinner must deal with is that God is omnipresent. In Jeremiah 23:23–24, the LORD says, "Am I a God at hand, declares the LORD, and not a God far away? Can a man hide himself in secret places so that I cannot see him? Declares the LORD. Do I not fill heaven and earth declares the LORD?" God is always present everywhere. There is nothing in heaven or on earth that is hidden from His sight. Therefore, since God is always present everywhere, He is aware and sees all sins. No sin is hidden from His sight. Therefore, since God can see all sin as He's omnipresent, He must punish all sins because He is an eternal, loving, just, good, faithful, immutable, omniscient, and omnipresent God.

A ninth attribute of God that a sinner must deal with is that God is holy. God's holiness can often be misunderstood. In the New Testament, the word for *holy* is *hágios,* which means "different (unlike)," "other (otherness)," or "set apart (distinguished/distinct)." In the Old Testament, the word for *holy* is *qodesh*, which means "apartness" or "sacredness." The meaning of this attribute as it relates to God is that He is unlike everything else.

One could ask the question, "What is closer to God, the archangel Michael or a golden retriever?" A very good theological answer would be neither. For example, if someone climbs Mt. Everest and all human population is at sea level, how much closer is the person at the top of Mt. Everest to the sun than the rest of the population that is at sea level? The obvious answer is that the person at the top of the mountain and those at sea level are both so far away from the sun that neither are considered even close to the sun. Any difference in proximity to the sun is completely negligible. In the same way, God's most distinguishable characteristic is that He is unlike any other. Isaiah 45:5 is a verse speaking of the Lord's holiness as God where it says, "I am the LORD, and there is no other; apart from me there is no God" and Isaiah 44:6 says, "Thus says the LORD, the King of Israel and his Redeemer, the LORD of hosts: 'I am the first and I am the last; besides me there is no god.'" The Triune God is the only God. God the creator is Lord over His creation and He is the one and only true and living God (1 Thessalonians 1:9). He is totally separate in terms of all of His attributes, which include his self-existence, sovereignty, immutability, self-sufficiency, omnipotence, omniscience, omnipresence, wisdom, faithfulness, goodness, justice, mercy, graciousness, love, and glory. In Matthew 5:48, Jesus says, "You therefore must be perfect, as your heavenly Father is perfect." It is quite clear, that man has fallen, doesn't meet God's required level of holiness and perfection, and must be punished according to his sin and fallenness. Therefore, God must punish sin because He is an eternal, loving, just, good, faithful, immutable, omniscient, omnipresent, and holy God.

The Bad News—Hell

Since we've established that sin must be punished, we will need to understand God's punishment for sin. This will lead us to the doctrine of hell (3). The doctrine of hell is quite possibly one of the least favorite and covered doctrines. It is a doctrine that must be covered. The doctrine of hell will make the glory of the gospel and Christ shine even brighter. The bad news of hell is more than bad news. The bad news of hell is terrifying. The bad news from God about hell is the worst news possible for man.

So, what is *hell*? First, we should know that *hell* is a place of fire. John the Baptist warned that hell was a place of fire. In Matthew 3:10, John the Baptist said, "Even now the axe is laid to the root of the trees. Every tree therefore that does not bear good fruit is cut down and thrown into the fire." Therefore, we can understand that *hell* is a place of fire for the unrepentant sinner.

Second, we should know that *hell* is a place of judgment. John the Baptist also said, "I baptize you with water for repentance, but he who is coming after me is mightier than I, whose sandals I am not worthy to carry. He will baptize you with the Holy Spirit and fire." Without making this verse too complicated, we should understand that Christ is the one who will baptize with the Holy Spirit, which means when someone puts saving faith in Christ, they will receive the Holy Spirit and be put into the body of Christ. Conversely, those who never put saving faith in Christ will be baptized with fire or, rather, judged and damned. In Revelation 20:10, it says, "And I saw the dead, the great and the small, standing before the throne, and the books were opened; and another book was opened, which is the book of life; and the dead were judged from the things which were written in the books, according to their deeds." Therefore, we can understand that *hell* is a place of judgment for unrepentant men who have sinned against God.

Third, we should understand that hell is eternal. John the Baptist also said in Matthew 3:12, "His winnowing fork is in His hand, and He will clear His threshing floor and gather His wheat into the barn, but the chaff He will burn with unquenchable fire." The wheat represents believers, but the chaff represents the unrepentant. Note that John says He will burn up the unrepentant with unquenchable fire. *Asbestos* has been translated to *unquenchable* and means "inextinguishable" or "unquenchable." Therefore, we can understand that the fires of hell will last forever and will never be extinguished.

Fourth, we should note that one sin is enough to send someone to hell. Jesus states that just one sin is worthy of sending man to hell. In Matthew 5:22, Jesus said, "But I say to you that everyone who is angry with his brother will be liable to judgment; whoever insults his brother will be liable to the council; and whoever says, 'You fool!' will be liable to the hell of fire." Likewise, James says in James 2:10, "For whoever keeps the whole law but fails in one point has become guilty of all of it." Additionally, Paul says of those who are unable to keep the law are cursed where he says in Galatians 3:10, "For all who rely on the works of the law are under a curse, as it is written: 'Cursed is everyone who does not continue to do everything written in the Book of the Law.'" Thus, we should understand that one sin is worthy of someone being cast into hell.

Fifth, we should note that Jesus warns that hell must be avoided at all costs. In Matthew 5:29–30, He says, "If your right eye causes you to sin, tear it out and throw it away. For it is better that you lose one of your members than that your whole body be thrown into hell. And if your right hand causes you to sin, cut it off and throw it away. For it is better that you lose one of your members than that your whole body go into hell." Here, Christ gives two warnings which strengthen the emphasis that hell must be avoided at any cost. Thus, we can understand that hell must be so horrible, that man must do everything to avoid going there. John Calvin has said this of hell, "Now, because no description can deal adequately with the gravity of God's vengeance against the wicked, their torments and tortures are figurately expressed to us by physical things, that is, by darkness, weeping, and gnashing of teeth (Matthew 8:12, 22:13), unquenchable fire (Matthew 3:12, Mark 9:43, Isaiah 66:24), an undying worm gnawing at the heart (Isaiah 66:24). By such expressions the Holy Spirit certainly intended to confound all our senses with dread." Martin Luther says something similar where he says, "Hell will be a particular place, where those will be who are condemned to hell or to the eternal wrath of God . . . No doubt it now is, and will be, far worse than anyone is able to describe, picture, or think it to be."

Sixth, we should note that *hell* is a place of weeping and gnashing of teeth. In Matthew 8:12, it says, "But the sons of the kingdom will be cast out into the outer darkness; in that place there will be weeping and gnashing of teeth." There is no joy in hell. There is no hope in hell. There is no hope of repentance. There is simply all eternity to weep over your condition and gnash your teeth in anger toward God.

Seventh, let's note that *hell* is a place of destruction. In Matthew 7:13, it says, "Enter through the narrow gate, for the gate is wide and the way is broad that leads to destruction, and there are many who enter through it (Matthew 7:13). *Destruction* is translated from the original word *apóleia*, which means "cut off, completely severed" or, properly, "loss of well-being." Hell is not a place where one will go to be annihilated or go out of existence. No, they will go there to be eternally destroyed.

Eighth, let's note that hell destroys the whole person. In Matthew 10:28, Jesus says, "Do not fear those who kill the body but are unable to kill the soul; but rather fear Him who is able to destroy both body and soul in hell." When Jesus is talking about *body and soul*, He is speaking of the totality of a person which includes body, soul, and spirit. In other words, *hell* will be a place where man can feel the full physical, emotional, and spiritual torments of God's wrath.

Ninth, let's note that *hell* is a furnace of fire. Jesus didn't give the idea that hell would be a place that was just merely warm, fairly hot, or a place with a couple pretty hot campfires that you would sit around. No, He says in Matthew 13:42, "And throw them into the fiery furnace. In that place there will be weeping and gnashing of teeth." If you think of a furnace, you can very easily think of lifting the lid of the furnace and throwing something in to be consumed by the fire. When you open the lid of the furnace, you get a blast of heat and quickly close it because of the intense heat. In the very same way, the fires of hell are described as a concentrated, closed system of unbearable fire.

Tenth, let's note that hell is inescapable. In Luke 16, we understand from the story that Jesus told of the rich man and Lazarus that hell is inescapable. In Luke 16:26, Abraham says to the rich man, "And besides all this, between us and you a great chasm has been set in place, so that those who want to go from here to you cannot, nor can anyone cross over from there to us." Although the damned will desire to escape the torments and fires of hell, they will not be able to do so.

Eleventh, let's note that hell is full of excruciating pain with no reprieve. In Luke 16:24, it says of the rich man, "So he called to him, 'Father Abraham, have pity on me and send Lazarus to dip the tip of his finger in water and cool my tongue, because I am in agony in this fire.'" The word *agony* comes from *odunaó,* which can mean "very painful physical or mental pain." What makes the physical and mental pain even worse is that there is not one millisecond of reprieve as the pain and agony goes on day and night forever and ever (Revelation 20:10).

Twelfth, let's note that there is a tormenting mental anguish for the sinner. In Luke 16:25, Abraham says to the rich man, "Child, remember that during your life you received your good things, and likewise Lazarus bad things; but now he is being comforted here, and you are in agony." All unbelievers will have the haunting memories of their wasted life and squandered opportunities to respond to Jesus Christ in repentance and faith. The mental anguish of their neglect and rejection of the Son of God will be their eternal regret.

Thirteenth, let's note that *hell* is a place of furious fire. In Hebrews 10:27, the author says this, "But a fearful expectation of judgment, and a fury of fire that will consume the adversaries." *Fury* has been translated from *zelos,* which means "zeal, enthusiasm" or, properly, "to boil" or "burning emotion." It carries with it the sense of a wild fire. Hell is filled with a wild, concentrated fire. If God can create a finite object, such as the sun, which has a core temperature of 27 million degrees Fahrenheit, what does the infinite fire and wrath of an infinite God look like? John Macarthur has said of hell, "Hell will not be a place, as some jokingly envision, where the ungodly will continue to do their thing while the godly do theirs in heaven. Hell will have no friendships, no fellowship, no camaraderie, no comfort. It will not even have the debauched pleasures in which the ungodly love to revel on earth. There will be no pleasure in hell of any kind or degree—only torment, "Day and night forever and ever" (Revelation 20:10).

Fourteenth, let's note that *hell* is blackest darkness and outer darkness. Jude says this in verse 13 of a false teacher's end destiny, "Wild waves of the sea, casting up their own shame like foam; wandering stars, for whom the black darkness has been reserved forever." Jesus says the same thing of this darkness in Matthew 22:13, where He says, "Then the king said to the servants, 'Bind him hand and foot, and throw him into the outer darkness; in that place there will be weeping and gnashing of teeth.'" In hell, there is the constant mental and emotional despair of living in perpetual darkness.

Fifteenth, let's note that hell is for the unbelievers. In Revelation 20:15, it says, "And if anyone's name was not found written in the book of life, he was thrown into the lake of fire." Hell is not for the person who repented and put their faith in Christ. Hell is for all those who never came to Christ in a saving way and they will be cast into hell.

Sixteenth, just as there are rewards for all the redeemed (1 Corinthians 3:10–15, Revelation 22:12), there are personal punishments for the damned. In Romans 2:6–8, it says, "He will render to each one according to his works: to those who by patience in well-doing seek for glory and honor and immortality, he will give eternal life; but for those who are self-seeking and do not obey the truth, but obey unrighteousness, there will be wrath and fury." For every lie there is an equal punishment for the condemned. For every sexual sin, there is an equal punishment for the condemned. For every covetous sin, there is an equal punishment for the condemned. The terrifying thought of being in a furious and fiery furnace that is perpetually blackest darkness where all your sins are paid back in full measure is a terrifying thought to ponder.

Finally, and somberly, let's note that hell will be heavily populated. In Matthew 7:13, Jesus says, "Enter through the narrow gate; for the gate is wide and the way is broad that leads to destruction, and there are many who enter through it." A large majority of humanity is headed to hell. Charles Spurgeon said this of hell, "Oh what would the damned in hell give for a sermon, could they but listen once more! They would consent, if it were possible, to bear ten thousand years of hell's torments, if they might but once more have the Word presented to them! If I had a congregation such as that would be, of men who have tasted the wrath of God, of men who know what an awful thing it is to fall into the hands of an angry God, how would they lean forward to catch every word."

Thus, we can develop a proper definition of *hell,* which could be as follows: ***Hell*** **is a place of God's full wrath and is a place of blackest darkness, filled with furious and concentrated fire everywhere, where there is weeping and anger against God for the unrepentant Christ-rejecting and Christ-neglecting sinners where they will spend all eternity paying for every sin they've ever committed with no hope of escape, and only the expectation of excruciating torments to their body, soul, and spirit and an undying conscience that will haunt them day and night, forever and ever, with no reprieve.** Let us end here in our sober contemplation of sin, death, and hell. There is bad news that we must grasp before we ever consider the good news of God's gospel. The soul-sobering reality of hell should cause anyone and everyone to test whether they be in the faith. When we contemplate the good news, let us always keep in mind the bad news. The bad news heightens the good news of Christ. The bad news inextricably and unequivocally should heighten our love for the Lord. The bad news will multiply a thousandfold a verse such as Romans 5:8, "But God demonstrates his own love toward us, in that while we were still sinners, Christ died for us."

The Inerrant, Infallible, Inspired, Authoritative, and All Sufficient Word of God

Romans 1:2—which he promised beforehand through His prophets in the Holy Scriptures

In Romans 1:2, we find that God promised His gospel in the Old Testament through the prophets and in the Holy Scriptures. So, what does this mean? First let's understand that God promised good news. Next, we see that that the promise came through His prophets in the Holy Scriptures. Notice here that God is the possessor of the prophets. God did not choose Nadab and Abihu (Leviticus 10:1–5). God did not choose Jannes and Jambres (2 Timothy 3:8). God did not choose the prophets of Baal on Mount Carmel (1 Kings 18). God did not choose the sons of Eli, Hophni and Phinehas (1 Samuel 2:12–36). God did not choose the false prophets who prophesied to King Ahab (1 Kings 21). God did not choose the false prophets during Jeremiah's time (Jeremiah 6:13–17, 23:9–32). God did not choose the false prophets during Isaiah's time (Isaiah 44:24–26). God did not choose the false prophets during Ezekiel's time (Ezekiel 13:1–16). No, God's prophets were chosen by Him to declare His Word through Scripture.

Second, let's note that God's prophets gave this promise of the gospel through Holy Scripture. In the original language, *Holy Scripture* comes to us as *graphais hagiais. Graphais* properly means "writing" and, as we learned earlier, *hagiais* means "different (unlike)," "other (otherness)," or "set apart (distinguished/distinct)." God promised this gospel through words. God promised His gospel through words that can be understood, interpreted, and studied. These are not ideas. These are not emotions or feelings. No, God promised His gospel through His prophets on words that can be understood, interpreted, and studied. So, what Holy Scripture is Paul talking about when he says we can see the gospel in these holy writings? Let's explore what this means as the Old Testament Scriptures promised the good news of Christ (4).

- God promised that Christ would be the seed of a woman (Genesis 3:15) and was fulfilled in Galatians 4:4.
- God promised that Christ would be of the seed of Abraham (Genesis 17:7, 22:18) and was fulfilled in Galatians 3:16.
- God promised Christ would be of the seed of Isaac (Genesis 21:12) and was fulfilled in Hebrews 11:17–19.
- God promised Christ would be of the seed of David (Psalm 132:11, Jeremiah 23:5) and was fulfilled in Acts 13:23 and Romans 1:3.
- God promised Christ would be born of a virgin (Isaiah 7:14) and was fulfilled in Matthew 1:22–23 and Luke 2:7.
- God promised Christ would be called Immanuel (Isaiah 7:14) and was fulfilled in Matthew 1:22–23.
- God promised Christ would be born in Bethlehem Ephrathah of Judah (Micah 5:2) and was fulfilled in Matthew 2:1 and Luke 2:4–6.

- God promised that persons would come to adore Christ and give Him gifts (Psalm 72:10) and was fulfilled in Matthew 2:1–11.
- God promised the killing of the children of Bethlehem (Jeremiah 31:15) and was fulfilled in Matthew 2:16–18.
- God promised Christ would be called out of Egypt (Hosea 11:1) and was fulfilled in Matthew 2:15.
- God promised Christ would be preceded by John the Baptist (Isaiah 40:3, Malachi 3:1) and was fulfilled in Matthew 3:1 and Luke 1:17.
- God promised Christ would be anointed with the Spirit (Psalm 45:7, Isaiah 11:2, 61:1) and was fulfilled in Matthew 3:16, John 3:34, and Acts 10:38.
- God promised Christ would be a prophet like Moses (Deuteronomy 18:15–18) and was fulfilled in Acts 3:20–22.
- God promised Christ would be a priest in the order of Melchizedek (Psalm 110:4) and was fulfilled in Hebrews 5:5–6.
- God promised Christ would enter public ministry (Isaiah 61:1–2) and was fulfilled in Luke 4:16–21, 43.
- God promised Christ's public entrance in Jerusalem (Zechariah 9:9) which was fulfilled in Matthew 21:1–5.
- God promised Christ's lowliness (Isaiah 53:2) and was fulfilled in Mark 6:3 and Luke 9:58.
- God promised Christ would be meek (Isaiah 42:2) and was fulfilled in Matthew 12:15–16, 19.
- God promised Christ would be tender and compassionate (Isaiah 40:11, 42:3) and was fulfilled in Matthew 12:15, 20 and Hebrews 4:15.
- God promised Christ would be without deceit (Isaiah 53:9) and was fulfilled in 1 Peter 2:22.
- God promised Christ would be full of zeal (Psalm 69:9) and was fulfilled in John 2:17.

- God promised Christ would preach by parables (Psalm 78:2) and was fulfilled in Matthew 13:34–35.
- God promised Christ would work miracles (Isaiah 35:5–6) and was fulfilled in Matthew 11:4–6 and John 11:47.
- God promised Christ would be scorned (Psalm 22:6, 69:7, 9, 20) and was fulfilled in Romans 15:3.
- God promised Christ would be rejected by His brothers (Psalm 69:8, Isaiah 63:3) and was fulfilled in John 1:11, 7:3.
- God promised Christ would be a stone of stumbling to the Jews (Isaiah 8:14) and was fulfilled in Romans 9:32 and 1 Peter 2:8.
- God promised Christ would be hated by the Jews (Psalm 69:4, Isaiah 49:7) and was fulfilled in John 15:24–25.
- God promised Christ would be rejected by the Jewish rulers (Psalm 118:22) and was fulfilled in Matthew 21:42 and John 7:48.
- God promised the Jews and Gentiles would combine against Christ (Psalm 2:1–2) and was fulfilled in Luke 23:12 and Acts 4:27.
- God promised Christ would be betrayed by a friend (Psalm 41:9, 55:12–14) and was fulfilled in John 13:18, 21.
- God promised Christ's disciples would forsake Him (Zechariah 13:7) and was fulfilled in Matthew 26:31, 56.
- God promised Christ would be sold for thirty pieces of silver (Zechariah 11:12) and was fulfilled in Matthew 26:15.
- God promised Christ's price would be given for the potter's field (Zechariah 11:13) and was fulfilled in Matthew 27:7.
- God promised Christ would suffer intensely (Psalm 22:14–15) and was fulfilled in Luke 22:42, 44.
- God promised Christ would suffer for others (Isaiah 53:4–6, 12) and was fulfilled in Matthew 20:28.

- God promised Christ would be patient and silent under suffering (Isaiah 53:7) and was fulfilled in Matthew 26:63, 27:12–14.
- God promised Christ would be struck on the cheek (Micah 5:1) and was fulfilled in Matthew 27:30.
- God promised Christ's appearance would be marred (Isaiah 52:14, 53:3) and was fulfilled in John 19:5.
- God promised Christ would be spit on and flogged (Isaiah 50:6) and was fulfilled in Mark 14:65 and John 19:1.
- God promised Christ's hands and feet being nailed to the cross (Psalm 22:16) and was fulfilled in John 19:18, 20:25.
- God promised Christ would be forsaken by God (Psalm 22:1) and was fulfilled in Matthew 27:46.
- God promised Christ would be mocked (Psalm 22:7–8) and was fulfilled in Matthew 27:39–44.
- God promised Christ would be given gall and vinegar to drink (Psalm 69:21) and was fulfilled in Matthew 27:34.
- God promised Christ's garments would be divided and lots cast for His clothing (Psalm 22:18) and was fulfilled in Matthew 27:35.
- God promised Christ would be numbered with the transgressors (Isaiah 53:12) and was fulfilled in Mark 15:28.
- God promised Christ would make intercession for His murderers (Isaiah 53:12) and was fulfilled in Luke 23:34.
- God promised Christ's death (Isaiah 53:12) and was fulfilled in Matthew 27:50.
- God promised that none of Christ's bones would be broken (Exodus 12:46, Psalm 34:20) and was fulfilled in John 19:33, 36.
- God promised Christ being pierced (Zechariah 12:10) and was fulfilled in John 19:34, 37.
- God promised Christ would be buried with the rich (Isaiah 53:9) and was fulfilled in Matthew 27:57–60.

- God promised Christ's flesh would not see decay (Psalm 16:10) and was fulfilled in Acts 2:31.
- God promised Christ would be resurrected from the dead (Psalm 16:10) and was fulfilled in Luke 24:6, 31, 34.
- God promised Christ's ascension (Psalm 68:18) and was fulfilled in Luke 24:51 and Acts 1:9.
- God promised Christ would be sitting at the right hand of God (Psalm 110:1) and was fulfilled in Hebrews 1:3.
- God promised Christ would exercise the priestly office in heaven (Zechariah 6:13) and was fulfilled in Romans 8:34.
- God promised Christ would be the chief cornerstone of the church (Isaiah 28:16) and was fulfilled in 1 Peter 2:6–7.
- God promised that Christ would be king (Psalm 2:6) and was fulfilled in Luke 1:32 and John 18:33–37.

As you can see, God's promise of the gospel is found in the writings of the prophets in Scripture. It has been estimated that for eight prophecies to be fulfilled in Christ, the likelihood or mere chance is 10^17. Expanding on this is that for 48 prophecies to be fulfilled in Christ, this would carry a mathematical chance of 10^157 which is 157 zeros. God's Word is not a stick, it's a sword that penetrates and pierces (Hebrews 4:12, Acts 2:37). God's Word is not asleep or idle, it is alive and active (Hebrews 4:12). God's Word is not indecisive, it judges thc thoughts and attitudes of men (Hebrews 4:12). God's Word never fails (Luke 1:37). God's Word is not frail, it's a fire that refines and reveals (Jeremiah 23:29, Psalm 12:6, Luke 1:37). God's Word is not helpless, it's a hammer that is powerful to save and sanctify (Jeremiah 23:29, 1 Corinthians 1:18, John 17:17). God's Word does not end, it endures for eternity (1 Peter 1:25). God's Word does not fail to fully predict, it foreordains and fulfills prophecy (Acts 2:23). God's Word is not treachery that can't be trusted, it is truth that is trustworthy (John 17:17). Therefore, not only do we see the unbelievable foreknowledge and sovereignty of God fulfilling prophecy, but we also understand how crucial the Holy Scripture is to the gospel and, more specifically as we'll learn, how it declares Jesus Christ. Scripture points to Jesus Christ! The Old Testament predicts Him, the gospels reveal Him, Acts proclaims Him, the Epistles explain Him, and Revelation anticipates Him. The gospel rests on the sturdy foundation of the Old Testament which point to Jesus Christ. Thus, we come to understand that an **essential component of the gospel is the Holy Scriptures of the Bible which are the authoritative, inspired, inerrant, and infallible Word of God needed to point to the person and work of Jesus Christ and show man how to be reconciled with God**. Paul says it well in 2 Timothy 3:16, "All Scripture is breathed out by God and profitable for teaching, for reproof, for correction, and for training in righteousness."

The Person of Christ

Romans 1:3—concerning his Son, who was descended from David according to the flesh

We have come to understand that the gospel is owned and authored by God. We have come to understand that the good news is only understood when considering the bad news of sin, death, and hell. We have come to understand that the gospel was promised by God through the Holy Scriptures and the Holy Scriptures are needed to point to the person and work of Jesus Christ and show man how to be reconciled with God. We will now become even more focused and concentrated as this gospel points us to someone.

As we see, in verse 3, the gospel of God is concerned with a person. The gospel of God is concerned with a person who is God's son. The gospel is concerned about God's son, Jesus Christ. This gospel does not concern the prophet Muhammad of Islam. This gospel does not concern the false god, Allah of Islam. This gospel does not concern Buddha. This gospel does not concern Sun Myung Moon. This gospel does not concern Mary Baker Eddy. This gospel does not concern Ron Hubbard. This gospel does not concern Joseph Smith. This gospel does not concern the false god, Vishnu of Hinduism. This gospel does not concern the false god, Brahman of Hinduism. No, this gospel is all about God's son, Jesus Christ.

Notice the brilliance of Paul in verse 3 as he claims this is the Son of God which is a claim to deity. Notice the brilliance of Paul in verse 3 that he also claims that the Son of God was descended from the physical lineage of David according to the flesh. Paul has just made a very important Christological statement which is an essential component of the gospel. The Christological and foundational statement that Paul makes is that **the person of Jesus Christ is an essential component of the gospel**. Jesus Christ is the sum and substance of the gospel. Jesus Christ is the Alpha and the Omega of the gospel. Jesus Christ is the priority and preeminence of the gospel.

So, what about the person of Jesus should be understood? First, as we already mentioned, Jesus is God as He is the Son of God (Romans 1:3). Peter makes this great confession in Matthew 16:16 and is confirmed by Christ where it says, "Simon Peter replied, 'You are the Christ, the Son of the living God.'" Paul makes the same claim to Jesus' deity where he says in Colossians 1:15, "He is the image of the invisible God, the firstborn of all creation" and, in Colossians 1:19, he also says, "For in Him all the fullness of God was pleased to dwell," and makes a similar statement in Colossians 2:9, "For in Him the whole fullness of deity dwells bodily." Likewise, the author of Hebrews says of Jesus, the Son of God, in Hebrews 1:3, "He is the radiance of the glory of God and the exact imprint of His nature, and he upholds the universe by the word of His power. After making purification for sins, He sat down at the right hand of the Majesty on high." Thus, we see Jesus as the Christ, the Son of the Living God.

Second, because Jesus is God He is also coequal and coeternal with God the Father and God the Holy Spirit. In John 5:17–18, after Jesus healed the invalid, Jesus makes a statement of being equal with the Father where it says, "But Jesus answered them, 'My Father is working until now, and I am working.' This was why the Jews were seeking all the more to kill Him, because not only was He breaking the Sabbath, but He was even calling God His own Father, making Himself equal with God." In John 10:30, Jesus makes another statement of being coequal with the Father where He says, "I and the Father are one." Jesus reiterates this same point but states it in another way where He says about the work He is doing in John 10:38, "But if I do them, even though you do not believe me, believe the works, that you may know and understand that the Father is in me and I am in the Father." Jesus makes another claim to coequality with the Father in John 14:10, where He says, "Do you not believe that I am in the Father and the Father is in me? The words that I say to you I do not speak on my own authority, but the Father who dwells in Me does His works." The point is that Jesus, being God, is coequal and coeternal with the Father. Jesus is saying He is one in essence with Father. Additionally, we should see that Jesus is the only begotten Son of God (John 3:16). The word "only begotten" has been translated from monogenés which properly means "one-and-only", "one of a kind", literally "one of a class and the only of its kind". Jesus is the only one-of-a-kind Son of God. Jesus is not a created being. We can know that Jesus is not a created being as He is the Son of God and, as we learned earlier, God is immutable and eternal. God cannot get better, for if He could get better, He would not be God. God can't get worse, because if He became worse, He would be less than God. Jesus is not a created being as God is eternal and God is immutable. God doesn't become more, and God doesn't become less. Additionally, another attribute of God is the aseity of God, or rather, God is self-sufficient and exists of and from Himself by His own self and self-will. John 1:4

captures the aseity of God and Jesus where it says, "In him was life, and the life was the light of men." This is simply stating that all created life came from Him because He is the source of all life, or rather, He is completely self-sufficient and self-existent in and of Himself and needs nothing. The one who is self-sufficient and self-existent in and of Himself cannot be created as He is eternal and is the origin and source of all life. Therefore, Jesus is the co-eternal, co-equal, and only begotten Son of God.

Third, we should see Jesus as the Christ or Messiah. As we saw above, Peter makes the confession that Jesus is the Son of God and He's also the Christ or the Messiah. Note in John 1:41, Andrew tells his brother Simon, or Peter, "We have found the Messiah" (which means "Christ"). There was much doubt about who Jesus was because the Jewish leaders were claiming that Jesus was driving out demons by Beelzebul (Matthew 12:24), whole towns such as Chorazin, Bethsaida, and Capernaum had rejected Him (Matthew 11:20–24), Jesus was not assuming the role of king when the people were trying to take Him by force to make Him king (John 6:15), and Jesus was being rejected by many followers, especially after His teaching on being the Bread of Life (6:66). Although Jesus was performing many miracles and signs along with His teaching, there was still doubt over who He was. Peter's confession was a culmination of the two and a half years of traveling with Christ and his great confession was that Jesus is the Christ or the Messiah. Paul's statement in Romans 1:3 "concerning his Son" carries the full weight of Peter's great confession concerning Jesus as Christ, Jesus as God, and Jesus as the Son of God as Paul calls Jesus "Christ" in Romans 1:4, 6.

Jesus is the Anointed One of God where He proclaims that He is the fulfillment of Isaiah's prophecy in Luke 4:18-19 when He says, "The Spirit of the Lord is upon me, because he has anointed me to proclaim good news to the poor. He has sent me to proclaim liberty to the captives and recovering of sight to the blind, to set at liberty those who are oppressed, to proclaim the year of the Lord's favor." He is the promised Messiah. He is the promised Messiah. He is the Prophet that was foretold of in Deuteronomy 18. He is the eternal King as Paul says in 1 Timothy 1:17, "To the King of the ages, immortal, invisible, the only God, be honor and glory forever and ever. Amen" and in 1 Timothy 6:15 where he also says, "he who is the blessed and only Sovereign, the King of kings and the Lord of lords." He is the eternal Savior as the angel declares in Luke 2:11, "For unto you is born this day in the city of David a Savior, who is Christ the Lord." He is the eternal High Priest as the author of Hebrews says in Hebrews 7:24, 26, "but he holds his priesthood permanently, because he continues forever... for it was indeed fitting that we should have such a high priest, holy, innocent, unstained, separated from sinners, and exalted above the heavens." He is the Creator and Sustainer of the universe (John 1:1-14. He is the eternal Savior. He is the Creator of the universe (John 1:1-14, Hebrews 1:1-3, Colossians 1:16-17, 1 Corinthians 8:6). The person of Jesus is that He is the Christ, the promised Jewish Messiah, the only begotten Son of the Living God (John 3:16) which makes Him God and equal with God the Father and God the Holy Spirit. The disciples initially made the claim of Jesus, "Some say John the Baptist" which alone is an eternally fatal understanding. The disciples also made the claim of Jesus, "Some say Elijah" which alone is an eternally fatal understanding. The disciples also made the claim of Jesus, "Jeremiah or one of the prophets" which alone is an eternally fatal understanding. Napoleon said of Jesus, "I know men, and Jesus Christ is no mere man." True, but this statement alone is an eternally fatal understanding. Pilate said of Jesus, "He's a man without fault." True, but this statement alone is an eternally fatal understanding. Diderot said, "He's the unsurpassed." True, but this statement alone is an eternally fatal understanding. Strauss said, "He's the highest model of religion." True, but this statement alone is an eternally fatal understanding. John Stuart Mill, the philosopher, said, "He's the guide of humanity." True, but this statement alone is an eternally fatal understanding. Lecky said, "He's the highest pattern of virtue." True, but this statement alone is an eternally fatal understanding. Renan, the French atheist, said; "He's the greatest among the sons of men." True, but this statement alone is an eternally fatal understanding. Close is not good enough when understanding the person of Jesus Christ (5).

Fourth, Paul's second statement in verse 3 says of Jesus, "who was descended from David according to the flesh." There are two powerful points in this statement. First, Jesus is the promised Messiah that came from the physical lineage of David (Matthew 1:1–16, Luke 3:23–38) which was promised in Psalm 132:11, Jeremiah 23:5, and 2 Samuel 2:8–17, 27–29. Jesus came according to the Messianic line. As we noted before, He is the Son of God, and we can now understand He is the Son of David. Second, Jesus was born of a virgin (Matthew 1:23). This means that Jesus was physically born into this world (Matthew 1:25). Jesus was the Word made flesh (John 1:14). Jesus was made man (Philippians 2:7-8). Paul tells Timothy this truth about Jesus' humanity as the God-man in 1 Timothy 2:5, "For there is one God, and there is one mediator between God and men, the man Christ Jesus".

Fifth, of what importance is it that Jesus was the Son of God and the Son of Man as it relates to the gospel? Why is it important to the gospel that Jesus be truly God and truly man? The fact that Jesus is God and man helps us understand an age-old question. In Numbers 14:18, it says, "The LORD is slow to anger and abounding in steadfast love, forgiving iniquity and transgression, but he will by no means clear the guilty, visiting the iniquity of the fathers on the children, to the third and the fourth generation." In Exodus 34:7, it says something similar, "keeping steadfast love for thousands, forgiving iniquity and transgression and sin, but who will by no means clear the guilty, visiting the iniquity of the fathers on the children and the children's children, to the third and fourth generation."

The question is, "How can sinful man be reconciled to a holy God"? The question is, "How can God punish transgressors and sinful men and yet somehow forgive transgressors and sinful men?" The question is, "How is God able to be just and punish sin, yet be the justifier of sinful men?" As we learned earlier, man's sin is incurable. Man can't reach up to the heights of heaven and earn God's favor. No, God needed to leave heaven and come to do the work that man couldn't do. Jesus had to become a man because the wages of sin is death (Romans 6:23) and God cannot die as God is eternal. Therefore, Jesus needed to be a man to die. Jesus needed to be a sinless man to take on the curse of the law and die (Galatians 3:13, Romans 8:3). The Son of God needed to become the Son of David to die in our place and make the only atonement for man's sin where it says in Romans 8:3, "For God has done what the law, weakened by the flesh, could not do. By sending his own Son in the likeness of sinful flesh and for sin, he condemned sin in the flesh". The Son of God needed to become a Son of Man to be the mediator between God and man (1 Timothy 2:5). A *mediator* intervenes to restore peace between two parties. As we saw above, these two parties were at enmity with each other and were unreconcilable. The mediator must stand in the middle and be equal to both sides. Jesus had to be truly God in order to represent God to man and He needed to be truly man to represent man to God. No one else could have stood between both parties. No angel could have mediated between God and man. No prophet could have mediated between God and man. Only God could take the wrath of God. Only God could live a sinless life. **Thus, the person of Jesus is essential to the gospel. The person of Jesus is He is the Christ, the Creator of the universe, the promised Jewish Messiah, the only begotten Son of the Living God which makes Him God and equal with God the Father and God the Holy Spirit who was born of a virgin and became man and is, thus, truly God and truly man.**

The Work of Christ

Romans 1:4—and was declared the Son of God in power according to the Spirit of holiness by his resurrection from the dead, Jesus Christ our Lord

Jesus' teaching and miracles were impossible to ignore. In His teaching He made several claims to deity as well as being the Messiah. Though not an exhaustive list, here are a few claims He made. He claimed to be the Bread of Life (John 6:35, 41, 48, 51), which was a claim that He came from heaven which pointed to the need of man to accept His work on the cross. Jesus claimed to be Lord of the Sabbath (Matthew 12:8), which was a claim to be Lord over everything of the Sabbath (Leviticus 23:3), which included the Passover and the Festival of Unleavened Bread (Leviticus 23:4–8), the Offering of Firstfruits (Leviticus 23:9–14), the Festival of Weeks (Leviticus 23:15–22), the Festival of Trumpets (Leviticus 23:23–25), the Day of Atonement (Leviticus 23:26–32), and the Festival of Tabernacles (Leviticus 23:33–44). Jesus was essentially claiming to be Lord over the entire Levitical system, which was a claim to deity as God gave the Jews the Levitical system. Jesus claimed to be the Light of the World (John 8:12), which was a claim to be Messiah and a light of salvation for His people (Isaiah 60:19–22) as well as for the whole earth (Isaiah 42:6–7, Isaiah 49:6). Jesus claimed to be the Gate for the sheep (John 10:7, 9), which indicated that although the shepherd led the sheep out of the sheep pen, He is the entrance to the pen that leads sheep to proper pasture and He serves as the sole means to approach the Father so His sheep could partake of God's promised salvation. Jesus claimed to be the Good Shepherd (John 10:11, 14), which was a claim of being the Lord (Psalm 23:1–6, Ezekiel 34:1–31, Isaiah 40:10–11). Jesus claimed to be the Resurrection and the Life (John 11:25), which meant He had power over death and power to raise people to life.

The claim to be the Resurrection was a claim to deity as only God could raise people from the dead (Job 19:25–27, Daniel 12:1–3). Jesus claimed to be the Way, the Truth, and the Life (John 14:6), which was an emphatic statement that He was the only means of approach to the Father. Jesus claimed to be the Messiah in Matthew 16:16–17, which was a claim to be the promised Savior of the Jews. Jesus made many claims to deity which were supported by His many miracles that He performed.

Jesus' miracles and life validated all His claims. For example, we see that Jesus proved He could be tempted at all points like man, yet he was without sin (Matthew 4:1-11, Hebrews 4:15). We see that Jesus healed great crowds and then taught by His own divine authority (Matthew 4:23-25, 7:28-29). We see Jesus calling Matthew, the tax collector, to be one of His disciples which proved that He could forgive the worst of sinners (Matthew 9:9-13). Jesus consistently pointed to His works as testimony to His teaching and claims. John 5:36 captures this wondrously where Jesus says this after healing the invalid at Bethesda, "I have a testimony weightier than that of John. For the works that the Father has given me to finish – the very works that I am doing – testify that the Father has sent me." Additionally, after Jesus heals the blind man and claims to be the Good Shepherd, He says this about His works which validate His claims in John 10:25, "Jesus answered, "I did tell you, but you do not believe. The works I do in my Father's name testify about me". Chapter 3 will highlight more on the significance of Jesus' miracles and claims which will help us understand how the false teachers consistently denied the person and work of Jesus.

One of the signs that Jesus promised He would perform to demonstrate that He was the Christ, the Son of the Living God, was He would be resurrected from the dead. He promised that He would give them the sign of Jonah (Matthew 12:38–42, 16:4; Luke 11:29), which was a predictive prophecy. It was a predictive prophecy given in picture rather than in word. As Jonah spent three days and three nights in the belly of the great fish, so Jesus spent three days and three nights in the heart of the earth. It looked like the end of Jonah, but it wasn't. It looked like the end of Jesus, but it wasn't. Jonah was buried in the depths; Jesus was buried in the depths. Jonah came out; Jesus came out. This was a picture of Jesus' resurrection. Jesus said in John 2:19, "Destroy this temple, and in three days I will raise it up." Jesus was again, speaking of His death and resurrection. Jesus reasoned with and taught His disciples that He needed to be killed and raised to life on the third day (Matthew 16:21–22, 17:22–23, 20:17–19; Mark 8:31, 9:30–32, 10:32–34; Luke 9:21–22, 9:43–45, 18:31–34). Jesus proclaimed that He had power to lay down His life and resurrect himself where He said in John 10:17–18, "For this reason the Father loves me, because I lay down my life that I may take it up again. No one takes it from me, but I lay it down on my own accord. I have authority to lay it down, and I have authority to take it up again. This charge I have received from my Father."

If Jesus could not resurrect Himself, it would prove He was not one with the Father (John 5:17–18). If Jesus could not resurrect Himself, He would be a lying prophet about His resurrection (Matthew 16:21–22, 17:22–23, 20:17–19; Mark 8:31, 9:30–32, 10:32–34; Luke 9:21–22, 9:43–45, 18:31–34). If Jesus could not resurrect Himself, it was evidence He was not the Son with whom the Father was well pleased (Matthew 3:17). If Jesus could not resurrect Himself, it was evidence that He was not anointed by the Holy Spirit (Luke 4:18–21). All of Jesus' works, teaching, and life were validated by His resurrection and proved that He was the Christ the Son of the Living God. This is what Romans 1:4 is saying. Without the Resurrection, all of this would have meant nothing. If Jesus would have died and not risen, He would not have been the Resurrection and the Life (John 11:25). If Jesus had not risen, He would have been like any other man who dies and does not come back to life (Psalm 90:1–12, Ecclesiastes

7:2). If Jesus had not risen, all His claims and miracles would have amounted to nothing as even Moses and Elisha were able to perform miracles but could not raise themselves from the dead. Without the resurrection, Jesus' claims and work would be invalidated. Siddhartha Gautama of Buddhism could not resurrect himself from the dead. Kong Qiu of Confucianism could not resurrect himself from the dead. Lao Tzu of Taoism could not resurrect himself from the dead. Joseph Smith of Mormonism could not resurrect himself from the dead. Muhammed of Islam could not resurrect himself from the dead. Mary Baker Eddy of Christian Science could not resurrect herself from the dead. Charles Taze Russell of the Jehovah's Witnesses could not resurrect himself from the dead. If Christ could not resurrect Himself from the dead, Paul would be exactly right about the Christian faith where he says this in 1 Corinthians 15:16-17, "For if the dead are not raised, not even Christ has been raised. And if Christ has not been raised, your faith is futile and you are still in your sins."

However, Jesus' work on the cross was accepted. Jesus' resurrection was proof positive that His salvific work was accepted by God. Christ's resurrection was God's apologetic on the sufficiency of Christ's substitutionary death on the cross for sinners. The resurrection was God's ultimate validation of Jesus' person and work on the cross. Jesus raised himself from the dead (John 10:17–18), God the Father raised Jesus from the dead (Galatians 1:1), the Holy Spirit raised Jesus from the dead (Romans 8:11). All three persons of the Godhead raised Jesus from the dead (Acts 2:24). God approved of Jesus' work by raising Jesus from the dead. The angel said this about Christ's resurrection to the women who were visiting the tomb in Luke 24:5-7, "Why do you seek the living among the dead? He is not here, but has risen. Remember how he told you, while he was still in Galilee, that the Son of Man must be delivered into the hands of sinful men and be crucified and on the third day rise." Paul told Timothy a very similar statement about the importance of the resurrection and lineage of Jesus where he says in 2 Timothy 2:8, "Remember Jesus Christ, risen from the dead, the offspring of David, as preached in my gospel." Paul also makes this important statement on the significance of Christ's resurrection and the implications for all those who come to faith in Christ in 1 Corinthians 15:20-21, "But in fact Christ has been raised from the dead, the firstfruits of those who have fallen asleep. For as by a man came death, by a man has come also the resurrection of the dead."

So what did Jesus' perfect work secure? In verse 3, Paul spoke of Jesus' deity and humanity. In verse 4, he has fast-forwarded to Christ's resurrection. So, what is Paul trying to do by claiming Jesus' deity and human birth and then going directly to the resurrection? He is capturing the entire life and work of Christ. Paul is saying that this gospel is about the person of Jesus (Romans 1:3) and the work of Jesus (Romans 1:4). **Therefore, an essential component to the gospel includes Jesus' work**. This includes His teaching, His miracles, His sinless life, His death, His resurrection, His ascension, His present enthronement, and Second Coming. So, how is one to understand Jesus' work that was validated by the Resurrection? Jesus' work can be summed up in eight words: *Propitiation, Reconciliation, Redemption, Expiation, Regeneration, Justification, Glorification,* and *Domination.*

The first word is *propitiation,* which is translated from the word *hilastérion. Hilastérion* means a sin offering, by which the wrath of the deity shall be appeased; a means of propitiation. As we learned earlier, God hates sin. God hates wickedness. God is angry with the wicked every day. God abhors sin and the wicked. God sees sin as filthy and defiling. God sees sin as open hostility toward Him as if two parties are at war with each other. God is pictured as aiming deadly weapons at the wicked and ready to destroy them. God's fierce anger toward sin and the wicked is one of swallowing them up in the fire of His wrath. God considers sin an abomination. God considers sin evil. God considers sin wicked. God simply hates sin with all His being.

Therefore, God needed a way to punish sin. God needed a way to propitiate or appease His righteous wrath toward sin and man. If there's anything that can be learned from the Old Testament Levitical system, it is that the sacrifice of goats, calves, bulls, and heifers never brought the Jews into the presence of God. Ceremonial washings never brought the people into the presence of God. Grain and fellowship offerings never brought the people into the presence of God. Good works never brought the people into the presence of God. However, we see the God–man, Jesus Christ, who was able to act as a mediator between both parties who were at enmity with each other, God and man. Animals couldn't step in and mediate. Angels couldn't step in and mediate. No, only one person, the Lord Jesus Christ who would be the sinless sacrifice to represent man to God and God to man could mediate between both parties. In Matthew 3:15, as Jesus was discussing the need for His baptism with John the Baptist, Jesus said, "'Let it be so now, for thus it is fitting for us to **fulfill all righteousness**.' Then he consented." In Matthew 5:17, Jesus said something similar where Jesus said, "Do not think that I have come to abolish the Law or the Prophets; I have not come to abolish them but to **fulfill them**." Jesus also said something similar to His disciples after His resurrection where He said, "These are My words that I spoke to you while I was still with you, that everything written about Me in the law of Moses and the Prophets and the Psalms **must be fulfilled.**" Jesus' work required that He fulfill the law and the prophets by living a sinless life and meeting all the requirements of God's law and prophecy. In fact, in Matthew 22:37-38, Jesus was asked what is the greatest commandment and He replied, "You shall love the Lord your God with all your heart and with all your soul and with all your mind." Therefore, we can and should know that there was not one millisecond where Christ did not fulfill this commandment perfectly. On the other hand, we should see that there's not one millisecond that man has ever perfectly obeyed this. Jesus lived a perfect and sinless life and the entirety of His life was one of loving the Lord perfectly with all His heart, soul, mind and strength in complete obedience to God's law.

In 2 Corinthians 5:21, it says, "For our sake he made him to be sin who knew no sin, so that in him we might become the righteousness of God." Therefore, we know that the sin offering had to be sinless which speaks to Christ's sinless life. So, what does it mean that Christ was made sin? Does it mean that when Christ was on the cross, He became defiled and corrupted? That He became in His nature something vile, loathsome, and sinful? So how did Christ become sin? Let's think about how Christ makes sinners righteous when they believe the gospel. The moment a person believes in the gospel and is saved, they do not become a righteous being. That is to say, the moment they believe, they are not so transformed in their nature that they become perfectly righteous and never again sin. We are not infused with a special grace that causes us never to sin. What happens is the moment that someone repents and believes in Christ, they are forensically and legally declared righteous before the throne of God. It is a legal declaration before the throne of God that is not based on one's merits or works, but is based upon the virtue and merit of Jesus Christ and God treats us as perfectly righteous in Christ. Therefore, we can understand how God made Christ to be sin. When Jesus Christ was on the cross, His nature did not become polluted. He did not become some vile being. No, what happened was that the sins of His people were imputed to Him and before the throne of God, He was considered and declared guilty and He was treated by God as guilty. He always was and is and will be the spotless Lamb of God. However, on the cross, the sins of His people were imputed to Him. He was legally declared guilty and then God treated Him as a righteous God should treat the wicked. Upon the cross, the Father treated His Son as the infidel, as the sinner, and as the lawbreaker.

Paul refers to Christ's sacrificial work where it talks about Christ being a propitiation in Romans 3:25, "whom God says of Jesus, "whom God put forward as a propitiation by His blood to be received by faith. This was to show God's righteousness, because in His divine forbearance He had passed over former sins." Of Jesus' death on the cross, Isaiah describes the Suffering Servant being crushed for sin where it says in Isaiah 53:10, "Yet it was the LORD's will to crush him and cause him to suffer, and though the LORD makes his life an offering for sin, he will see his offspring and prolong his days, and the will of the LORD will prosper in his hand." Additionally, in Galatians 3:13 it talks about Christ becoming a curse where it says, "Christ redeemed us from the curse of the law by becoming a curse for us – for it is written, "Cursed is everyone who is hanged on a tree."

So what does it mean when Jesus was crushed? What does it mean that Jesus became a curse? What is a curse? A curse is the opposite of a blessing. Every curse pronounced in the Bible was to fall on Jesus upon the cross. For example, in Matthew 5, we see what it means to be blessed in the Beatitudes. For example, we see that those who are blessed will inherit the kingdom of heaven (Matthew 5:3). However, because Christ became a curse He was punished as one who is refused entrance into the Kingdom of heaven. Those who are blessed will be comforted (Matthew 5:4). However, because Christ became a curse, He suffered divine wrath and was punished with divine pain and misery. Isaiah 53:5 details Christ suffering divine wrath, pain and misery where it says, "But he was pierced for our transgressions; he was crushed for our iniquities; upon him was the chastisement that brought us peace, and with his wounds we are healed." We see that the blessed shall be satisfied (Matthew 5:6). However, the cursed die miserable and wretched. Those who are blessed will receive mercy (Matthew 5:7). However, because Christ became a curse, we see that Christ died miserable and wretched. Isaiah 53:8 captures this where the Suffering Servant is given over to mistrials and is sentenced to death as though He was the wicked one where it says, "By oppression and judgment he was taken away; and as for his generation, who considered that he was cut off out of the land of the living, stricken for the transgression of my people?". Because Christ became a curse, He received divine justice without pity. Isaiah 53:10 speaks of the Suffering Servant receiving divine justice with no pity where it says, "Yet it was the will of the LORD to **crush him; he has put him to grief**; when his soul makes an offering for guilt". Those who are blessed shall see God (Matthew 5:8). However, because Christ became a curse, He was completely cut off from God's presence, thus God showed up in darkness and judgment at Calvary where God treated Christ as the infidel (Mark 15:33). Isaiah 53:12 speaks of Christ bearing sin and being treated as a transgressor where it says, "because he poured out his soul to death and **was numbered with the transgressors;** yet he bore the sin of many, and makes intercession for the transgressors." Those who are blessed shall be called sons of God (Matthew 5:9). However, because Christ became a curse, He was cut off from God as one bearing disgrace. Psalm 22:1 captures Christ being forsaken and cut off where the Psalmist says, "**My God, My God, why have you forsaken me?** Why are you so far from saving me, from the words of my groaning?" Here, we see very clearly what it meant for Jesus to be cursed and crushed.

Jesus offered himself up as a sinless offering to God the Father so that God the Father could place all the sins of God's people on Jesus and curse Jesus as if He was the vile sinner. Upon that cross, Jesus suffered the wrath of God for His elect (John 10:11). All those in hell are the only ones who have an idea of what Jesus suffered on the cross and know what it is to be cursed. It wasn't the nails, the flogging, the crown of thorns, the punching, and beatings that Jesus was dreading. Even in the first century there were Christians who were killed by being hung on a tree and being lit on fire and they went to their deaths singing hymns of praise to God. Jesus wasn't dreading the physical beatings. No, it was the full cup of wrath and righteous anger of God toward sin that Jesus was dreading (Matthew 26:39). God didn't unload a rifle firing squad on His Son. God didn't unload a nuclear bomb on His Son. God didn't unload the full heat of the sun on His Son. No, God unloaded something far more terrifying than all of these combined. God unloaded His full unbridled wrath on His only begotten Son. Only the eternal Son of God could take the wrath from His Father. Only the Son of God could be presented as a sinless propitiation. Only the eternal Son of God could suffer the eternal punishment we deserve. Only the Son of God and Son of Man could propitiate the righteous anger of God toward man. In Romans 2:5 it says this about God's wrath towards man, "But because of your hard and unrepentant heart you are storing up wrath for yourself on the day of wrath when God's righteous judgment will be revealed." Therefore, we can and should know that every sin a man commits is like stacking up the wrath of God for that man on the day of judgment. For example, and since we know that hell is a furnace of fire, it would not be out of line to imagine that if a man heard the gospel and rejected the gospel at age 18, the Lord would be just in sentencing that man to suffer in 1 million degree Fahrenheit hellfire for all eternity. The next year, this same man at the age of 19 years hears the gospel again and neglects it and so the Lord would be just in sentencing that man to suffer 1 trillion degree Fahrenheit hellfire for all eternity as he is storing up more wrath for himself. The next year at the age of 20 years, this same man hears the gospel again and neglects it and so the Lord would be just in sentencing that man to suffer in 1 quintillion degree Fahrenheit hellfire for all eternity as he continues to store up wrath for himself on the day of judgment. Therefore, we should try and comprehend something of what Christ suffered as He took the full cup and unbridled wrath of God for the sins of His people. The example listed above of a man suffering 1 quintillion degree Fahrenheit hellfire for his sins falls woefully and pathetically short of describing the wrath of

God toward man's sin. God's wrath is far greater and far more terrible than we can imagine. Therefore, we should never forget and always seek to fathom the incomprehensible worth of Jesus Christ's substitutionary work on the cross for sinners. Not only did He suffer the wrath of God for one man, but He has also suffered the wrath of God for the sins of a great multitude of humanity as it says in Revelation 7:9, "After this I looked, and behold, a great multitude that no one could number, from every nation, from all tribes and peoples and languages, standing before the throne and before the Lamb, clothed in white robes, with palm branches in their hands". Romans 5:1 says, "Therefore, since we have been justified by faith, we have peace with God through our Lord Jesus Christ." Romans 8:1 says, "There is therefore now no condemnation for those who are in Christ Jesus." Every drop of wrath for those whom the Son of God died was satisfied and placated at Calvary. There is not one drop of wrath left for those in Christ Jesus. The wrathful cannon of God has been unloaded and emptied on the Son of God who loved us and gave Himself up for us (Galatians 2:20).

Upon the cross and before yielding up His spirit, Jesus said, "It is finished." "It is finished", is translated from *tetelestai* which means "to end", "to bring to conclusion", "to accomplish", "to fulfill", or "to finish". Please note that Jesus didn't say, "I am finished". No! He said, "It is finished." His perfect propitiating and sin bearing substitutionary work was complete. Jesus paid the full price for sin. Jesus took the whole wrath of God. There is not one sin of God's people that was not punished at Calvary. There is not one sin of God's people that the Father did not lay on His only begotten Son. God's justice was fully satisfied. In the secular sense, *tetelestai* was used to signify the full payment of a debt. The parchment on which the debt was recorded was stamped with the word *tetelestai* which meant the debt had been paid in full. Charles Spurgeon has said of this word, "an ocean of meaning in a drop of language, a mere drop. It would need all the other words that ever were spoken, or ever can be spoken, to explain this one word. It is altogether immeasurable. It is high; I cannot attain to it. It is deep; I cannot fathom it. It is finished is the most charming note in all of Calvary's music. The fire has passed upon the Lamb. He has borne the whole wrath that was due to His people. This is the royal dish of the feast of love." A.W. Pink has said of *tetelestai*, "Eternity will be needed to make manifest all that *tetelestai* contains." A.C. Gaebelein has said of *tetelestai*, "Never before and never after was ever spoken one word which contains and means so much. It is the shout of the mighty Victor. And who can measure the depths of this one word!".

For those who have come to Jesus Christ in repentance and faith, they are no longer enemies of God. There is no more punishment for sin to those who are in Christ Jesus. There was one perfect sacrifice that was able to propitiate the righteous anger and wrath of God toward sin and this propitiating sacrifice is never to be repeated (Hebrews 9:25-27). The author of Hebrews says this beautifully in Hebrews 9:28 where he says, "so Christ, having been offered once to bear the sins of many, will appear a second time, not to deal with sin but to save those who are eagerly waiting for Him."

The second word is *reconciliation. Reconciliation* is translated from *katallassó. Katallassó* is a compound word with *kata* being an intensifying prefix that means "to bring down to an exact point" and *allássō* means to "to change." Properly, this word means "to decisively change, as when two parties reconcile when coming to the same position" or "changing from enmity to friendship." In 2 Corinthians 5:19, Paul says, "That is, in Christ God was reconciling the world to himself, not counting their trespasses against them, and entrusting to us the message of reconciliation." In Romans 5:10–11, Paul says, "For if while we were enemies we were reconciled to God by the death of His Son, much more, now that we are reconciled, shall we be saved by his life. More than that, we also rejoice in God through our Lord Jesus Christ, through whom we have now received reconciliation." Additionally, in Colossians 1:21–22, Paul says, "And you, who once were alienated and hostile in mind, doing evil deeds, he has now reconciled in his body of flesh by his death, in order to present you holy and blameless and above reproach before him."

Even if God punished Christ for our sins, man would still not be reconciled and made right with God. Man would have his sins forgiven but not have the Godly righteousness needed to enter heaven. How we were reconciled to Christ speaks of the substitutionary atonement of Christ being punished in our place and Christ imputing His righteousness to us. In 2 Corinthians 5:21, it says, "For our sake he made him to be sin who knew no sin, so that in him we might become the righteousness of God." This is essentially saying that all of man's sin was laid on Christ and all of Christ's righteousness would be given to man for those who come to Jesus in repentance and faith. Romans 4:5 says, "And to the one who does not work but believes in him who justifies the ungodly, his faith is counted as righteousness." Romans 5:19 says something very similar where Paul says, "For as by the one man's disobedience the many were made sinners, so by the one man's obedience the many will be made righteous." The message of the gospel is the work of Christ's sacrifice for sin brought reconciliation between God and sinners. No more does man have to war against God. Man can now be at peace with God through the reconciliation of Christ who suffered for the sins of man and gives His righteousness to men who come to Him in repentance and faith.

Because of this reconciliation we have an all-new relationship with God and there is something quite amazing that occurs. There is a complete change in relationship which includes becoming children of God (1 John 3:1, Romans 8:16), having right standing with God (Romans 3:22–28), being adopted into the family of God (Ephesians 1:5), being given the Holy Spirit as a deposit guaranteeing our promise of glorification (2 Corinthians

1:22), being raised up with Christ and seated in the heavenly realm (Ephesians 2:6), being made coheirs with Christ (Romans 8:17), receiving Christ as our Great High Priest (Hebrews 4:14), receiving God as our Father (Romans 8:15), receiving Christ as our brother (Hebrews 2:11–12), and receiving eternal life (John 17:3). Thus, we see the reconciliation which gives us a new relationship with God.

The third word is *redemption* and comes from *apolutrósis,* which means "release effected by payment of ransom; redemption, deliverance" or, properly, "buying back from, repurchasing (winning back) what was previously forfeited (lost)." The *gospel* is the story of Jesus paying a ransom to buy back a people from the slave market of sin upon Calvary. The price was high. The price could not be paid with bulls, rams, goats, or birds. The price could not be paid with man's good works. The price could not be paid with circumcision. The cost to buy back Christ's bride was Jesus' shed blood on the cross. Paul speaks of how this redemption occurred in Galatians 3:13, where he says, "Christ redeemed us from the curse of the law by becoming a curse for us—for it is written, 'Cursed is everyone who is hanged on a tree.'" Peter also speaks of how this redemption occurred where he says in 1 Peter 1:18–19, "Knowing that you were ransomed from the futile ways inherited from your forefathers, not with perishable things such as silver or god, but with the precious blood of Christ, like that of a lamb without blemish or spot." So, not only did God propitiate the righteous anger of God and reconcile man to God and God to man, He also redeemed us and we are now slaves to Christ as Paul says in Romans 1:1.

The fourth word is *expiation*, which is translated from *aphiémi. Aphiémi* means to "send away; release." This word speaks of forgiveness of sins. Christ's death on the cross propitiated God's righteous anger, reconciled God to man, redeemed man from sin, death, and hell, and forgave man his sins. How forgiven can man be through Jesus' sacrificial death on the cross? Psalm 103:12

says, "As far as the east is from the west, so far has he removed our transgressions from us." Isaiah 1:18 speaks of this forgiveness of sins as well where it says, "Come now, let us reason together says the LORD: though your sins are like scarlet, they shall be as white as snow; though they are red like crimson, they shall become like wool." In Ephesians 1:7, Paul says, "In him we have redemption through his blood, the forgiveness of our trespasses, according to the riches of his grace." In Hebrews 8:12, where the Hebrew author is speaking of the New Covenant, he says this about the forgiveness of sins, "For I will forgive their wickedness and will remember their sins no more." John the Baptist said in John 1:29, Jesus was "the Lamb of God who takes away the sin of the world." Micah 7:19 says of how far He'll take our sins from us where he says, "You will cast all our sins into the depths of the sea." Therefore, the cross allowed for God to forgive sins, to remember them no more, to remove them from us as far as the east is from the west, to throw them in the depths of the sea, and to make us spotless. Not one sin will be charged to the account of those who are in Christ Jesus. Not one sin shall be brought up against God's chosen in judgment (Romans 8:33–34). What a wonder to hear the Savior say, "All is forgiven." What a wonder to hear the Savior say, "Never will I remember your sins again."

The fifth word is *regeneration,* which can also be called the new birth, being born again, or being born from above. In John 3, Jesus has a conversation with Nicodemus and He gives a definition of being born from above in John 3:5, where He says to Nicodemus, "Truly, truly, I say to you, unless one is born of water and the Spirit, he cannot enter the kingdom of God." This is a reference to Ezekiel 36:25–27, where the LORD says, "I will sprinkle clean water on you, and you shall be clean from all your uncleanness, and from all your idols I will cleanse you. And I will give you a new heart, and a new spirit I will put within you. And I will remove the heart of stone from your flesh and give you a heart of flesh. And I will put my Spirit within you, and cause you to walk in my statues and be careful to obey my rules." When the LORD is saying He will give a new heart and a new spirit, the LORD is essentially saying that He is going to completely change the intellect, emotion, and volition of man. The amazing work of the LORD to completely change man's nature, change man's intellect, change man's affections, and change man's volition to embrace Christ are truly stunning. Not only does God make this promise in Ezekiel 36, but He also makes it elsewhere in the Old Testament. The LORD promises an amazing salvific work in the New Covenant in verses such as Ezekiel 11:19–20, Jeremiah 24:7, Jeremiah 32:38–40, Ezekiel 36:24–27, and Jeremiah 31:33–34. Notice all of the monergistic actions that the LORD is going to perform in salvation. Look at the "they will be My people, and I will be their God" statements. Let's put all of these verses together in one statement to get an understanding of the awesome regenerating work of the LORD which, thus, enables man to repent and trust in Jesus Christ:

> And **I will give them one heart**, and **put a new spirit within them**. And **I will remove the heart of stone from their flesh** and **give them a heart of flesh**, so that they will walk in My statutes, and keep My ordinances and do them. Then they will be My people, and I shall be their God (Ezekiel 11:19–20). **I will also give them a heart to know Me**, for I am the LORD; and they will be My people, and I will be their God, for they will return to Me wholeheartedly (Jeremiah 24:7). They shall be My people, and I will be their God; and **I will give them one heart and one way**, so that they will fear Me always, for their own good and for the good of their children after them. **I will make an everlasting covenant** with them that **I will not turn away from them, to do them good**; and **I will put the fear of Me in their hearts**, so that they will not turn away from Me (Jeremiah 32:38–40). For **I will take you from the nations**,

> and gather you from all the lands; and **I will bring you into your own land.** Then **I will sprinkle clean water on you, and you will be clean; I will cleanse you from all your filthiness and from all your idols.** Moreover, **I will give you a new heart and put a new spirit within you**; and **I will remove the heart of stone from your flesh and give you a heart of flesh.** And **I will put my Spirit within you and bring it about that you walk in My statutes, and are careful and follow my ordinances** (Ezekiel 36:24–27). **For this is the covenant which I will make with the house of Israel** after those days, "Declares the LORD: "**I will put My law within them and write it on their heart**; and **I will be their God**, and they shall be My people. They will not teach again, each one his neighbor and each one his brother, saying, 'Know the LORD,' for they will all know Me, from the least of them to the greatest of them," declares the LORD, "For **I will forgive their wrongdoing**, and **their sin I will no longer remember"** (Jeremiah 31:33–34).

In John 3:8, Jesus says this with regard to the sovereign monergistic and transforming work of the Holy Spirit in regeneration, "The wind blows where it wishes, and you hear its sound, but you do not know where it comes from or where it goes. So it is with everyone who is born of the Spirit." Just as man can't start the wind, stop the wind, influence the wind, or control the wind, so it is with the Spirit. Man simply has no role in the regenerating work of the Holy Spirit and the Spirit operates freely and totally by Divine will. So it is with everyone born of the Spirit. Another way of restating this is, when the Spirit operates, you will know that there was work done by the Spirit. When the Spirit operates, it will be obvious that a work of God was done to change a man. When the Spirit operates, you will see a man with a new nature and new affections. The man will have a new intellect or rather, the mind of Christ (Jeremiah 31:33-34, 1 Corinthians 2:16). The man will have a new heart of flesh that responds to God's Word and bears fruit (Ezekiel 11:19, Matthew 13:23, Mark 4:20, Luke 8:15, 11:28). The man will be given a heart and a new spirit to know God (Ezekiel 11:20, 1 John 2:3). The man will have a heart with one way or rather, a dedicated and pure heart for God (Jeremiah 32:39, Matthew 5:8). The man will fear the Lord (Jeremiah 32:40, Matthew 10:28). The man will be cleansed from his sins and will have an ongoing work of God to cleanse him from sin (Ezekiel 36:25, 1 John 3:3). The man will have God's law written on his heart, or rather, will love God's law (Jeremiah 31:33-34, John 14:15, 1 John 5:3-5). You will not know where the Spirit came from or went, but it will be obvious that someone was operated on by the Spirit. Just as we can't control a tornado or a hurricane, so we cannot control the Spirit. Just as when there's been a tornado or a hurricane, we will see the evidence of it. So it is with the Spirit. When the Spirit operates, there will be evidence of regeneration and new life. This is not hypothetical. This is actual. A definition for *regeneration* would be able to be developed thoroughly by expositing (John 3:1–10). In the absence of being able to do so, a good definition of *regeneration* would be as follows: ***Regeneration* is the sovereign monergistic work of God the Holy Spirit in giving spiritual life to spiritually dead and sinful man so that man is enabled to repent and respond in saving faith (conversion) to Jesus Christ.** Jesus' propitiating, reconciliating, redeeming, and expiating work secures regeneration for those for whom He died.

The apostle Peter was certainly in awe of this new birth or regeneration when he says this in 1 Peter 1:3, "Blessed be the God and Father of our Lord Jesus Christ! According to his great mercy, he has caused us to be born again to a living hope through the resurrection of Jesus Christ from the dead." The apostle John marvels over this gift of regeneration where he says in 1 John 3:1, "See what kind of love the Father has given to us, that we should be called children of God; and so we are. The reason why the world does not know us is that it did not know him." Paul has a likewise astonishment over the second birth in Titus 3:4–6, where he says, "But when the kindness and love of God our Savior appeared, he saved us, not because of righteous things we had done, but because of his mercy. He saved us through the washing of rebirth and renewal by the Holy Spirit, whom he poured out on us generously through Jesus Christ our Savior."

The sixth word is *justification,* which is translated from *dikaioó. Dikaioó* means "made right, righteous," "conformed to a proper standard," or "made right, judicial approval." As we've mentioned above, Jesus took upon himself the sins of man and the punishment that we deserved and then imputed His perfect righteousness to those who would come to Him in repentance and faith. Therefore, because of this justification through faith, man is seen not only as having been forgiven his sins, but also being clothed in the righteousness of Christ (Galatians 3:26–27). Those who are in Christ can stand before God's throne of judgment with confidence that they will be judged as perfectly righteous in Christ (Romans 8:33-34).

The seventh word is *glorification.* Not only has Jesus satisfied the righteous anger of God to man, reconciled man to God and God to man, paid the ransom price to purchase man from the slavery of sin, death, and hell, forgiven man his sin, given man new birth or regeneration, and given man right standing with God, He has also promised that He will bring us to heaven to be with Him forever. In John 14:2–3, Jesus makes this promise to His disciples where He says, "In my Father's house are many rooms. If it were not so, would I have told you that I go to prepare a place for you? And if I go and prepare a place for you, I will come again and will take you to myself, that where I am you may be also." In Romans 8:29–30, Paul affirms the same thing where he says, "For those whom he foreknew he also predestined to be conformed to the image of his Son, in order that he might be the firstborn among many brothers. And those whom he predestined he also called, and those whom he called he also justified, and those whom he justified he also glorified." The author of Hebrews says something similar of those Old Testament saints who had faith in God where the author says in Hebrews 11:16, "Instead, they were longing for a better country—a heavenly one. Therefore, God is not ashamed to be called their God, for he has prepared a city for them." Again, Jesus in His High Priestly prayer, prays for the glorification of all believers to be with Him where He is where He prays this in John 17:24, "Father, I desire that they also, whom you have given me, may be with me where I am, to see my glory that you have given me because you loved me before the foundation of the world." Jesus' work on the cross has propitiated God's wrath for our sins, reconciled sinners to God, redeemed us from sin, death, and the devil, forgave us of all our sins, given us new birth, justified us and given us right standing before God, and promised glorification which guarantees God bringing us to heaven to live with Him forever.

The eight word is domination. Christ triumphed over sin, death, and the devil at Calvary. Colossians 2:13-15 captures this wondrously where Paul says, "And you, who were dead in your trespasses and the uncircumcision of your flesh, God made alive together with him, having forgiven us all our trespasses, by canceling the record of debt that stood against us with its legal demands. This he set aside, nailing it to the cross. He disarmed the rulers and authorities and put them to open shame, by triumphing over them in him. Paul says something similar in 1 Corinthians 15:54-57 where he says, "'Death has been swallowed up in victory.' 'Where, O death, is your victory? Where, O death, is your sting?' The sting of death is sin, and the power of sin is the law. But thanks be to God! He gives us the victory through our Lord Jesus Christ." Finally, just before Jesus' ascension into heaven and His great commission, He confirms his dominance by stating, "All authority in heaven and on earth has been given to me." 1 John 3:8 says this about Christ's dominating work, "The reason the Son of God appeared was to destroy the works of the devil." Christ has all Christ has all authority and has triumphed over His enemies. The end is written and Jesus will return as the conquering King to throw His enemies into the lake of fire (Revelation 20:14-15).

Not only does Jesus' work include His resurrection, but it also includes His ascension into heaven where it says in Luke 24:51, "While he blessed them, he parted from them and was carried up into heaven." Again, the author of Hebrews says this on Christ's ascension where he speaks of Christ's priesthood in Hebrews 8:1, "Now the point in what we are saying is this: we have such a high priest, one who is seated at the right hand of the throne of the Majesty in heaven". Peter says this of Christ's ascension in 1 Peter 3:22, "who has gone into heaven and is at the right hand of God, with angels, authorities, and powers having been subjected to him." Christ's work also includes His second coming. Jesus says of His second coming in Revelation 22:12-13, "Behold, I am coming soon, bringing recompense with me, to repay each one for what he has done. I am the Alpha and the Omega, the first and the last, the beginning and the end." Again, Jesus speaks of His second coming in Matthew 24:42-44, "Therefore keep watch, because you do not know on what day your Lord will come. But understand this: If the owner of the house had known at what time of night the thief was coming, he would have kept watch and would not have let his house be broken into. So you also must be ready, because the Son of Man will come at an hour when you do not expect him." Christ's work also includes His final judgment. Christ will come back to bring all of His own to be with Him, but He will also judge the world in righteousness and administer His wrath. In Matthew 25:31-34,41 it says this of God's final judgment, "When the Son of Man comes in his glory, and all the angels with him, then he will sit on his glorious throne. Before him will be gathered all the nations, and he will separate people one from another as a shepherd separates the sheep from the goats.

And he will place the sheep on his right, but the goats on the left. Then the King will say to those on his right, 'Come, you who are blessed by my Father, inherit the kingdom prepared for you from the foundation of the world... Then he will say to those on his left, 'Depart from me, you cursed, into the eternal fire prepared for the devil and his angels.'"

For those that would contend that one can lose their salvation or lose saving faith must answer several questions regarding the propitiating, reconciling, expiating, redeeming, regenerating, justifying, glorifying, and dominating work of Jesus. This list is not exhaustive, but only contains a small amount of disturbing conclusions one must make if man can lose salvation or saving faith:

- If someone has been justified by faith but can lose their salvation, did Jesus' work on the cross partially or fully propitiate the wrath of God on that person's behalf (1 Peter 2:24, Hebrews 7:27)? Did Jesus' work on the cross partially redeem us or fully redeem us (Hebrews 9:12)? Did Jesus' work on the cross forgive all of our past, present, and future sins or partially forgive our sins (Hebrews 8:12)?
- If one has been justified by faith and Jesus has eternally redeemed that one (Hebrews 9:12), what sin was not propitiated and paid for that caused Jesus to lose one of His own? What price did the devil pay to get that person back into the dominion of darkness? How did someone lose saving faith when they were eternally redeemed and paid for with the precious blood of Jesus Christ (1 Peter 1:18-19)? What price is higher than the sacrificial blood of Christ to ransom one from the kingdom of light back to the dominion of darkness (Colossians 1:13-14)?
- Since Jesus died for all the sins of His people (John 10:15, Isaiah 53:11, Hebrews 10:10), what sin did God the Father

forget to lay on Christ? God the Father would have sinned by not placing all of the sins of God's people on His Son as His Son would not have fully paid for all the sins of God's people and man would still be left with sin that would need to be punished. Additionally, Jesus would have sinned and lied on the cross when He said, "tetelestai" or "it is finished" if the price for sin was not fully paid for (John 19:30).

- If one has been justified by faith but can lose their salvation, then this means that Jesus has failed and sinned as our Great High Priest as Hebrews 7:25 says He forever lives to make intercession for His people. If we were justified and legally declared righteous before the throne of God, then Jesus would have failed in His intercession if one can lose their right standing and justification before God.
- Since Jesus said He would not lose any the Father had given Him and no one can snatch God's people out of the Father's hand (John 6:37-40, 10:28-29), Jesus would be a sinner if He didn't do the Father's will and eternally lost someone whom He justified. Therefore, the Father would also be a sinner if He chose a savior who justified, reconciled, redeemed sinners, and made them children of God but then eternally lost those He had formerly justified, reconciled, redeemed, and made children of God. Additionally, as Jesus is the author and perfector of our faith (Hebrews 12:2), Jesus would be a sinner as the saving faith He authored was a faith that failed.
- If Jesus has given us new birth (John 3:1-10) of an imperishable seed (1 Peter 1:23), how is it that someone could lose their salvation as the new birth is imperishable? How could one become a child of God through the new birth (John 3:1-10) but then become a son of disobedience again (Ephesians 2:3) as this person has been given eternal and imperishable life?

- When we are justified by faith, we are given the Holy Spirit and sealed with the Holy Spirit as a deposit guaranteeing what is to come (2 Corinthians 1:20-22). At what point does God take the Holy Spirit away from His children and take away their justification or right standing before Him and transfer His children from the kingdom of light back to the dominion of darkness? At what point does the guaranteed deposit of the Holy Spirit become a fake and broken promise where the Holy Spirit leaves a child of God?

In just a few short points, we can see that those who would argue that one can lose their salvation indirectly attack the propitiating, redeeming, expiating, reconciling, justifying, regenerating, glorifying, and dominating work of Jesus. Additionally, not only do they indirectly attack the work of Christ, but they also attack the attributes of God.

Therefore, we can see what a glorious gospel this is! What great news this is from heaven! Jesus needed to be born of a virgin (Matthew 1:23), so we could be born of God (John 3:3, 7). Jesus needed to be born a man (Matthew 1:23), so we could be born again (John 3:3, 7). Jesus needed to be the Son of Man (Luke 19:10), so that we could be sons of God (1 John 3:1). Jesus needed to be rejected by God (Isaiah 53:3), so we could be resurrected by God (1 Corinthians 15:52). Jesus needed to be despised (Isaiah 53:3), so we would not be damned (Romans 1:18–32). Jesus needed to be crushed by God (Isaiah 53:5, 10), so we would not be cursed by God (Galations 3:13). Jesus needed to be crucified (Isaiah 53:5), so we could be justified (Romans 3:24). Jesus needed to be forsaken (Matthew 27:46), so we could be forgiven (Isaiah 53:12). Jesus suffered (Isaiah 53:11), so we would be saved (Matthew 1:23). Jesus needed to suffer the wrath of God (Isaiah 53:10), so He could show forth the riches of God (Ephesians 2:7). Jesus needed to be resurrected (Isaiah 53:11), so we could be perfected (Hebrews 10:14). Jesus needed to bear reproach (Hebrews 13:13), so we could be redeemed (Romans 3:24). Jesus offered himself as a sacrifice (Hebrews 9:26), so we could be saints (2 Corinthians 5:21). This is the gospel of the person and work of Jesus Christ, the Son of the Living God. Thus, we see that the gospel is about **the person of Jesus which is He is the Christ, the Creator of the universe, the promised Jewish Messiah, the only begotten Son of the Living God which makes Him God and equal with God the Father and God the Holy Spirit who was born of a virgin and became man and is, thus, truly God and truly man.** We also have learned about the work of Jesus. Thus, we see **the work of Jesus is that Jesus lived a sinless life and fulfilled all righteousness found in the law and prophets and declared Himself to be the Christ, the only begotten Son of the Living God through His teaching, which was attested to by His miracles. Jesus offered himself as a spotless and blameless sacrifice for sin to propitiate the righteous anger of God by taking all the sins of God's people and, thus, the full wrath of God that was due to man. His sacrifice propitiated the righteous anger of God and reconciled and brought peace from man to God and God to man. His substitutionary sacrifice and death also redeemed sinful man to Holy God by forgiving man's sin and imputing Christ's righteousness to man. Jesus was resurrected from the dead on the third day by His own power, by God the Father and God the Holy Spirit, which affirmed His person, His teachings, and salvific work for sinners. He ascended to the right hand of the Father and is empowered with all authority to bring about the plan of salvation for all His people by causing them to be born again and justified by His grace. He will also return to bring all of His own to heaven with Him to be glorified while also judging and condemning Satan, demons, and sinful man.**

As Paul concludes verse four, he concludes by saying, "Jesus Christ our Lord." Jesus is His saving name which means "Jehovah saves." Matthew 1:21 says, "You shall call his name Jesus, for he will save his people from their sins." As we learned earlier, we are being saved by God from God. We are being saved by Jesus Christ who is true God and true Man from the wrath of God against sin. Only God could save us from Himself. Only God could save us from His wrath. The name Christ, as we learned earlier, is "the Anointed One." Jesus is the Anointed One in the power of the Holy Spirit (Luke 4:18–21). Jesus was anointed by the Holy Spirit to carry out his salvific work here on earth. Jesus is the Christ. The title Lord is His sovereign name. The title *Lord* means "master" and denotes someone one who has absolute ownership rights. Jesus said in Matthew 28:18, "All authority in heaven and on earth has been given to me." Paul affirms this in Ephesians 1:20–21 where he says, "He exerted when he raised Christ from the dead and seated him at his right hand in the heavenly realms, far above all rule and authority, power and dominion, and every name that is invoked, not only in the present age but also in the one to come." Jesus possesses all authority to bring about the plan of salvation for all His people for His glory!

The Subjective Response to the Person and Work of Jesus Christ

Romans 1:5—through whom we have received grace and apostleship to bring about the obedience of faith for the sake of his name among all the nations

Paul is seeking to remind his listeners that all saving grace comes through Jesus. Likewise, Paul seeks to remind the Romans that all ministry comes through the Lord Jesus Christ who is the head of the church (Ephesians 1:22) and has given His church gifts such as apostles, prophets, evangelists, shepherds, and teachers (Ephesians 4:11). Grace has all come through the Lord Jesus Christ. All saving grace, all ministerial grace, all spiritual grace, all heavenly grace comes through the Lord Jesus Christ. This should draw us to the undeniable assertion that Jesus is the very center and circumference of the gospel. Jesus is the very sum and substance of the gospel. Jesus is the priority and preeminence of the gospel. The gospel all centers on the person and work of Jesus Christ.

We have discussed the objective facts of the person and work of Jesus and now Paul transitions to the subjective response to the person and work of Jesus Christ. If you know all the objective truth about Christ, what good does that do you if you don't know how to respond to Christ? If you know the objective truth about Jesus' person and work, how do you obtain the benefits of what Jesus did? Unfortunately, this is where many churches have lost it. Some churches would teach that you respond to the person and work of Jesus by coming to Him in faith, but you must also bring good works to inherit salvation. Some churches would teach that you respond to the person and work of Jesus by being baptized to inherit salvation. Some churches would teach that you respond to the person and work of Jesus by mental assent or believing and agreeing to the objective facts of Jesus, but there is no need to repent to inherit salvation. Some churches would teach that you respond to the person and work of Jesus by becoming a church member to inherit salvation. Some churches would teach that you respond to the person and work of Jesus by praying the sinner's prayer to inherit salvation. Some churches would teach that if you responded to an altar call, you have inherited salvation. Since there is much confusion in Christianity, we will take our time to thoroughly understand Christ's gospel call to follow Him in saving faith.

In another book, I wrote on the call to saving faith and included HARD and EASY verses regarding salvation. In dealing with this subjective response to the objective facts of the person and work of Jesus, it is helpful to categorize salvation verses to see the complexity of responding to the person and work of Jesus and trying to understand the subjective response to Jesus as it relates to salvation. The Bible commands that we believe. The Bible commands that we repent. The Bible commands that we have faith in Jesus Christ. The Bible tells us to call on the name of the Lord. The Bible sets forth hard conditions on what it means to be Christ's disciple or to come to Him in saving faith. I will pair them in groups of three to compare the "EASY," "HARD," and "VERY HARD" sayings. I will also highlight terms such as *believe, repent, call,* and *faith.*

- EASY—John 1:12–13—Yet to all who did receive him, to those who **believed** in his name he gave the right to become children of God—children born not of natural descent, nor of human decision or a husband's will, but born of God
- HARD—Matthew 11:20—Then Jesus began to denounce the cities in which most of his miracles had been performed, because they did not **repent**
- VERY HARD—Matthew 10:37–39—Whoever loves father or mother more than me is not worthy of me, and whoever loves son or daughter more than me is not worthy of me. And whoever does not take his cross and follow me is not worthy of me. Whoever finds his life will lose it, and whoever loses his life for my sake will find it.
- EASY—John 3:16—For God so loved the world that he gave his one and only Son, that whoever believes in him shall not perish but have eternal life.
- HARD—Matthew 3:1–2—In those days John the Baptist came, preaching in the wilderness of Judea and saying, "**Repent**, for the kingdom of heaven has come near."
- VERY HARD—Matthew 16:24–26—Then Jesus told his disciples, "If anyone would come after me, let him deny himself and take up his cross and follow me. For whoever would save his life will lose it, but whoever loses his life

for my sake will find it. For what will it profit a man if he gains the whole world and forfeits his soul? Or what shall a man give in return for his soul?"

- EASY—John 3:18—Whoever **believes** in him is not condemned, but whoever does not believe stands condemned already because they have not believed in the name of God's one and only Son.
- HARD—Matthew 3:8-9—Produce fruit in keeping with **repentance**. And do not presume to say to yourselves, 'We have Abraham as our father,' for I tell you, God is able from these stones to raise up children for Abraham.
- VERY HARD—Mark 8:34–37—And calling the crowd to him with his disciples, he said to them, "If anyone would come after me, let him deny himself and take up his cross and follow me. For whoever would save his life will lose it, but whoever loses his life for my sake and the gospel's will save it. For what does it profit a man to gain the whole world and forfeit his soul? For what can a man give in return for his soul?
- EASY—John 3:36—Whoever **believes** in the Son has eternal life, but whoever rejects the Son will not see life, for God's wrath remains on them.
- HARD—Matthew 4:17—From that time on Jesus began to preach, "**Repent**, for the kingdom of heaven has come near."
- VERY HARD—Luke 9:23–25—And he said to all, "If anyone would come after me, let him deny himself and take up his cross daily and follow me. For whoever would save his life will lose it, but whoever loses his life for my sake will save it. For what does it profit a man if he gains the whole world and loses or forfeits himself?"

- EASY—John 5:24—Very truly I tell you, whoever hears my word and believes him who sent me has eternal life and will not be judged but has crossed over from death to life.
- HARD—Matthew 11:21–24— "Woe to you, Chorazin! Woe to you, Bethsaida! For if the miracles that were performed in you had been performed in Tyre and Sidon, they would have **repented** long ago in sackcloth and ashes. But I tell you, it will be more bearable for Tyre and Sidon on the day of judgment than for you."
- VERY HARD—Luke 14:26–27, 33—"If anyone comes to me and does not hate his own father and mother and wife and children and brothers and sisters, yes, and even his own life, he cannot be my disciple. Whoever does not bear his own cross and come after me cannot be my disciple. So therefore, any one of you who does not renounce all that he has cannot be my disciple."
- EASY—John 6:29—The work of God is this: to believe in the one he has sent
- HARD—Mark 1:4–5—And so John the Baptist appeared in the wilderness, preaching a baptism of **repentance** for the forgiveness of sins. The whole Judean countryside and all the people of Jerusalem went out to him. Confessing their sins, they were baptized by him in the Jordan River.
- VERY HARD—John 12:24–26—Truly, truly, I say to you, unless a grain of wheat falls into the earth and dies, it remains alone; but if it dies, it bears much fruit. Whoever loves his life loses it, and whoever hates his life in this world will keep it for eternal life. If anyone serves me, he must follow me; and where I am, there will my servant be also. If anyone serves me, the Father will honor him.
- EASY—John 7:38—Whoever **believes** in me, as Scripture has said, rivers of living water will flow from within them.
- HARD—Luke 13:3—I tell you, no! But unless you **repent**, you too will all perish.

- VERY HARD—Philippians 3:7–9—But whatever gain I had, I counted as loss for the sake of Christ. Indeed, I count everything as loss because of the surpassing worth of knowing Christ Jesus my Lord. For his sake I have suffered the loss of all things and count them as rubbish, in order that I may gain Christ and be found in him, not having a righteousness of my own that comes from the law, but that which comes through faith in Christ, the righteousness from God that depends on faith.
- EASY—John 6:47—Very truly I tell you, the one who **believes** has eternal life.
- HARD - Luke 13:5 – I tell you, no! But unless you **repent**, you too will all perish.
- VERY HARD—Matthew 10:37–39—Whoever loves father or mother more than me is not worthy of me, and whoever loves son or daughter more than me is not worthy of me. And whoever does not take his cross and follow me is not worthy of me. Whoever finds his life will lose it, and whoever loses his life for my sake will find it.
- EASY—John 11:25–26—Jesus said to her, “I am the resurrection and the life. The one who **believes** in me will live, even though they die; and whoever lives by **believing** in me will never die.”
- HARD—Mark 1:15—“The time has come,” he said. “The kingdom of God has come near. **Repent** and **believe** the good news!”
- VERY HARD—Matthew 16:24–26—Then Jesus told his disciples, “If anyone would come after me, let him deny himself and take up his cross and follow me. For whoever would save his life will lose it, but whoever loses his life for my sake will find it. For what will it profit a man if he gains the whole world and forfeits his soul? Or what shall a man give in return for his soul?”

- EASY—John 12:36—**Believe** in the light while you have the light, so that you may become children of light.
- HARD—Luke 3:3—He went into all the country around the Jordan, preaching a baptism of **repentance** for the forgiveness of sins.
- VERY HARD—Mark 8:34–37—And calling the crowd to him with his disciples, he said to them, "If anyone would come after me, let him deny himself and take up his cross and follow me. For whoever would save his life will lose it, but whoever loses his life for my sake and the gospel's will save it. For what does it profit a man to gain the whole world and forfeit his soul? For what can a man give in return for his soul?"
- EASY—John 12:46—I have come into the world as a light, so that no one who **believes** in me should stay in darkness.
- HARD—Luke 3:8—Produce fruit in keeping with **repentance**. And do not begin to say to yourselves, "We have Abraham as our father. For I tell you that out of these stones God can raise up children for Abraham."
- VERY HARD—Luke 9:23–25—And he said to all, "If anyone would come after me, let him deny himself and take up his cross daily and follow me. For whoever would save his life will lose it, but whoever loses his life for my sake will save it. For what does it profit a man if he gains the whole world and loses or forfeits himself?"
- EASY—Acts 10:43—All the prophets testify about him that everyone who **believes** in him receives forgiveness of sins through his name.
- HARD—Luke 10:13— "Woe to you, Chorazin! Woe to you, Bethsaida! For if the miracles that were performed in you had been performed in Tyre and Sidon, they would have **repented** long ago, sitting in sackcloth and ashes."
- VERY HARD—Luke 14:26–27, 33—"If anyone comes to me and does not hate his own father and mother and wife

and children and brothers and sisters, yes, and even his own life, he cannot be my disciple. Whoever does not bear his own cross and come after me cannot be my disciple. So therefore, any one of you who does not renounce all that he has cannot be my disciple."

- EASY—Romans 3:22—This righteousness is given through **faith** in Jesus Christ to all who **believe**.
- HARD—Acts 17:30 – In the past God overlooked such ignorance, but now he commands all people everywhere to **repent**.
- VERY HARD—John 12:24–26—Truly, truly, I say to you, unless a grain of wheat falls into the earth and dies, it remains alone; but if it dies, it bears much fruit. Whoever loves his life loses it, and whoever hates his life in this world will keep it for eternal life. If anyone serves me, he must follow me; and where I am, there will my servant be also. If anyone serves me, the Father will honor him.
- EASY—Romans 4:23–24—The words "it was credited to him" were written not for him alone, but also for us to whom God will credit righteous—for us who **believe** in him who raised Jesus our Lord from the dead.
- HARD—Acts 20:21—I have declared to both Jews and Greeks that they must turn to God in **repentance** and have **faith** in our Lord Jesus.
- VERY HARD—Philippians 3:7–9—But whatever gain I had, I counted as loss for the sake of Christ. Indeed, I count everything as loss because of the surpassing worth of knowing Christ Jesus my Lord. For his sake I have suffered the loss of all things and count them as rubbish, in order that I may gain Christ and be found in him, not having a righteousness of my own that comes from the law, but that which comes through faith in Christ, the righteousness from God that depends on faith.

- EASY—Romans 10:4—Christ is the culmination of the law so that there may be righteousness for everyone who **believes.**
- HARD—Romans 2:4—God's kindness is intended to lead you to **repentance.**
- VERY HARD—Matthew 10:37–39—Whoever loves father or mother more than me is not worthy of me, and whoever loves son or daughter more than me is not worthy of me. And whoever does not take his cross and follow me is not worthy of me. Whoever finds his life will lose it, and whoever loses his life for my sake will find it.
- EASY—Romans 10:9–11—If you declare with your mouth, "Jesus is Lord," and **believe** in your heart that God raised him from the dead, you will be saved. For it is with your heart that you **believe** and are justified, and it is with your mouth that you profess your **faith** and are saved. As Scripture says, "Anyone who **believes** in him will never be put to shame."
- HARD—Luke 15:7—I tell you that in the same way there will be more rejoicing in heaven over one sinner who **repents** than over ninety-nine righteous persons who do not need to **repent.**
- VERY HARD—Matthew 16:24–26—Then Jesus told his disciples, "If anyone would come after me, let him deny himself and take up his cross and follow me. For whoever would save his life will lose it, but whoever loses his life for my sake will find it. For what will it profit a man if he gains the whole world and forfeits his soul? Or what shall a man give in return for his soul?"
- EASY—Romans 10:17—Consequently, **faith** comes from hearing the message, and the message is heard through the word about Christ.

- HARD—Luke 15:10—In the same way, I tell you, there is rejoicing in the presence of the angels of God over one sinner who **repents**.
- VERY HARD—Mark 8:34–37—And calling the crowd to him with his disciples, he said to them, "If anyone would come after me, let him deny himself and take up his cross and follow me. For whoever would save his life will lose it, but whoever loses his life for my sake and the gospel's will save it. For what does it profit a man to gain the whole world and forfeit his soul? For what can a man give in return for his soul?"
- EASY—Romans 1:17—For in it the righteousness of God is revealed from **faith** for **faith**, as it is written, "The righteous shall live by **faith**."
- HARD—Luke 24:47—and **repentance** for the forgiveness of sins will be preached in his name to all nations, beginning at Jerusalem
- VERY HARD—Luke 9:23–25—And he said to all, "If anyone would come after me, let him deny himself and take up his cross daily and follow me. For whoever would save his life will lose it, but whoever loses his life for my sake will save it. For what does it profit a man if he gains the whole world and loses or forfeits himself?"
- EASY—Romans 3:22—the righteousness of God through **faith** in Jesus Christ for all who **believe**. For there is no distinction
- HARD—Acts 2:38—Peter replied, "**Repent** and be baptized, every one of you, in the name of Jesus Christ for the forgiveness of your sins. And you will receive the gift of the Holy Spirit."
- VERY HARD—Luke 14:26–27, 33—"If anyone comes to me and does not hate his own father and mother and wife and children and brothers and sisters, yes, and even his own life, he cannot be my disciple. Whoever does not bear

his own cross and come after me cannot be my disciple. So therefore, any one of you who does not renounce all that he has cannot be my disciple."

- EASY—Romans 3:25—whom God put forward as a propitiation by his blood, to be received by **faith**. This was to show God's righteousness, because in his divine forbearance he had passed over former sins
- HARD—Acts 3:19—**Repent**, then, and turn to God, so that your sins may be wiped out, that times of refreshing may come from the Lord.
- VERY HARD—John 12:24–26—Truly, truly, I say to you, unless a grain of wheat falls into the earth and dies, it remains alone; but if it dies, it bears much fruit. Whoever loves his life loses it, and whoever hates his life in this world will keep it for eternal life. If anyone serves me, he must follow me; and where I am, there will my servant be also. If anyone serves me, the Father will honor him.
- EASY—Romans 3:26—it was to show his righteousness at the present time, so that he might be just and the justifier of the one who has **faith** in Jesus
- HARD—Acts 5:31—God exalted him to his own right hand as Prince and Savior that he might bring Israel to **repentance** and forgive their sins.
- VERY HARD—Philippians 3:7–9—But whatever gain I had, I counted as loss for the sake of Christ. Indeed, I count everything as loss because of the surpassing worth of knowing Christ Jesus my Lord. For his sake I have suffered the loss of all things and count them as rubbish, in order that I may gain Christ and be found in him, not having a righteousness of my own that comes from the law, but that which comes through faith in Christ, the righteousness from God that depends on faith.
- EASY—Romans 3:28—for we hold that one is justified by **faith** apart from works of the law

- HARD—Acts 11:18—When they heard this, they had no further objections and praised God, saying, "So then, even to Gentiles God has granted **repentance** that leads to life."
- VERY HARD—Matthew 10:37–39—Whoever loves father or mother more than me is not worthy of me, and whoever loves son or daughter more than me is not worthy of me. And whoever does not take his cross and follow me is not worthy of me. Whoever finds his life will lose it, and whoever loses his life for my sake will find it.
- EASY—Acts 2:21—And it shall come to pass that everyone who **calls upon the name** of the Lord shall be saved.
- HARD—2 Corinthians 7:10—Godly sorrow brings **repentance** that leads to salvation and leaves no regret, but worldly sorrow brings death.
- VERY HARD—Matthew 16:24–26—Then Jesus told his disciples, "If anyone would come after me, let him deny himself and take up his cross and follow me. For whoever would save his life will lose it, but whoever loses his life for my sake will find it. For what will it profit a man if he gains the whole world and forfeits his soul? Or what shall a man give in return for his soul?"
- EASY—Romans 10:13—For "everyone who **calls on the name** of the Lord will be saved."
- HARD—Acts 14:15—Friends, why are you doing this? We too are only human, like you. We are bringing you good news, tell you **to turn** from these worthless things to the living God.
- VERY HARD—Mark 8:34–37—And calling the crowd to him with his disciples, he said to them, "If anyone would come after me, let him deny himself and take up his cross and follow me. For whoever would save his life will lose it, but whoever loses his life for my sake and the gospel's will save it. For what does it profit a man to gain the whole

world and forfeit his soul? For what can a man give in return for his soul?"

- EASY—Ephesians 2:8—For by grace you have been saved through **faith**. And this is not your own doing; it is the gift of God.
- HARD—Luke 5:32—I have not come to call the righteous but sinners to **repentance.**
- VERY HARD—Luke 9:23–25—And he said to all, "If anyone would come after me, let him deny himself and take up his cross daily and follow me. For whoever would save his life will lose it, but whoever loses his life for my sake will save it. For what does it profit a man if he gains the whole world and loses or forfeits himself?"
- EASY—Romans 5:1—Therefore, since we have been justified by **faith**, we have peace with God through our Lord Jesus Christ.
- HARD—Matthew 19:21—Jesus said to him, "If you would be perfect, **go, sell what you possess** and **give to the poor**, and you will have treasure in heaven; and come, follow me."
- VERY HARD—Luke 14:26–27, 33—"If anyone comes to me and does not hate his own father and mother and wife and children and brothers and sisters, yes, and even his own life, he cannot be my disciple. Whoever does not bear his own cross and come after me cannot be my disciple. So therefore, any one of you who does not renounce all that he has cannot be my disciple."
- EASY—Romans 3:30—since God is one—who will justify the circumcised by **faith** and the uncircumcised through **faith**.
- HARD—Mark 10:17–21—Looking at him, Jesus showed love to him and said to him, "One thing you lack: **go and sell all you possess and give to the poor**, and you will have treasure in heaven; and come, follow me."

- VERY HARD—John 12:24–26—Truly, truly, I say to you, unless a grain of wheat falls into the earth and dies, it remains alone; but if it dies, it bears much fruit. Whoever loves his life loses it, and whoever hates his life in this world will keep it for eternal life. If anyone serves me, he must follow me; and where I am, there will my servant be also. If anyone serves me, the Father will honor him.

- EASY—Romans 4:5—And to the one who does not work but believes in him who justifies the ungodly, his **faith** is counted as righteousness
- HARD—Luke 18:22—When Jesus heard this, he said to him, "One thing you still lack. **Sell all you have and distribute to the poor**, and you will have treasure in heaven; and come, follow me."
- VERY HARD—Philippians 3:7–9—But whatever gain I had, I counted as loss for the sake of Christ. Indeed, I count everything as loss because of the surpassing worth of knowing Christ Jesus my Lord. For his sake I have suffered the loss of all things and count them as rubbish, in order that I may gain Christ and be found in him, not having a righteousness of my own that comes from the law, but that which comes through faith in Christ, the righteousness from God that depends on faith.

We can sometimes think of salvation as being easy to understand. However, as we've seen above, we're dealing with many verses that describe the subjective response to the person and work of Jesus. For example, what does it mean to believe? What does it mean to have faith? What does it mean to repent? What does it mean to call on the name of the Lord? What is being said in the "VERY HARD" verses? As we seek to understand the subjective response to Christ's person and work, let us understand the importance of properly understanding the call or response to saving faith as all the benefits of Jesus' person and work are of no benefit unless we respond according to God's terms, which is that which "bring about the obedience of faith." We will look at Luke 14:26–33 to help us understand believing, repentance, calling on the Lord's name, faith, and the conditions the Bible defines in coming to and following after Jesus in saving faith (6).

Luke 14:26—If anyone comes to me and does not hate his own father and mother and wife and children and brothers and sisters, yes, and even his own life, he cannot be my disciple.

Jesus never hid His cost of discipleship and the demand that was required to follow Him. Jesus never hid His call of believing in Him in the fine print. His call to being a disciple was always front-loaded in His messages. In fact, Jesus was never seeking to make following Him easy. If you look at Jesus' call to discipleship, you could never accuse Him of trying to build a large crowd with His message or terms of entering the kingdom. Jesus calls for cross bearers and not merely cross wearers. We will either be abandoned to Christ or abandoned by Christ. We cannot have Christ on our own terms. There is no crown without first bearing a cross. There is no religion without repentance. There is no blessedness without brokenness. There is no salvation without sacrifice. There is no church without commitment. There is no heaven without holiness. Jesus will now turn to the large crowd and set forth His terms of discipleship, or rather, entrance into the kingdom of God. Let's pay close attention. The One who issues the call sets the terms.

Jesus starts by evangelistically inviting all people to come to Him. Just as He said in John 7:37, "On the last and greatest day of the feast, Jesus stood and cried out, saying, 'If anyone is thirsty, let him come to me and drink.'" Jesus, the narrow gate (Matthew 7:13–14, John 10:7, 9), is explaining how to enter through the narrow gate, or rather, enter the kingdom of God. However, everyone is required to enter into the kingdom of God on Jesus' terms. It's important to notice the word *disciple*. *Disciple* is translated from the word *mathétés*. *Mathétés* means "a learner, a disciple, and pupil." Properly, this is a learner or follower of Christ who learns the doctrines of Scripture and the lifestyle required to follow Christ. Jesus is saying that if you want to be a follower, a believer, or a disciple of His, then they must enter the kingdom of God on His terms.

First, Jesus is going to begin with relationships. Jesus' words would certainly shock people when He said, "If anyone comes to Me and does not hate his own father, mother, wife, children, brothers, and yes, even his own life, he cannot be My disciple." Let's note that Jesus is not calling for His disciples to hate anyone. Jesus is not calling us to suddenly turn on those we love and have an evil disposition toward those that are closest to us. Cross-referencing this verse helps to draw out what Jesus is saying. In Matthew 10:37, Jesus says, "The one who loves father or mother more than Me is not worthy of Me; and the one who loves son or daughter more than Me is not worthy of Me." In Matthew 5:43, Jesus says, "You have heard that it was said, 'Love your neighbor and hate your enemy.' But I tell you, love your enemies and pray for those who persecute you, that you may be children of Your Father in heaven. He causes his sun to rise on the evil and the good, and sends rain on the righteous and the unrighteous." God also says in the Fourth Commandment, "Honor your father and your mother." Additionally, Jesus, when being tested, states in Matthew 22:39 that the second greatest commandment is "Love your neighbor as yourself." It is clear that Jesus is not calling for hate. Jesus commands that we love our enemies, love our neighbor as ourselves, and honor our father and mother.

What Jesus is doing is showing contrast or preference. He uses this same method of showing preference in Matthew 6:24, where He says, "No one can serve two masters. Either you will hate one and love the other, or you will be devoted to the one and despise the other. You cannot serve both God and money." As in

Jesus' example of serving both God and money, Jesus is simply saying that both God and money cannot have the same top priority as you will ultimately love one more than the other. Jesus is purposefully creating extremes. He is pitting one's affections of one's most loved ones against one's affections to Himself. Jesus is saying is that if you want to be His disciple then your affections for Him must be far greater than the love for those in your closest concentric circle. Your affections must be far greater for Him that, by comparison, it seems as hate toward others. For example, if Christ were to call you to leave a church that taught a false gospel, but you had other family members that were still in the church that taught the false gospel and your family wanted you to stay, you would leave the church that taught the false gospel because your affections toward Jesus far exceed those of your family.

Jesus starts with the people that mean most to you. Jesus starts with your father, mother, wife, and children. **Christ is calling for your total allegiance and affection. Your allegiance and affections toward Him must be far greater than the affections and allegiance you have with the people that are most important to you**. Jesus makes a shocking statement at the end of this verse. Jesus says, "*ou dynatai einai mou mathetes.*" *Ou* means "no" or "not." *Dynatei* means "to be able" or "to have power." *Einai* means "to be." *Mou* is a personal pronoun and means "I." *Mathetes* is a disciple or learner, specifically, a follower or learner of Christ. So, let's put this statement together and understand what Jesus is saying in a few different ways:

- If anyone comes to Me and has greater affections for his father, mother, wife, children, or brothers and sisters, he is not able to be My disciple.
- If anyone comes to Me and sees his father, mother, wife, children, or brothers as more important than Me, he has no ability to be My disciple.

- If anyone comes to Me and finds any relationship more important than their relationship with Me, they are not one of My disciples.
- If anyone comes to Me and has a relationship or allegiance to anyone that is more important to them than Me, you are not in My kingdom.

It's also important to note here that Jesus is not saying, you may be able to be My disciple. No, He is stating that you cannot be His disciple. *May* is a word of permission. *Cannot* is a word of ability. Jesus is requiring absolute allegiance and affection over every relationship you have on this earth. When it comes down to listening to your mother and father or listening to Jesus, which one will it be? Do you have more affections and allegiance to your wife or Jesus? Jesus is asking whether you've done your searching and seeking and found Him to be of greater importance than your closest relationship. If not, you're simply not a disciple of His and you've made an eternally fatal assessment.

Note that in Matthew 10:37, instead of *hate* he says, *worthy*. *Axios* can also mean "worthy, worthy of, deserving, or suitable." Another way of describing this word is to weigh in, assigning the matching value or *worth-to-worth* (i.e., as the assessment in keeping with how something "weighs in" on God's balance scale of truth). Jesus says that if you love anyone in this world more than Him, you're simply just not worthy to be His disciple.

Jesus really starts intensifying His call as He lays down another term of becoming His disciple. He says that we must hate our own life. Jesus demands that you evaluate your own life and determine whether submitting and committing your life to Him is more valuable than keeping it. Jesus was never shy about calling people to evaluate their lives and asking them to determine if their current relationships, personal interests, personal hobbies, personal sins, or personal belongings were more important than Him. To further clarify Jesus' call of hating one's own life, we can look to other portions of Scripture to understand this call of "hating yourself" as He is not advocating suicide, self-mutilation, or anything of this nature.

Jesus' calls to discipleship or saving faith often included a command to deny yourself which could also be understood as "hating your own life" as noted in Luke 14:26. Denying yourself and hating yourself have the same connotation. In Luke 9:23, Jesus calls for self-denial where He says, "Whoever wants to be my disciple must deny themselves and take up their cross daily and follow me. For whoever wants to save their life will lose it, but whoever loses their life for me will save it." In Matthew 16:24, Jesus calls for self-denial again where He says, "Whoever wants to be my disciple must deny themselves and take up their cross and follow me. For whoever wants to save their life will lose it, but whoever loses their life for me will find it." In Mark 8:34–35, Jesus calls for self-denial where He says, "Whoever wants to be my disciple must deny themselves and take up their cross and follow me. For whoever wants to save their life will lose it, but whoever loses their life for me and for the gospel will save it." In Matthew 10:39 Jesus calls for losing your life or self-denial in a different way where He says, "Whoever finds their life will lose it, and whoever loses their life for my sake will find it." In John 12:25, Jesus calls for hating one's life or self-denial where He says, "Anyone who loves their life will lose it, while anyone who hates their life in this world will keep it for eternal life." Jesus said several times that one must "*deny themselves.*" This word is very strong and in the original language is *aparneomai*. *Aparneomai* means "to deny, disown, repudiate, forsake, or reject." This same word is used when Jesus told Peter he would deny Him three times. Just as Peter said, "I don't know the man," so Jesus calls us to say the same thing to our lives which is to say to ourselves, "I don't know the man. I'm sold out, submitted, and committed to Jesus." Additionally, when Jesus calls for one to "lose your life," this carries the same meaning as "denying yourself" or "hating yourself." **When Jesus is telling you to deny yourself or hate yourself, He is saying that you must repent of your sins, say goodbye to your worldly desires and pride, and say goodbye to self-will in exchange for His yoke, His will, and His rule over your life.** In other words, Jesus is calling men everywhere to look at their sin, look at their life, and make a judgment call. Is Jesus Christ important enough to submit, commit, and entrust your life to? If not, then "*ou dynatai einai mou mathetes*" or "You cannot be my disciple."

Let's notice that Jesus is giving a call to get to know Him. A faithful gospel call will explain the punishment of sin, death, and hell and also include the person of Jesus, the work of Jesus, and then give the evangelistic call to come to and follow after Jesus in repentance and faith. Jesus is inviting us to get to know Him. Just like when you are dating and getting to know someone in the hope of making the final decision to get married, so a similar analogy could be made here. Jesus is inviting you to see His person, which includes being the second person of the Godhead, the Son of God, the Christ, or the Messiah who was promised in the Old Testament. Jesus is true God and true man. Jesus was born of a virgin. Jesus is the Great I AM, the Judge, the only Savior, and more. Jesus is inviting you to see His work which includes His sinless life, His miracles which attest to His deity and Messiahship, His death on the cross for the sins of His people, and His imputed righteousness that He gives to all those who come to Him in saving faith. He is inviting you to see His resurrection which confirms His victory over all powers. He is inviting you to view His ascension into heaven and His current enthronement at the right hand of God. He is inviting you to see His High Priestly work in heaven, the guarantee of eternal life for all that come to Him, and more. Jesus is not calling us to decide without getting to know Him or His work. Just as we would take time to get to know someone before we decide to marry that person, so Jesus invites us to get to know Him. Jesus is inviting us to learn about Him and seek Him through the Scriptures. This is no blind date. This is no quick commitment. Jesus gives the invitation to know His person and work and then commands and demands an answer.

Let's notice that if you have come to Jesus and conclude that the created things in your life are more important than the Creator, than you have made a disastrous judgment. If you don't see the weight of your sins and condemnation as a big deal, then Christ is not a big deal to you. If you have not seen your personal sin as the priority that needs to be immediately and urgently addressed, then Christ has no meaning to you.

- Man calls sin an accident. God calls sin an abomination.
- Man calls sin a blunder. God calls sin blasphemy.
- Man calls sin an error. God calls sin enmity.
- Man calls sin a fascination. God calls sin a fatality.
- Man calls sin an infirmity. God calls sin iniquity.
- Man calls sin a trifle. God calls sin a transgression.
- Man calls sin a mistake. God calls sin madness.
- Man calls sin weakness. God calls sin wickedness.
- Man calls sin an oops. God calls sin an offense.

Let's also notice that the attitude when coming to Jesus is incredibly important. Jesus describes the person who has come to the end of themselves and have seen their sins as great and seen Christ as greater. Jesus talks about this person in the Beatitudes in Matthew 5:3–6. Matthew 5:3–6 describes repentance and turning to God! Jesus starts out in verse 3 where He says, "Blessed are the poor in spirit, for theirs is the kingdom of heaven." *Blessed* here refers to "those who have divine favor with God." The original word *makarios* is translated to "blessed" in the English language. *Makarios* means "blessed or happy." The reason these individuals are happy or blessed is because they have divine favor or God's grace. Here is how you can think about the repentant attitude which marks those who enter the kingdom of God. These first four Beatitudes mark the repentant attitudes of those who enter into the kingdom of God and the attitudes that characterize the Christian walk of life.

- Matthew 5:3—Blessed are the poor in spirit, for theirs is the kingdom of heaven.
    - *Ptóchos* has been translated to "poor," but it means beggarly poor of one who crouches and cowers because all he can do is to hold out his hand. It is the extreme opposite of rich. In other words, Jesus is saying, blessed are those who are so spiritually bankrupt in their spirit and realize they have no right to stand before God. Blessed are those who are so troubled and anguished in their spirit that all they can do is crouch and ask for mercy from God. These people are blessed for theirs is the kingdom of God. Isaiah 57:15 is another excellent cross-reference on poor in spirit where the LORD says, "I live in a high and holy place, but also with the one who is contrite and lowly in spirit, to revive the spirit of the lowly and to revive the heart of the contrite." Isaiah 66:2 is an excellent cross-reference that talks about the poor in spirit where the LORD says, "These are the ones I look on with favor: those who are humble and contrite in spirit, and who tremble at my word."
- Matthew 5:4—Blessed are those who mourn, for they will be comforted.
    - *Pentheó* has been translated "mourn" and it means mourning as if grieving over a death. This mourning is so severe that it takes possession of a person and cannot be hidden. This is not talking about those who mourn over losing a job or a loved one. It cannot mean that because even people in false religions mourn over such things. No, Jesus is saying that those who mourn, weep, and wail over their own personal sins

against God have divine favor. Those who will mourn over how they have sinned against God will be comforted. Those who will say the same thing about their sin, as what God says about sin, will be comforted by God. Joel 2:12–13 is an excellent cross-reference for mourning over sin, "'Even now,' declares the LORD, 'return to me with all your heart, with fasting and weeping and mourning.' Rend your heart and not your garments. Return to the LORD your God, for he is gracious and compassionate, slow to anger and abounding in love, and he relents from sending calamity."

- Matthew 5:5—Blessed are the meek for they shall inherit the earth.
    - First, the word *meekness* does not mean weakness. No, this word carries with it the idea of submission unto a master. It could also be thought of as strength under control. This is a person who will no longer exercise untamed power, self-will and control but will submit to a master. This word was used to describe breaking in a horse. Before breaking in a horse, the horse would buck, bite, and kick, but after the horse had been broken in and the bit and bridle put into its mouth, it would be considered "meeked." This is not to say the horse lost its power, but rather, the power remained and was directed by its master. So it is with those who enter the kingdom. They come in submission to God. They are meeked because of their sin and submit to the Lord Jesus Christ. These are the weary, burdened, and heavy ladened who bow the head, submit the will, and take Christ's yoke (Matthew 11:28-30). Those who are meek shall inherit the earth. Those who are meek because of their sin and submit to the authority of Jesus Christ shall inherit "a new heaven and a new earth" (Revelation 21:1).

- Matthew 5:6—Blessed are those who hunger and thirst for righteousness, for they will be satisfied.
    - Thinking of hunger and thirsting is hard in the United States or in First World countries. Most people have never experienced this in their lives. However, for those who have been so hungry where they have no strength, have body aches, and body pains, they would know what this means. Likewise, those who are so deprived of water where they have dryness of throat, where they have no strength, and where they experience dehydration would know of this thirsting. Jesus is saying those who hunger and thirst for righteousness in such a way have divine favor from God. In other words, those who hunger and thirst for the righteousness that can only be found in Jesus Christ will be satisfied. Not only will they hunger and thirst for the righteousness of Christ for their justification before God, they will also be hungering and thirsting for more righteousness to be conformed to the image of the Son of God in their sanctified walk with the Lord.

Matthew 5:3–6 is one of the clearest descriptions of true repentance where the sinner is intellectually aware of their personal spiritual bankruptcy before God (Matthew 5:3), they mourn over their sin against God and have Godly sorrow (Matthew 5:4, 2 Corinthians 7:10), they are meek and submissive under the Lord (Matthew 5:5), and they turn to Jesus for the righteousness they do not possess (Matthew 5:6). The original word for repentance in Greek is translated from *metanoeo* which means, "to change one's mind" or "a change of mind". However, when this change of mind occurs, it is radical. When this change of mind occurs or when there is true repentance, the person realizes they've been wrong about sin, the person realizes they have been wrong about God, the person realizes they have been wrong about salvation, the person realizes they have been wrong about their standing before God, the person realizes they have a wrong worldview and much more. This change of mind drives them to this Beatitude attitude. Thus, a good definition of repentance is: ***Repentance* is a gift from God where the sinner understands his sin against God (intellect), has Godly sorrow and mourns over his sin against God (emotions and affections), and turns away from his sin and toward God for righteousness (will or volition)**. This is the person who has come to the end of themselves, and this is their attitude when entering the kingdom of God. These people have submitted and committed everything to Christ. They deny themselves. They are broken over sin. They long for Jesus and the righteousness He provides. This is the tax collector in Jesus' parable in Luke 18, where the tax collector stood at a distance and would not even look up to heaven, but said, "God have mercy on me the sinner." This is the person that cowers to God in spirit and only asks for mercy and never for justice. This is the attitude of repentance, self-denial, and self-hate that Christ is calling for. If there is just sorrow over sin but no turning from the sin towards God, this is a *false repentance*. If there is sorrow over sin and a turning from the sin but no turning to God, this is mere *moral reform* (Matthew 12:43-45) and not true repentance. Jesus is calling for a radical repentance and allegiance to Him, but as He moves on, His cost and terms of becoming a disciple become even more demanding.

Luke 14:27—Whoever does not carry his own cross and come after Me cannot be My disciple.

Crucifixion was considered one of the most brutal and shameful modes of death. It likely had origins with the Assyrians and Babylonians and was eventually introduced to Rome by the Phoenicians in the third century BC. The Romans perfected crucifixion for five hundred years until it was abolished by Constantine I in the fourth century AD. Death could take from six hours to several days and could be due to after effects of compulsory scourging, maiming, hemorrhage, and dehydration causing hypovolemic shock. Death could also be precipitated by cardiac arrest. The attending Roman guards only left the site after the victim had died and would either break the victim's legs, stab the heart or chest with spears, or build a fire at the foot of the cross to asphyxiate the victim. Those who were crucified included slaves, disgraced soldiers, Christians, foreigners, and, very rarely, Roman citizens. The Jews knew what Jesus was talking about when Jesus said, "Whoever does not carry his own cross and come after Me cannot be my disciple." They had seen crucifixion before. They knew it was the death of deaths. They knew the cross meant agony. They knew the cross meant suffering. They knew the cross meant torture. They knew the cross meant shame. They knew the cross meant certain death.

Jesus' invitation to carry one's cross is an invitation to not only deny yourself, but to die to yourself. This is a death to self-will. This is a death to personal sins. This is a willingness to give your life to Christ even if it calls for death. This is a death to the lust of the flesh, the lust of the eyes, and the pride of life. This is not perfection, but it is the call to daily die to yourself. In fact, in Luke 9:23, Jesus says, "Whoever wants to be my disciple must deny themselves and take up their cross and follow me daily." This is an ongoing death to self. This is a daily death to self. Not only is this an open invitation, it's also a command. Notice that He invites everyone, but He still requires all His disciples to bear a cross and to do it daily. This is a call to supreme loyalty and faith in Christ to give your life to Him daily, and if He so chooses for your life, to die for Him.

Are you willing to so identify with Christ through faith that it costs you everything? Is following Christ worth losing your relationships, your personal interests, your belongings? Will you give up everything to gain Christ like Paul did (Philippians

3:4–9)? Is picking up your cross and identifying with Jesus worth the agony, worth the persecution, worth the shame, worth death? Christ may not require that you sell your house, sell your car, give up your job, but if that is in His plan, are you willing to pay the price? Is Christ worth this cost? Make a careful assessment. Notice that He once again says, "*ou dynatai einai mou mathetes.*" Whoever does not carry his own cross and come after Christ "cannot be His disciple." These are absolute terms. There is no negotiating with Jesus Christ. These are the terms of entrance into the kingdom. If entrance into the kingdom is just "believing" or "mental assent" to facts, then Jesus is a liar. Jesus is stating His terms of entrance into the kingdom of God. Jesus is defining the call to saving faith. Christ called men to follow Him under these terms. Christ laid down the terms and conditions for entrance into His kingdom. His disciples must do the same as well.

Jesus also gives two parables in Matthew 13:44–46, those of the Hidden Treasure and the Pearl. In Matthew 13:44, he says, "The kingdom of heaven is like treasure hidden in a field. When a man found it, he hid it again, and then in his joy went and sold all he had and bought the field." This is speaking of a man who finds Jesus Christ, the forgiveness of sins, and eternal life. The man is filled with joy inexpressible and sells everything to buy the field. This more specifically talks about the joy and price people are willing to pay to enter the kingdom of God. This is the most valuable possession in the world that is worth the cost of a personal cross, denying yourself, repenting of sins, and submitting and trusting in Christ.

In Matthew 13:45–46, Jesus says, "Again, the kingdom of heaven is like a merchant looking for fine pearls. When he found one of great value, he went away and sold everything he had and bought it." There are differences in each parable, but the underlying theme is that those who have found the forgiveness of sins, Jesus Christ, and eternal life will pay the price because what they have found is so much more valuable than anything else in this life. This is the cross-carrying, self-denying, repentant faith that Jesus is calling for. Jesus is describing the sinner who is destitute, who finds the Savior, and loses their life to gain Him. Thus, we see that entrance into the kingdom is one of both sorrow and brokenness over sin, but also one of joy inexpressible over having Christ.

A book that would be of great value to Christians would be *Foxe's Book of Martyrs* (7), where it describes the killing of Christians from the Apostolic Age through the 1800s. You can see very clearly in the Early Church and throughout the Christian Era that the disciples of Christ knew the terms of discipleship and the cost of following Christ:

- Charles Emmanuel II issued several edicts and published them in 1655 aimed at eliminating Protestants and Waldensians in his territory. Those who would not renounce the faith and convert to Roman Catholicism were removed from their homes and left to die in the cold weather, were shot by troops, and beaten severely. In one village, they cruelly tormented 150 women and children after the men fled, beheading the women, and dashing out the brains of the children.
- During the 1655 edict, there was a woman named Sarah Ratignole des Vignes who was sixty. She was seized by some soldiers, they ordered her to say a prayer to some saints, which she refusing, they thrust a sickle into her belly, ripped her up, and then cut off her head.
- During the 1655 edict, Magdalen Bertino was stripped stark naked, her head tied between her legs, and thrown down a precipice.
- During this same time period, Francis Gros, the son of a clergyman, had his flesh slowly cut from his body into small pieces, and put into a dish before him; two of his children were minced before his sight; and, his wife was

made to watch these cruelties to her husband and children. The tormentors tired of the cruelties and cut off the heads of the husband and wife and gave the flesh of the whole family to dogs.

- John Rogers suffered martyrdom at the hands of Queen Mary in England. He warned the people of the pestilence of popery, idolatry, and superstition and, eventually, was imprisoned for preaching the gospel of Christ. On February 4, in 1555, Rogers was led to the stake to be burned from Newgate Prison. When called to recant he said, "That which I have preached I will seal with my blood." His wife and children met him on the way to his execution as he went toward Smithfield, the place of execution, but he constantly and cheerfully took his death with wonderful patience, in the defense and quarrel of the gospel of Christ as he was burned to ashes.
- William Hunter had been trained in the doctrines of the Reformation and refused to take communion at Mass. He was unwavering in his commitment to participate in this and held to his convictions. The bishop asked again if he would recant and when William would not, he was sentenced to be burned. On coming to the stake, he knelt down and read Psalm 51 and came upon these words, "The sacrifices of God are a broken spirit; a broken and contrite heart, O God, Thou will not despise." He refused the queen's pardon and when brought to the smothering smoke he said, "Lord, Lord, Lord receive my spirit." Thus, he yielded up his life for the truth, sealing it with his blood to the praise of God.

This has always been the call to saving faith and following Christ. It is to repent from your sins, deny yourself, pick up your cross, submit your life to Christ, and trust in Christ as Lord and Savior for salvation. Additionally, Jesus says that this will be your daily way of life if you follow Him (Luke 9:23). Jesus is defining saving faith or entrance into His kingdom and Jesus says anything short of this is not saving faith and you are not a disciple if you don't come to Him on His terms.

Luke 14:28–30—For which one of you, when he wants to build a tower, does not first sit down and calculate the cost, to see if he has enough to complete it? Otherwise, when he has laid a foundation and is not able to finish, all who are watching it will begin to ridicule him, saying, "This person began to build and was not able to finish!"

Jesus here is calling people to count the cost to follow Him. He has laid down His terms for being His disciple. He is asking everyone to stop and consider the cost. He does not want a quick decision. He does not want to coerce anyone. He is not guaranteeing what will happen in the next five, ten, or twenty years. He is simply stating that you will need to carefully consider whether you're willing to commit to Him. In an ultimate shame and honor society, such as the Jewish culture, they would have understood this parable. They would know that it would be foolish to start to build a building without first determining whether they could finish. The one who had not carefully counted the costs and decided to build without considering the costs, would ultimately lead to great shame. Is it worth losing your life to gain Jesus? Christ is calling everyone to consider the cost of following Him as it requires a death to oneself and a submission and trust in Him.

Luke 14:31–32—Or what king, when he sets out to meet another king in battle, will not first sit down and consider whether he is strong enough with ten thousand men to face the one coming against him with twenty thousand? Otherwise, while the other is still far away, he sends a delegation and requests terms of peace.

The King will return one day, and He will not be coming as the suffering servant, but as the conquering King. This King will come to judge and wage war (Revelation 19:11). This King will come with His armies (Revelation 19:14). This King will strike down nations with His Word (Revelation 19:15). This King will tread upon His enemies with the wrath of God (Revelation 19:15). This King will kill and destroy His enemies (Revelation 19:21). This King will come with a wrath so horrible that people will cry for mountains and rocks to fall on them rather than suffer the wrath of the Lamb (Revelation 6:16–17). This is the King that is coming, and He has made terms of peace.

Jesus is saying that the king with ten thousand men should see that he is outnumbered and outmatched against the King with twenty thousand men. Jesus is stating that the king with ten thousand men should request terms of peace from the King with twenty thousand men. Psalm 2 pictures this beautifully where the nations are seen raging against the LORD and against the One enthroned in heaven. At the end of Psalm 2 in verse 12 the psalmist says this, "Kiss the Son, lest he be angry, and you perish in the way, for his wrath is quickly kindled. Blessed are all who take refuge in him." Psalm 2:12 is a picture of someone coming to the throne and submitting to the LORD. The psalmist is picturing a dignitary receiving the humble kiss of an inferior submitting and pledging allegiance. Jesus Christ has made terms of peace with mankind. Christ's terms of peace are stated in Luke 14:26–33 and further clarified in Matthew 5:3–6, 10:37–39, 13:44–46, 16:24–26; Mark 8:34–35; Luke 9:23–26, 18:9–14; and, John 12:24–26. He is coming against His enemies with strength and force. There is still time for the sinful man to come to terms of peace with this King. You don't want to meet this Judge in His courtroom without coming to His terms of peace. You don't want to be relying on your baptism when you meet this King. You don't want to be relying on good works when you meet this King. You don't want to be relying on your confirmation when you meet this King. He has offered His terms of peace. This includes repentance, submission of your life, and trust in Him alone. Faith alone in Him justifies, but the gospel presentation is not complete without talking about the response of repentance and submission to Christ.

Luke 14:33—So then, none of you can be My disciple who does not give up all his own possessions.

Jesus has addressed relationships in verse 26. He has addressed crossbearing, self-denial, submission, and trust in verse 27. He has addressed the need for careful consideration in verses 28–30. He has addressed making the decision to come to terms of peace with God in verses 31–32. Jesus is now talking about possessions. As mentioned above, He may not ask you to give up everything, but you must be willing to give up everything if He calls you. In fact, in this life He may give you an abundance or more than you need. However, He may require everything of you. Regardless of what He decides, are you willing to give up everything for Him? Therefore, Jesus Christ is calling you to become an owner of nothing and a steward of everything. Thus, we see that Christ is asking for total allegiance and trust with your personal relationships, personal life, and possessions.

Repentance is a gift (Acts 5:31, 11:18; 2 Timothy 2:25). Faith is a gift (Ephesians 2:8–9, Romans 5:15). Who could possibly respond to Christ's call to discipleship? Who can possibly respond in faith? Who can possibly be saved? Someone asked Jesus in Luke 13:23, "Lord, are only a few people going to be saved?" This is an extreme call to faith. How can it be that anyone would come to Christ on these terms of discipleship? The answer can be found in John 3:3, "Jesus responded and said to him, "Truly,

truly, I say to you, unless someone is born from above he cannot see the kingdom of God." Only those born from above can respond to this call to discipleship in repentance and faith.

Paul gives an account of his conversion to Christ. He starts by giving an account of his BC or "Before Christ" days where he recalls in Philippians 3:4–6: "Though I myself have reason for confidence in the flesh also. If anyone else thinks he has reason for confidence in the flesh, I have more: circumcised on the eighth day, of the people of Israel, of the tribe of Benjamin, a Hebrew of Hebrews; as to the law, a Pharisee; as to zeal, a persecutor of the church; as to righteousness under the law, blameless."

As you can see, before his conversion, Paul was an outwardly moral Pharisee, had great zeal for God's Word, and was externally blameless. However, Paul transitions from his "Before Christ" days to his conversion in verses 7–9:

"But whatever gain I had, I counted as loss for the sake of Christ. Indeed, **I count everything as loss** because of the surpassing worth of knowing Christ Jesus my Lord. For his sake **I have suffered the loss of all things and count them as rubbish, in order that I may gain Christ and be found in him, not having a righteousness of my own that comes from the law, but that which comes through faith in Christ, the righteousness from God that depends on faith.**"

The apostle Paul, who taught the great doctrine of justification by faith, goes on to describe the call of saving faith in Philippians 3. Here, Paul looks at his religious rituals and ceremonies. Paul looks at his national heritage. Paul looks at his family relations. Paul looks at his external righteousness. Paul looks at all of this and counts it all as rubbish or *skybala* in the original language, which can refer to "refuse or dung." Paul did his accounting. Paul saw his liabilities and his assets. Paul put all his religious rituals, rites, and accomplishments on one side and Jesus Christ on the other side and found Christ was everything and everything else was dung. Christ's call to saving faith was the same call that Paul answered. Paul evaluated everything in his life and gave it up for Christ. The same apostle who wrote thirteen books of the New Testament and explained the doctrine of justification by faith is the same apostle who knew the call to saving faith and surely proclaimed this same call to saving faith in Christ.

When looking at "believe," "repent," "call upon the name," and "faith" verses, one must also take a careful look at other portions of Scripture where Jesus is very specific on His terms of entrance into the kingdom of God. The call to saving faith can be found in verses such as Matthew 10:37–39, 13:44–46; Mark 8:34–35; Luke 9:23–26, 14:25–33, 18:9–14; and, John 12:24–26. Luke 14:25–33 is one of the greatest gifts and passages in Scripture to help us understand Jesus' call to saving faith. When looking at the "EASY" salvation Scriptures, it's very easy to come up with a doctrine of justification by believing or "mental assent" to Jesus and the gospel. However, if you just look at the "HARD" and "VERY HARD" verses, it's very easy to mistakenly preach a "works gospel." Both the "EASY," "HARD," and "VERY HARD" portions of Scripture must be used together to understand the call to saving faith. Stressing the intellectual, emotional, and volitional element of saving faith is vitally important just as much as teaching that faith and repentance are gifts that God gives. Luke 14:25–33 helps us understand the Lord's conditions to entering into the kingdom of God, becoming a disciple of Christ, or believing. Thus, saving faith and entering into the kingdom of God could be expressed as follows: ***Saving faith* is a gift from God where a sinner has knowledge of Jesus' person and work where a sinner will respond to Christ's person and work by denying themselves, picking up their cross, submitting and committing their life to Jesus, and trusting in Him only for salvation.**

Jesus is the friend of sinners (Matthew 11:19). Jesus calls all men to Himself as in Matthew 11:28–30, "Come to me, all who are weary and burdened, and I will give you rest. Take my yoke upon you and learn from me, for I am gentle and humble in heart, and you will find rest for your souls. For my yoke is easy, and my burden is light." Jesus again affirms in John 6:37 that He will accept and save sinners where He says, "All those the Father gives me will come to me, and whoever comes to me I will never drive away." God rejoices over redeeming the lost (Luke 15:1-32). Jesus is rich in mercy (Ephesians 2:7). Jesus came to save sinners (Luke 5:32). Jesus calls all men unto Himself. The call to salvation is open to everyone regardless of age, income, gender, nationality, ethnicity, and more. However, let us note that when we come to Jesus, Jesus has set forth the cost and terms of entrance into His kingdom. So let's put this all together. In John 3:3, Jesus told Nicodemus, "Truly, truly, I say to you, unless someone is born again he cannot see the kingdom of God." We gave a definition of regeneration, or being born from above, which is: ***Regeneration* is the sovereign monergistic work of God the Holy Spirit in giving spiritual life to spiritually dead and sinful man so that man is enabled to repent and respond in saving faith (conversion) to Jesus Christ**. In Mark 1:15, Jesus says, "The kingdom of God has come near. Repent and believe the good news!" Thus, given our definitions of *repentance* and *saving faith*, here is how Christ calls all men to enter into the kingdom of God: ***Repentance* is a gift from God where the sinner understands his sin against God (intellect), has godly sorrow and mourns over his sin against God (emotions and affections), and turns away from his sin and toward God for righteousness (will or volition). *Saving faith* is a gift from God where a sinner has knowledge of Jesus' person and work where a sinner will respond to Christ's person and work by denying themselves, picking up their cross, submitting and committing their life to Jesus, and trusting in Him only for salvation**. Although there is much that could be discussed on the doctrine of assurance of salvation, such as the First Book of John, evidence of entering the kingdom of God and being in union with Christ will be a lifelong walk of bearing fruits of repentance and saving faith. As Paul says in Colossians 2:6, "So then, just as you received Christ Jesus as Lord, continue to live your lives in him."

Thus, we can see, **the subjective response of repentance and faith to the objective person of Jesus and objective work of Jesus is an essential component of the gospel**. For without this understanding, all the salvific work of Jesus is of no benefit to us. Repentance and faith is the subjective response to the objective person and work of Jesus. Now that we understand the bad news and have an understanding of the good news, we can put together a definition the gospel.

- The bad news is that man has sinned, which is breaking God's law by either not doing what His law demands or doing what His law prohibits by any thought, word, deed, or intent. God's disposition toward sin is one of hatred, anger, abhorrence, defilement, wickedness, evil, hostility, and is warfare against Him. Man is incapable of curing his problem with sin. Man cannot propitiate the righteous anger of God, redeem himself, earn forgiveness, or be made right with God on his own merits. God's attributes such as being eternal, loving, just, good, faithful, omniscient, and immutable demand that God must punish sin. The punishment of sin is hell, which is a place of God's full wrath and a place of blackest darkness, filled with furious and concentrated fire everywhere, where there is weeping and anger against God for the unrepentant Christ-rejecting and Christ-neglecting sinners where they will spend all eternity paying for every sin they've ever committed with no hope of escape, and only the expectation of excruciating torments to their body, soul, and spirit and an undying conscience that will haunt them day and night, forever and ever, with no reprieve.
- The good news or the gospel is the good news of salvation that God has authored and owns. God had promised this

plan of salvation through His prophets and Holy Scripture and has fully revealed the good news of salvation through Scripture which is the authoritative, inspired inerrant, and infallible Word of God. The good news concerns the person and work of Jesus Christ. The person of Jesus is He is the Christ, the Creator of the universe, the promised Jewish Messiah, the only begotten Son of the Living God, which makes Him God and equal with God the Father and God the Holy Spirit. Jesus was born of a virgin and conceived by the Holy Spirit and became a man and is, thus, truly God and truly man and can represent God to man and man to God. The work of Jesus is that Jesus lived a sinless life and fulfilled all righteousness found in the law and prophets and declared Himself to be the Christ, the only begotten Son of the Living God through His teaching which was attested to by His miracles and the Holy Spirit. Jesus offered himself as a sinless, spotless, and blameless sacrifice for sin to propitiate the righteous anger of God by taking all the sins of God's people on Himself and, thus, the full wrath of God that was due to man. His sacrifice propitiated the righteous anger of God and reconciled and brought peace from man to God and God to man. His substitutionary sacrifice and death also redeemed sinful man to Holy God by forgiving man's sin and imputing His righteousness to man, so man could stand before God with the righteousness of Jesus Christ in judgment. Jesus was resurrected from the dead on the third day by His own power, by God the Father, and God the Holy Spirit which affirmed His person, His teachings, and salvific work for sinners. He ascended to the right hand of the Father and is empowered with all authority to bring about the plan of salvation for all His people by causing them to be born again and justified by His grace. He will also return to bring all of His own to heaven with Him to be glorified while also

> judging and condemning Satan, demons, and sinful man. The benefits of Christ's person and work are available to those who repent and put saving faith in Christ. *Repentance* is a gift from God where the sinner understands his sin against God (intellect), has godly sorrow and mourns over his sin against God (emotions and affections), and turns away from his sin and toward God for righteousness (will or volition). *Saving faith* is a gift from God where a sinner has knowledge of Jesus' person and work where a sinner will respond to Christ's person and work by denying themselves, picking up their cross, submitting and committing their life to Jesus, and trusting in Him only for salvation.

This is the gospel. This is the good news of salvation. As we transition to the last portion of verse 5, it's important to remember that we preach the gospel not only for the salvation of others, but for the glory of God. The last portion of Romans 1:5 says, "for the sake of his name among all the nations." When the LORD promises Israel's restoration in Ezekiel 36, He says in Ezekiel 36:23, "I will show the holiness of my great name, which has been profaned among the nations, the name you have profaned among them. Then the nations will know that I am the LORD, declares the Sovereign LORD, when I am proved holy through you before their eyes." When God saves a man, He is proven holy among men and the nations. That is to say that the salvific work of God is so holy and amazing, that although unregenerate man may not fully understand the salvation that took place, they will marvel and awe at the transforming, regenerative, and salvific work of God who puts the life of God in the soul of a man. Additionally, in Isaiah 48:11, when the LORD sees Israel's sinfulness and stubbornness and decides to delay his wrath and not destroy Israel He says, "For my own sake, for my own sake, I do this. How can I let myself be defamed? I will not yield my glory to another." God's name is glorified in His work of salvation.

As we look at the good news, we can now see that the attributes of God that were scary regarding sin, death, and hell are also wonderful and glorious. This gospel shows forth all of God's attributes in His self-existence, immutability, self-sufficiency, omnipotence, omniscience, omnipresence, wisdom, faithfulness, goodness, justice, mercy, graciousness, love, and glory. Because God is eternal, we can be assured that God took out His wrath on His eternal Son and know that there is no more wrath left for His children (1 Thessalonians 1:10). Because God is loving, we know that He will eternally love us as His children just as He loves His one and only Son (John 17:23). Because God is just, we can know that He has fully settled our accounts of sin on behalf of His Son (Romans 5:1). Because God is a good Father, we can know that He will never do that which is bad and leave one of His children, but will care for us as a tender Father (Galatians 4:6, Romans 8:15, Hebrews 12:4–13). Because He is faithful, we can know that He will keep His promise that He will be with us always to the very end of the age (Matthew 28:20). Because He is immutable, we can trust His Word and be confident that the gift of new birth He gave us will be carried out to completion (Philippians 1:6, James 1:17). Because God is omniscient, we can trust that He knows all things past, present, and future and will work out everything for our good (Romans 8:28). Because God is omnipresent, we know that He will never leave us or forsake us (Hebrews 13:5). Because God is omnipotent and nothing or no one is more powerful than God, we can know that neither death nor life, neither angels nor demons, neither the present nor the future, nor any powers, neither height nor depth, nor anything else in all creation, will be able to separate us from the love of God that is in Christ Jesus our Lord (Romans 8:38–39).

Romans 1:6—including you who are called to belong to Jesus Christ

There should be a distinction made when Paul is talking about being "called." The "call" in Scripture can refer to both the *general call* and the *effectual call*. The general call can be referred to the gospel being proclaimed to everyone such as in the Parable of the Great Banquet in Luke 14:23, "And the master said to the servant, 'Go out to the highways and hedges and compel people to come in, that my house may be filled.'" Jesus also gives a general call at the Feast of Booths where it says, in John 7:37, "On the last day of the feast, the great day, Jesus stood up and cried out, 'If anyone thirsts, let him come to me and drink.'" Likewise, Paul reiterated this same general call as he preached the gospel at Pisidian Antioch, saying in Acts 13:47, which is a quote from Isaiah 49:6, "I have made you a light for the Gentiles, that you may bring salvation to the ends of the earth." We are commanded to preach the gospel to everyone, and this is known as the *general call*.

Conversely, there is the *effectual call*. Theologians refer to the *effectual call* when the gospel is preached and the Word falls on the ears of its hearers, God works within the hearts of His elect, the Father calling them to His Son by the power of the Holy Spirit and the hearer responds to God's gospel invitation. John 6:65 certainly calls out the distinction between the general call and the effectual call where Jesus says, "This is why I told you that no one can come to me unless it is granted him by the Father." The call goes out, but the call is not effectual to everyone in bringing about the salvation of all people for there are those who reject the call (Acts 13:46) and those who neglect the call (Hebrews 2:3). Thus, it should be understood that the *effectual call* which Paul is referring to in Romans 1:6, is one that is effective to bring about the salvation to those who hear the gospel and respond.

Two doctrinal words that come to mind when describing the effectual call are *regeneration* and *conversion* (repentance and faith). As we learned earlier, ***Regeneration* is the sovereign monergistic work of God the Holy Spirit in giving spiritual life to spiritually dead and sinful man so that man is enabled to repent and respond in saving faith (conversion) to Jesus Christ.** It is the Father who effectually draws His own to Jesus through the power of the Holy Spirit. It is God the Holy Spirit who will change man from the inside (intellect, affections, and will) and make him a new person. Let's refresh our understanding of regeneration and see what the Holy Spirit does to man in Ezekiel 11:19–20, 36:24–27; and, Jeremiah 24:7, 31:33–34, 32:38–40. I will highlight the work that the Holy Spirit does in regeneration to see what a complete transformation He brings about in man:

And **I will give them one heart**, and **put a new spirit within them.** And **I will remove the heart of stone from their flesh** and **give them a heart of flesh**, so that they will walk in My statutes, and keep My ordinances and do them. Then they will be My people, and I shall be their God (Ezekiel 11:19–20). **I will also give them a heart to know Me**, for I am the LORD; and they will be My people, and I will be their God, for they will return to Me wholeheartedly (Jeremiah 24:7). They shall be My people, and I will be their God; and **I will give them one heart and one way**, so that they will fear Me always, for their own good and for the good of their children after them. **I will make an everlasting covenant** with them that **I will not turn away from them, to do them good**; and, **I will put the fear of Me in their hearts**, so that they will not turn away from Me (Jeremiah 32:38–40). For **I will take you from the nations**, and gather you from all the lands; and, **I will bring you into your own land**. Then, **I will sprinkle clean water on you, and you will be clean; I will cleanse you from all your filthiness and from all your idols**. Moreover, **I will give you a new heart and put a new spirit within you**; and, **I will remove the heart of stone from your flesh and give you a**

heart of flesh. And, **I will put my Spirit within you and bring it about that you walk in My statutes, and are careful and follow my ordinances** (Ezekiel 36:24–27). **For this is the covenant which I will make with the house of Israel** after those days, "Declares the LORD: '**I will put My law within them and write it on their heart**; and **I will be their God**, and they shall be My people. They will not teach again, each one his neighbor and each one his brother,' saying, "Know the LORD," for they will all know Me, from the least of them to the greatest of them,' declares the LORD, "for **I will forgive their wrongdoing**, and **their sin I will no longer remember"** (Jeremiah 31:33–34).

So, how does the *effectual call* relate to regeneration and conversion (repentance and faith)? Unless God the Holy Spirit regenerates a man and gives him spiritual life, the man is spiritually dead and will not respond to the gospel call. It would be the same scenario of calling to a dead man to stand up, to breathe, to talk, to open his eyes. The dead man can't do anything except stay dead. Only when God regenerates a man, will the man immediately respond in repentance and faith (conversion). Once the man is regenerated, he will deny himself, pick up his cross, submit and commit his life to Jesus, and trust in Christ alone for salvation or, rather, be converted to Christ. Paul links the *effectual call* to security of salvation when he says in Romans 8:29–30, "For those whom he foreknew he also predestined to be conformed to the image of his Son, in order that he might be the firstborn among many brothers. And those whom he predestined he also called, and those whom he called he also justified, and those whom he justified he also glorified." In Paul's mind, there is an unbreakable link in the salvific plan of God. God foreknew a people, God predestined those people, God effectually called those people, God justified those people, and God glorified those people. When Paul says, "You who are called to belong to Jesus Christ," he is speaking of this effectual call. If we have been effectually called by God to belong to Jesus, we should stop, ponder, and meditate on what out-of-this-world love God has for us (1 John 3:1). Thus, when Paul refers to us being "called," we should immediately think of God giving us new birth and granting us repentance and faith.

When coming to the close of understanding the bad news and the gospel, what should our attitudes be toward the gospel? We should believe the gospel (Mark 1:15). We should not be ashamed of the gospel (Romans 1:16). We should understand the gospel is the power of God to save mankind (Romans 1:16). We should be eager to preach the gospel (Romans 1:15). We should proclaim the gospel without fear (Philippians 1:14). We should defend the gospel (Philippians 1:16, Jude 3). We should live our lives in a manner worthy of the gospel (Philippians 1:27). We should seek to understand the gospel clearly (Acts 18:26). We should understand the gospel is not ours (Romans 1:1). We should fear preaching a wrong or false gospel (Galatians 1:8–9). We should fear preaching the gospel from wrong motives (Philippians 1:15). We should understand that God guarantees the success of His gospel for His Name's sake (Romans 1:5). We should give our lives for the gospel of God (Mark 8:35). We should give all glory to God for His gospel (Romans 11:36).

Chapter 2: Different Gospels Equal False Teachers

Galatians 1:8–9—But even if we or an angel from heaven should preach to you a gospel contrary to the one we preached to you, let him be accursed. As we have said before, so now I say again: If anyone is preaching to you a gospel contrary to the one you received, let him be accursed.

When thinking about the gospel of God, we've explored that there are many essential components to the gospel and labored to explain it. As you'll recall, before we worked through defining the gospel or good news, we needed to first define the bad news which included: **sin, death, and hell**. We needed to do this to help understand why the gospel is God's good news of salvation. For example, how would the gospel be impacted if we didn't talk about what sin was? How would the gospel be impacted if we didn't describe God's feeling toward sin? How would the gospel be impacted if we didn't talk about man's inability to cure sin? How would the gospel be impacted if we didn't talk about the punishment of sin? How would the gospel be impacted if there was no hell? How would the gospel be impacted if we didn't talk about the eternality of hell? How would the gospel be impacted if we didn't talk about the torments and fire of hell? Without understanding the bad news, we really don't have any context to help us understand why the gospel is good news.

After we defined the bad news, we set out to define essential components of the gospel as well which included the following: **owned and authored by God, found in Scripture, objective person of Jesus, objective work of Jesus**, and **subjective response of repentance and faith**. We needed to understand these essential components because if they are misunderstood, there is damage to the gospel. For example, how would the gospel be impacted if it wasn't God's gospel? How would the gospel be impacted if the gospel could be understood outside of Scripture? How would the gospel be impacted if Jesus was just a man and not God? How would the gospel be impacted if Jesus was God but not man? How would the gospel be impacted if Jesus wasn't conceived by the Holy Spirit and born to Mary? How would the gospel be impacted if Jesus wasn't sinless? How would the gospel be impacted if Jesus didn't die? How would the gospel be impacted if Jesus wasn't resurrected? How would the gospel be impacted if we left out His teaching work? How would the gospel be impacted if we left out His working of miracles? How would the gospel be impacted if we left out His claims to deity? How would the gospel be impacted if man wasn't commanded to repent? How would the gospel be impacted if we left out Christ's call to follow Him in discipleship or saving faith? How would the gospel be impacted if good works were required for salvation? How would the gospel be impacted if someone could be saved through baptism? How would the gospel be impacted if someone could be saved through circumcision? How would the gospel be impacted if someone could be saved through taking the Lord's Supper? As we move through the rest of the book, we will see that when these essential components to the gospel are attacked, twisted, misinterpreted, added to, or left out, we are left with a different gospel or a false gospel.

One of the purposes of this book is to not only define the gospel, but to also identify false teachers. In 1 John 1:8, John says of us, "If we say we have no sin, we deceive ourselves, and the truth is not in us." Even after man is regenerated and saved, he is still susceptible to sin and, thus, will not have a perfect understanding of the gospel or what happened to him at salvation. Additionally, man is still fallible after regeneration and is susceptible to teach error. Therefore, we can be certain that every man will have some error in his teaching. However, when looking at Scripture, the Bible consistently portrays false teachers as having false gospels and being those that lead people astray. Therefore, a starting point as a definition for a *false teacher* would be as follows: **a *false teacher* is one who holds to, unrepentantly, and persistently teaches and preaches a false gospel that damns men's souls by attacking, twisting, misinterpreting, adding to, or leaving out the essential components of the gospel or essential components of the bad news of sin, death, and hell** (Galatians 1:6–9, Matthew 15:14, 23:13–15, 2 Peter 2:1–2, Luke 11:52, 2 Peter 3:16, Jude 4). As we move through the book, this definition will be strengthened through Scripture and will give us a firm grasp of understanding what makes a false teacher. With this being said, let's review Galatians 1:6–9, which is one of the most severe warnings to anyone who would distort the gospel or preach another gospel.

Galatians 1:6—I am astonished that you are so quickly deserting him who called you in the grace of Christ and are turning to a different gospel.

Paul's letter to the Galatians opens with fierce declaration of divine punishment without any reservation. Paul is direct, confrontational, and frank about his forceful pronunciation of damnation on preaching another gospel. Paul doesn't open his letter with thanksgiving, commendation, or praise but immediately jumps into the heart of the issue which is the gospel. In Paul's letter to the Galatians, he stresses the doctrine of justification by faith in Christ. As we go through Galatians 1:6–9, we will pull from the subsequent chapters and verses in Galatians to get a full understanding of Paul's forceful denunciation of false teachers who give a false gospel.

Starting in verse 6, Paul says, "I am astonished you are so quickly deserting him who called you in the grace of Christ and are turning to another gospel." Paul was astonished that the Galatians were turning to another gospel. The word *astonished* comes from *thaumazó,* which means "to wonder or marvel" or "be astonished out of one's senses; awestruck." Paul was literally struck out of his mind that the Galatians were turning to a different gospel so quickly. Paul wasn't surprised that there was damning heresy coming into the church as this occurred very early on in the church.

Paul wasn't surprised by the false teachers, but he was struck out of his sense by the Galatians so quickly accepting a different gospel. So, why would Paul be so surprised by this? He gets right to the point in Galatians 3:2, where he says, "Let me ask you only this: Did you receive the Spirit by works of the law or by hearing with faith?" In other words, there were some there that received the Holy Spirit by believing the gospel. As we learned earlier, as the gospel is heard and understood, the Holy Spirit regenerates and gives spiritual life to a man and completely changes his affections and will to love Christ, and the man responds by repenting of his sins, denying himself, surrendering to Christ, trusting in Him alone, and is justified by faith. Although regeneration precedes conversion, conversion immediately follows regeneration. When this happens, there is a new man that emerges. In fact, Paul makes this very point where he tells them in Galatians 5:6, "For in Christ Jesus neither circumcision nor uncircumcision counts for anything, but only faith working through love," and, in Galatians 6:15, "For neither circumcision counts for anything, nor uncircumcision, but a new creation." Paul's point is that if you've been regenerated by the Holy Spirit and received the Holy Spirit and are now indwelt by the Holy Spirit, how did you receive the Holy Spirit? Did you receive the Holy Spirit by keeping the law? Did you receive the Holy Spirit by keeping a ritual? How did you undergo such a spiritual transformation from walking in the flesh (Galatians 5:16–21) to now walking in the Spirit (Galatians 5:22–25)? After asking them how they received the Spirit, he then explains that one is justified by faith and not by keeping the law (Galatians 3:5–9). Paul was surprised that there were some there that had been regenerated, were converted to Christ, were new creations, went from the kingdom of darkness to the kingdom of light, saw the power of the Holy Spirit in their life, and were now entertaining a false gospel which had no power to save.

In fact, Paul says that they are "quickly deserting him." *Tacheós* means "swiftly, promptly, speedily." *Metatithemi* means "to transfer or to go over to another party." We see who Paul says the Galatians are in the process of quickly deserting. It is God they are in the process of deserting because it is God's gospel. It is God who called them by grace. Rejecting the gospel is the very same thing as rejecting the One who authored the gospel. In this context, Paul seems to be talking about an *effectual call* and not a general call since he noted that there were those who had believed and received the Holy Spirit. We could paraphrase Paul's statement this way about quickly deserting the gospel for a different gospel:

- I'm struck out of my mind that you, who were called by God into the grace of Christ, are turning to a different gospel.
- I'm dumbfounded that you are so quickly deserting God's gospel after your spiritual transformation and are now turning to a different gospel.
- I'm awestruck that you are rapidly deserting God and His gospel after receiving the Holy Spirit for a different gospel.

Of course, we know that the true believers cannot lose their salvation (Romans 8:29–30), but it is to say that the Galatians were tolerating and accepting or even hearing a false gospel with an outrageous lack of discernment. In Galatians 5:9, Paul says, "A little leaven leavens the whole lump." He is essentially saying that false teaching and false gospels have a strong permeating affect. If you give ear to a false gospel or tolerate a false gospel in the church, it is going to have a devastating and permeating affect and work its way through the entire church. This permeating effect will not only impact the church but have a devastating effect on other doctrine as well. Paul is stating that he's shocked that they've tolerated this different gospel and are beginning to turn to it.

In fact, the Jerusalem Council had to deal with this heresy that came from the Judaizers, which taught that converts to Christianity had to first be circumcised and then observe rituals and ceremonies to be saved. When the Jerusalem Council deliberated the necessity of circumcision and ceremonies as necessary for salvation, it was around AD 50.

In Acts 15:1, it says that there were people that came from Judea to Antioch and were teaching the believers that unless they were circumcised according to the custom of Moses, they could not be saved. Paul and Barnabas had a sharp dispute with these Judaizers and were sent to Jerusalem to figure this matter out. Fast-forwarding to the Jerusalem Council, there were some believers who belonged to the Pharisees who said that the Gentiles must be circumcised and required to keep the law of Moses (Acts 15:5). Apparently, there was a lot of discussion and, finally, Peter stood up and addressed everyone where he said in Acts 15:7–9, "Brothers, you know that in the early days God made a choice among you, that by my mouth the Gentiles should hear the word of the gospel and believe. And God, who knows the heart, bore witness to them, by giving them the Holy Spirit just as he did to us, and he made no distinction between us and them, having cleansed their hearts by faith." After Peter reminds the assembly of the first conversion of the Gentiles that occurred in Acts 10–11, of which he was the gospel messenger and witnessed the conversion, he goes on to say in verse 10, "Now, therefore, why are you putting God to the test by placing a yoke on the neck of the disciples that neither our fathers nor we have been able to bear?" Both Peter and Paul had witnessed the Judaizers perverting the gospel early on where the Judaizers would claim that one needed to be circumcised and follow Jewish rituals to be saved.

As we learned in Acts 15:1, Paul was not afraid of confronting the error of a works-based gospel. Although Peter stands up at the Jerusalem Council and boldly says that circumcision has no saving value, Paul would correct Peter prior to the Jerusalem Council in Galatians 2 where Peter's actions affirmed the Judaizer's false gospel and threw other believers into confusion.

Apparently, there were men that were sent to the Galatian church by James who was a leader in the Jerusalem (Galatians 2:12). These men were claiming to be Christians, claiming allegiance to Christ, and said that they were being sent by James. The hypocrisy that Peter was showing was that he would withdraw from the Gentiles when the Judaizers came. The hypocrisy in this is that the Judaizers didn't associate with Gentiles as the Judaizers saw the Gentiles as unclean pagans. Furthermore, since the Judaizers believed that one needed to be circumcised and follow Jewish rituals to be saved, they would not have believed the Gentiles to be true converts. Thus, when Peter withdrew from the Gentiles, he was affirming through his actions that the Judaizers were correct in their teaching, which was absolutely devastating to the teaching of justification by faith.

The hypocrisy of Peter led other Jews astray as well such as Barnabas. Therefore, Paul's reaction to Peter was that Paul opposed Peter to his face where it says in Galatians 2:11, "But when

Cephas came to Antioch, I opposed him to his face, because he stood condemned." This was a strong reaction from Paul to Peter for Peter misleading others. The original word that has been translated to "opposed" is *anthistémi,* which carries the idea of "opposing someone and taking a complete stand against," "forcefully declare one's personal conviction," and was used as a military term to mean "to strongly resist an opponent." Paul even says that Peter stood "condemned," which is translated from *kataginóskó,* which means "to be decisively guilty on the basis of direct personal acquaintance." *Kataginóskó* is not the same word used for condemnation or final judgment which Paul uses in Romans as *katakrima.* Additionally, we know that Peter was not eternally condemned as Peter was an apostle and was recommissioned by the Lord.

Peter was knowingly wrong. Peter had enough time with the Lord to know that circumcision was not a means to salvation. Peter was warned to watch out for the teaching leaven of the Pharisees (Matthew 16:6, 12, Luke 12:1, Mark 8:15). Peter knew that he was supposed to be on guard against the false teaching hypocrisy of the Pharisees and by withdrawing from the Gentiles when the Judaizers came, Peter was affirming the teaching of the Judaizers through his withdrawal.

The false teaching that the Judaizers were propagating attacked the subjective response of repentance and faith to the objective person and work of Jesus. The Judaizers replaced repentance and faith in Christ with circumcision and ceremonies plus Christ. We should see how dangerous it is to tolerate a false gospel. We should see how dangerous it is to give cadence or acceptance to those who preach a false gospel. This example in the life of Peter and Paul is an example of dealing with one who is affirming a false gospel through their actions. When one either teaches a false gospel or affirms it, that person must be dealt with urgently, firmly, and boldly.

Galatians 1:7—not that there is another one, but there are some who trouble you and want to distort the gospel of Christ

As we learned, there is only one gospel which has been authored by God. Paul seeks to remind the Galatians of this when he says, "not that there is another." In verse 6, he calls the false gospel a different gospel or a *heteros* gospel, meaning "other or different." In verse 7, he is saying that there is "not another." Another is translated from *allos,* which means "another of the same kind" or "another of a similar type." In essence, he's saying that they are believing a different gospel, one of another kind, which is not the same kind as the true gospel. Paul is saying that either the "different gospel" or the *heteros euaggelion* or the "other gospel" or *allon euaggelion* are not gospels at all.

All of this confusion was causing the Galatians trouble. The word *tarassó* indicates that the Galatians were emotionally agitated and were inwardly perplexed. This same word is used to describe the disciples being disturbed when they saw Jesus walking on water (Matthew 14:26). It is also used when the disciples were troubled because Jesus let them know He would be with them for only a little while longer (John 14:1). This is to say that those who teach another gospel cause severe trouble by distorting or perverting the gospel. There are not only those outside of Christianity that teach another way to be saved, but there are also those in the church who teach different ways to be saved or different gospels.

As we see in verse 7, they "want to distort the gospel of Christ." *Distort* comes from *metastrephó,* which means "change," "corrupt," "pervert." This is not something passive. This is not some random mistake. No, the verse gives the idea that they are present tense, continuing and desiring to pervert the gospel of Christ. Even when someone comes and tries to correct them, they either ignore the warning or continue to believe the false gospel and continue propagating it because they've been deceived. Therefore, either by their ongoing and present tense ignorance or by their ongoing and present tense belief in the false gospel, these false teachers pervert the gospel. As we saw in the case of Peter and Paul, Peter was able to take the correction as evidenced by his statement in the Jerusalem Council. Peter corrected his mistake. However, this is not so with the false teacher who propagates a false gospel. They continue in their false teaching which perverts or corrupts the gospel. This is an important point to keep in mind when considering the definition of a false teacher that was provided earlier. As we noted earlier, all teachers in the church will have some error in their teaching. However, it is quite another thing when one teaches a false gospel, has been warned, has been given instruction, has been warned again, and refuses to repent and continues in teaching a false gospel.

As we've noted earlier, the Judaizers were tampering with the subjective response to the gospel. Instead of repentance and faith, they replaced it with circumcision and ceremony. When one tampers with one piece of the gospel, they end up destroying the rest of the gospel. For example, if someone claims that faith in Christ plus good works is needed for salvation, this attacks the salvific work of Christ. Paul says it much better when he says in Galatians 2:21, "For if righteousness could be gained through the law, Christ died for nothing!" Paul is essentially saying that if you rely on works, ceremonies, rituals, sacraments, and anything else, you proclaim that Christ died for nothing. If you say that you can be saved by an act or sacrament of baptism or the Lord's Supper, you proclaim Christ died for nothing! If you proclaim that one is saved through church membership, you attack the propitiating, reconciling, expiating, and redeeming work of Christ and proclaim that Christ died for nothing!

As Paul goes on in Galatians 3:10, he says, "For all who rely on works of the law are under a curse; for it is written, "Cursed be everyone who does not abide by all things written in the Book of the Law, and do them." In Galatians 3:13, Paul says, "Christ redeemed us from the curse of the law by becoming a curse for us—for it is written, "Cursed is everyone who is hanged on a tree." Therefore, if anyone believes they can have faith in Christ and baptism for salvation, they are cursed. If anyone believes they can have faith in Christ and circumcision for salvation, they are cursed. If anyone believes they can have faith in Christ and the Lord's Supper for salvation, they are cursed. If anyone believes they can have faith in Christ and confirmation for salvation, they are cursed. If anyone believes they can have faith in Christ and good works for salvation, they are cursed. So, let's understand this correctly. If anyone adds faith in Christ plus anything else for salvation, that person proclaims that Christ died for nothing, attacks the salvific work of Christ, and is under God's curse.

As Paul goes on in Galatians 5:2, he says, "Look: I, Paul, say to you that if you accept circumcision, Christ will be of no advantage to you." In other words, if one accepts circumcision as a means to salvation, all of Christ's person and work is of no profit for you. In putting Galatians 2:21, 3:10, 3:13, and 5:2, Paul is building a tremendous case where he is saying that if you respond to the person and work of Christ in any other way than repentance and faith in Christ, you proclaim that Christ died for nothing, you attack the salvific work of Christ, you are under a curse, and Christ's salvific work is of no profit to you.

Paul will intensify his argument as he'll state in Galatians 5:3–4, "I testify again to every man who accepts circumcision that he is obligated to keep the whole law." Paul is stating that if you take even one small step outside of repentance and faith in Christ, you are obligated to keep the whole law perfectly. In other words, if you want to put just one milligram of hope in your baptism, circumcision, good works, church membership, or law obedience plus Christ, you need to keep the whole law. You can almost hear Paul saying this, "OK, you want to rely on circumcision and Christ? Is this the path you want to take? If so, here's what you're in for. If you want to look to anything else other than Christ or Christ plus anything else, then this is what you've signed up for. You are on the hook for keeping all the Sabbaths, keeping all of the dietary restrictions, keeping the burnt offerings, keeping the sin offerings, keeping the grain offerings, keeping the guilt offerings, keeping the appointed Festivals (Passover and Unleavened Bread, Offering of Firstfruits, Weeks, Trumpets, Day of Atonement, Tabernacles), keeping restrictions on skin diseases, keeping the Ten Commandments, keeping the bodily discharge requirements, keeping the purification after childbirth, and everything else." If you put one foot outside of repentance and faith in Christ, then you are severed from Christ. *Severed* is a strong word which comes from *katargeo*, which means to "render inoperative, abolish." Just one foot outside of repentance and faith in Christ is to be severed and completely cut off from Christ.

Lastly, in Galatians 5:12, Paul says of those who would rely on circumcision, any means other than Christ, or Christ plus any other work or sacrament, "I wish those who unsettle you would emasculate themselves!" Galatia was adjacent to Phrygia. Phrygia was known for the worship of Cybele, a pagan goddess. The priests who worshipped Cybele who were very devout would castrate themselves and become eunuchs. This was absolute paganism. You can almost hear Paul saying this, "OK, if you want to teach that circumcision saves, then you may as well go all the way and chop off your genitalia and become a full-blown pagan, because that's what you will be. You will be in the same company of the worshippers of Cybele who castrate themselves to worship their god. You will be a full-fledged pagan." Under the inspiration of the Holy Spirit, Paul wrote this. This is the Spirit of God speaking these words which is the authoritative, inerrant, and infallible Word of God. Although the false gospel in Galatians had to do with a works-based gospel, these statements toward a false gospel applies to anyone who would either teach a false gospel or embrace it:

- If you proclaim that you can be saved by your works plus Christ, sacraments plus Christ, or anything else plus Christ, **you proclaim that Christ died for nothing and you attack the propitiating, reconciling, expiating, and redeeming work of Christ.** (Galatians 2:21)
- If you proclaim that you can be saved by your works plus Christ, sacraments plus Christ, or anything else plus Christ, **you are under God's curse.** (Galatians 3:10, 13)
- If you proclaim that you can be saved by your works plus Christ, sacraments plus Christ, or anything else plus Christ, **you are obligated to keep the whole law.** (Galatians 3:10, 13)
- If you proclaim that you can be saved by your works plus Christ, sacraments plus Christ, or anything else plus Christ, **then Christ's salvific work is of no benefit for you.** (Galatians 5:2)
- If you proclaim that you can be saved by your works plus Christ, sacraments plus Christ, or anything else plus Christ, **then you are severed and completely cut off from Christ.** (Galatians 5:3–4)
- If you proclaim that you can be saved by your works plus Christ, sacraments plus Christ, or anything else plus Christ, **then you may as well become a full-fledged pagan and worship a false god because you are not a believer in Christ.** (Galatians 5:12)

As we transition into Galatians 1:8–9, no wonder we see Paul's denunciation of those who preach a false gospel. No wonder we see his strong language and denunciation of false gospel preachers. No wonder we see such a strong curse given to false teachers who propagate a false gospel. These false teachers lead others into false religion or false Christianity. These false teachers proclaim Christ died for nothing, they put their followers under God's curse, they obligate their followers to keep the whole law, they render Christ as unprofitable to their followers, they completely sever their followers from Christ, and they turn their followers into full-fledged pagans.

Galatians 1:8–9—But even if we or an angel from heaven should preach to you a gospel contrary to the one we preached to you, let him be accursed. As we have said before, so now I say again: if anyone is preaching to you a gospel contrary to the one you received, let him be accursed.

There's a word that is of importance to understand which occurs twice, once in verse 8 and once in verse 9. This word is *anathema,* which means "a thing devoted to God for destruction." Paul uses this same word in 1 Corinthians 16:22, where he says, "If anyone does not love the Lord, he is to be accursed. Come Lord." Why do false teachers who propagate a false gospel deserve such a cursing? The answer becomes obvious as these false teachers will take the gospel which is owned and authored by God (Romans 1:1), will pervert and corrupt the true gospel into a false gospel (Galatians 1:7), and will ultimately damn men's souls and damn their own souls (Galatians 3:10, 13, 5:2–4, 12).

Paul uses hyperbole in verse 8, where he says, "Even if we or an angel from heaven should preach a gospel contrary to the one we preached, let him be accursed." Paul knew that false teachers would be disguised as shepherds (Matthew 7:15–20). Paul knew that there was a possibility that false teachers would look moral on the outside but were corrupt on the inside (Matthew 23:25–28). Paul knew that false teachers could spring up from inside the church (Acts 20:29–30). Paul knew that false teachers could come from outside the church (Acts 20:29). Paul knew that there was danger in tolerating a false gospel from the false teachers where he says in 2 Corinthians 11:4, "For if one comes and preaches another Jesus whom we have not preached, or you receive a different spirit which you have not received, or a different gospel which you have not accepted, this you tolerate very well." Paul knew that false teachers would teach different objective truths about the person of Jesus (2 Corinthians 11:4). Paul knew that false teachers would teach different objective truths about the work of Jesus (2 Corinthians 11:4). Paul knew that false teachers would have different and deceptive spirits (2 Corinthians 11:4). Paul knew that false apostles would be deceitful and would disguise themselves as apostles of Christ (2 Corinthians 11:13). Paul knew that Satan was in false religion and disguised himself as an angel of light (2 Corinthians 11:14). Paul knew that those who serve Satan would disguise themselves as servants of righteousness (2 Corinthians 11:15). Paul knew how deceptive false teachers could be with smooth and flattering speech (Romans 16:18). That is why Paul warned that even if the best looking, best sounding, most articulate, outwardly moral teacher proclaimed a different gospel, let that one be damned. Just because one carries the title of pastor, bishop, father, apostle, reverend, deacon, elder, or any other title does not make them a true gospel teacher. Paul is warning them of this danger. It's not that Paul or a heavenly angel would do this, but he was warning the Galatians to not let the messenger or the message deceive them. He was saying, don't believe any other gospel no matter how attractive the messenger or the message is because the one carrying the false gospel is to be *anathema*, he is to be damned and he damns men's souls.

Paul says again in verse 9, "As we have said before, so now I say again: If anyone is preaching to you a gospel contrary to the one you received, let him be accursed." Paul says this statement twice for more emphasis. When the writers would want to make a point emphatic, they would not use exclamation points, but would repeat a statement a second time. Paul is doubling down on the danger of accepting a false gospel. The false teachers who give the false gospels are *anathema* and curse and damn those who accept the false gospel. Let us be aware of the importance of knowing the true gospel so we can distinguish and identify when a false gospel is proclaimed. Paul gave this very charge to Timothy in 1 Timothy 4:16, where he says, "Pay close attention to yourself and to the teaching; persevere in these things, for as you do this you will save both yourself and those who hear you."

When understanding false gospels and false teachers, we can understand the following points from this chapter:

- A false teacher is one who holds to, unrepentantly, and persistently teaches and preaches a false gospel that damns men's souls by attacking, twisting, misinterpreting, adding to, or leaving out the essential components of the gospel or essential components of the bad news of sin, death, and hell. (Galatians 1:6–9, Matthew 15:14, 23:13–15, Jude 4, Luke 11:52, 2 Peter 2:1–2, 3:16)
- It is dangerous to tolerate a false gospel. (Galatians 1:6, 2:13, 5:9)
- A false gospel will lead to other errors. (Galatians 2:21, 5:9)
- A false gospel curses those who embrace it. (Galatians 3:10, 13)
- Those who embrace the false gospel are severed from Christ. (Galatians 5:3–4)
- A false gospel makes its hearers or believers full-fledged pagans. (Galatians 5:12)
- False teachers are closely linked to propagating false gospels. (Galatians 1–6)
- False teachers are anathema, cursed, damned. (Galatians 1:8–9)

Chapter 3: Woe to the False Teaching Gate Closers

Matthew 23:13—"But woe to you, scribes and Pharisees, hypocrites! For you shut the kingdom of heaven in people's faces. For you neither enter yourselves nor allow those who would enter to go in."

If you were to ask someone, "What is the most dangerous threat in our world?" You probably would get the following answers around the world: guns, cancer, corona virus, war in Ukraine, poverty, child abuse, spousal abuse, sexual abuse, physical abuse, food supply, communism, Russia, China, liberal politicians, and more. If you were to ask the Lord, "What is the most dangerous threat in our world?", aside from one's sin not being forgiven (Luke 13:3, 5), a likely answer would be the threat and danger of false teachers.

The teaching of God's Word to God's people has always been a serious matter. In Jeremiah 5:31, it says, "The prophets prophesy falsely, and the priests rule at their direction; my people love to have it so, but what will you do when the end comes?" The LORD is essentially saying that the prophets are speaking falsely, but pretending to speak for the LORD. Likewise, the priests ruled in the same manner. Both prophets and priests were self-willed and unsubmissive. The prophets did not speak God's Word and the priests did not do God's work. The LORD asks a very simple question, "What will you do when the end comes?" The undeniable answer is that when one prophesies falsely and spiritually rule with their own self-will and lead people astray, the end for the prophet and the people will be disastrous.

In Jeremiah 6:13–15, the LORD speaks through Jeremiah where Jeremiah says of the false prophets, "'For from the least to the greatest of them, everyone is greedy for unjust gain; and from prophet to priest, everyone deals falsely. They have healed the wound of my people lightly, saying, 'Peace, peace,' when there is no peace. Were they ashamed when they committed abomination? No, they were not at all ashamed; they did not know how to blush. Therefore they shall fall among those who fall; at the time that I punish them, they shall be overthrown,' says the LORD." The false prophets and false teachers did not deal seriously with the spiritual wound of sin and its effects. Instead of warning the people and turning them from sin, they told the people that there was peace with God when there was no peace. What is most striking is that you could see the false prophets were not ashamed. The false prophets couldn't even blush. The false prophets during Jeremiah's time did not even know how to be ashamed for leading their people astray.

In Jeremiah 8:10–12, the prophet makes a similar statement where he says, "Therefore I will give their wives to others and their fields to conquerors, because from the least to the greatest everyone is greedy for unjust gain; from prophet to priest, everyone deals falsely. They have healed the wound of my people lightly, saying, 'Peace, peace,' when there is no peace. Were they ashamed when they committed abomination? No, they were not at all ashamed; they did not know how to blush. Therefore they shall fall among the fallen; when I punish them, they shall be overthrown, says the LORD." Once again, the false teachers aren't condemned for just minor errors in teaching. No, they are condemned for treating sin lightly and prophesying peace with God when there is no peace. You'll see in this verse as well that the false prophets were not even ashamed of leading people astray. They did not even know how to blush.

In Jeremiah 23:16–17, the LORD says, "Thus says the LORD of hosts: 'Do not listen to the words of the prophets who prophesy to you, filling you with vain hopes. They speak visions of their own minds, not from the mouth of the LORD. They say continually to those who despise the word of the LORD, "It shall be well with you" and to everyone who stubbornly follows his own heart, they say, 'No disaster shall come upon you.'" Here, again, you have false prophets who give false hopes and claim that all will be well with the LORD's people when it is not well. The false prophets are not making some minor doctrinal error, but rather they are knowingly giving a message of peace and comfort when there really should be a message of warning and judgment. Lastly, we see that this is not a temporary position but a fixed stance. The false prophets will not change and lead their followers to disaster.

In Ezekiel 13:9–12, the LORD speaks against the false prophets through Ezekiel where He says, "My hand will be against the prophets who see false visions and who give lying divinations. They shall not be in the council of my people, nor be enrolled in the register of the house of Israel, nor shall they enter the land of Israel. And you shall know that I am the LORD God. Precisely because they have misled my people saying, 'Peace, when there is no peace,' and because when the people build a wall, these prophets smear it with whitewash, say to those who smear it with whitewash that it shall fall! There will be a deluge of rain, and you, O great hailstones, will fall, and a stormy wind break out. And when the wall falls, will it not be said to you, 'Where is the coating with which you smeared it?'" The false prophets had lulled the people into false security. They gave phony "peace" promises while sin continued on the brink of God's judgment. They essentially erected a defective "wall" and whitewashed it to make it look good. Such an unsafe "wall" was doomed to collapse when God would bring His storm, or rather, when Israel would be invaded. The false teachers led the people astray, promised peace when God was angry with them, and continually and superficially addressed Israel's sin problem. In Ezekiel 13:16, He says, "Those prophets of Israel who prophesied to Jerusalem saw visions of peace for her when there was no peace, declares the Sovereign LORD." What a horrible and abominable thing it is to stand as God's representative and declare peace to God's people when there is no peace with God!

As we enter Matthew 23:13, we should note that this was the LORD's last sermon given during the last week of His life. Of importance notice, we should note that the LORD was not teaching about the kingdom, He was not teaching about salvation, He was not teaching about childlike faith. No, Christ gave a public sermon during the Passover week that was aimed at condemning false religious leaders. Christ did not give this sermon in the corner of a back room to His disciples. This sermon was preached to the crowds and to His disciples (Matthew 23:1). It is said about the Passover by the Jewish historian Josephus that the population could swell to two million people. This was a blistering sermon from Jesus on the danger of the false teaching that existed in Israel with the Pharisees and Sadducees. This sermon carries just as much weight today. Not only does this apply to false religious systems such as Hinduism, Confucianism, Buddhism, Taoism, Shintoism, Islam, and Judaism, but this sermon also carries the full weight and force of denunciation and condemnation today for those who would stand as representatives of Christ, but, in reality, are a gate-shutting false teacher that propagates a false gospel. We developed a definition of a *false teacher* in the previous chapter and, as we start this chapter, we will keep this definition at the forefront of our thoughts: **A *false teacher* is one who holds to, unrepentantly, and persistently teaches and preaches a false gospel that damns men's souls by attacking, twisting, misinterpreting, adding to, or leaving out the essential components of the gospel or essential components of the bad news of sin, death, and hell.**

As we noted earlier, the Lord uses blistering language in His final sermon. Jesus pronounces seven "woes" on the false teachers. Jesus calls the false teachers "hypocrites" seven times. Jesus calls the false teachers "blind" five times. Jesus will call them "double sons of hell" (Matthew 23:15). Jesus will tell the false teachers "they're full of hypocrisy and lawlessness" (Matthew 23:28). Jesus will call false teachers "serpents" (Matthew 23:33). Jesus will call the false teachers "broods of vipers" (Matthew 23:33). Jesus' sermon isn't just a blistering rageful condemnation of the false teachers, it's also mixed with sadness and empathy. In Matthew 23:37, He says, "O Jerusalem, Jerusalem, the city that kills the prophets and stones those who are sent to it! How often would I have gathered your children together as a hen gathers her brood under her wings, and you were not willing!" Jesus' righteous anger and wrath is mixed with deep sadness and sorrow. Although Jesus curses the false teachers, he laments over their unwillingness to repent and so we see a striking balance of holy indignation with holy compassion as Jesus will pronounce condemnation on the false teachers.

Matthew 23:13—"But woe to you scribes and Pharisees, hypocrites! For you shut the kingdom of heaven in people's faces. For you neither enter yourselves nor allow those who would enter to go in."

When dealing with this passage, there are a few words and phrases that must be understood to have a clear understanding of what Jesus is saying. In Matthew 23:13–36, Jesus announces seven woes upon the Pharisees. *Woe* is translated from *ouai* and this word can be said as "alas!" or "woe" and uttered in grief or denunciation. It is an onomatopoeic word (an imitation of the sound) which serves as an interjection expression or a cry of intense distress, displeasure, or horror. In the Septuagint, it can be a funeral lament, which is used eight times in this expression; it can mean a cry to get attention, which is used four times in this expression; or, it can mean an announcement of doom, which is used forty-one times in this expression. In William Barclay's commentary, he says of this word, "This is not the accent of one who is in a temper because his self-esteem has been touched; it is not the accent of one who is blazingly angry because he has been insulted. It is the accent of sorrow, the accent of one who offered men the most precious thing in the world and saw it disregarded. Jesus' condemnation of sin is holy anger, but the anger comes, not from outraged pride, but from a broken heart."

A second word that deserves our attention is the word *hypocrite*. The original word for *hypocrite* is *hupokritẻs* which is "an actor, a pretender," a "two-faced person," or "one whose profession does not match their practice" (i.e., says one thing but does another). This word originally carried the meaning of one who was an actor and then came to mean an actor in the worst sense of the term, a pretender, one who acts a part, one who wears a mask to cover his true feelings, one who puts on an external show while inwardly his thoughts and feelings are different.

A third phrase that would need to be understood is *the kingdom of heaven*. This phrase can be described as the "sphere of salvation," God's reign through God's people over God's place," "salvation," and more. Any of these descriptions would be appropriate. There is a kingdom which assumes there is a King. Since it is the kingdom of heaven, God is the King of heaven and, thus, the King over those who enter His kingdom. These individuals who enter the kingdom of heaven are those who have inherited eternal life and salvation. Hence, we understand the *kingdom of heaven* as those who inherit salvation and enter His kingdom. The *kingdom of God* expression carries the same meaning as the *kingdom of heaven* as it describes the spiritual realm over which the Lord reigns as King.

Now that we've understood some of these important words and phrases, we can gain a better understanding of what Jesus is saying. Jesus is pronouncing judgment on the scribes and Pharisees for being hypocrites. The Pharisees were the premier teachers in Israel. Pharisees were meticulous about preserving both the Old Testament Scripture as well as oral tradition. Pharisees also sat on the Sanhedrin, which was a Jewish ruling council. The Pharisees were responsible for the spiritual life and teaching of the Jews. Scribes were recognized as experts in Jewish law including both Scripture and traditional laws and regulations. They were members of a learned class who studied the Scriptures and served as copyists, editors, and teachers. Thus, they were considered to be experts in matters relating to divine revelation, especially in regard to the law of Moses. They would also teach, develop, and use the law in connection with the Sanhedrin and various local courts. Jesus called the Pharisees and scribes hypocrites because they were supposed to be the spiritual leaders of the Jews and those who would correctly interpret the Word of God. They were supposed to be those that would lead the people to God and not away from God. Essentially, Jesus is saying, "You play the part of God's teacher. You play the part of God's spokesman. You play the part of one who can interpret God's Word. You play the part of one who can lead people to God. However, you're a hypocrite. You are neither a teacher of God nor a spokesman of God. You can't interpret God's Word and you lead people away from God." Jesus is pronouncing judgment on their utter hypocrisy. They played the part of religious leaders who could lead people to God but were, in reality, diverting people away from God.

Jesus becomes very specific why the scribes and Pharisees are hypocrites when He says, "For you shut the kingdom of heaven in people's faces." This is very graphic language the Lord uses. Jesus is saying that they shut the kingdom of heaven in people's faces. This carries the idea that people are coming close to the kingdom of heaven and seeking it (Matthew 7:7). This carries the idea that people are seeking first the kingdom of God (Matthew 6:33, Luke 12:31). This carries the idea that many are agonizing to enter through the narrow door (Luke 13:24). This carries the idea that people have come to the Gate (John 10:7, 9). This carries the idea that people are seeking to enter through the narrow gate (Matthew 7:13–14). This carries the idea that when someone has come right up to Jesus who is the Gate, the narrow door, the narrow gate, entrance into the kingdom of heaven, and the only way to the Father (John 14:6), that the Pharisees shut up the kingdom of heaven just as men are about to enter.

We should note that this is a continual shutting of the door. The phrase *for you shut the king of heaven* is in the present tense. It's saying that this is a continual and perpetual behavior. This is not isolated. This is not random. No, this is willful, continual, deliberate, and purposeful shutting of the kingdom of heaven. Let's also notice that it says "before men's faces." The literal translation is *emprosthen tōn anthrópos. Emprosthen* means "in front" or "before the face." *Tōn* is a definite article and *anthrópos* is "men" or "mankind." The Pharisees and scribes are literally shutting up the kingdom of heaven right in man's face. As we noted above, this is an objective picture of someone earnestly seeking the Lord and coming right up to the line and having a door slammed in their face. This is a brutal picture of someone about to enter through a wide-open door and, then, having a false teacher continually slam the door shut right in the face of those entering. This is a graphic and violent picture of the effort that false teachers go to which keeps people out of the kingdom of heaven.

When we look at the last half of the verse, it says, "For you neither enter yourselves nor allow those who would enter to go in." As we learned earlier, false teachers are accursed and damned by God for a false gospel. They are accursed because they've given a false or a different gospel that damns men's souls. They are accursed because they make Christ's salvific work of no profit for those who are trying to enter the kingdom of God. They sever and completely cut people off from Christ and they make people full-fledged pagans. Once again, this is not random. This is not a mistake. This is not isolated. No, this is purposeful. This is deliberate. This is continual. This is habitual. This is constant. This is a fixed position. Jesus is talking in the present tense. These false teachers are purposefully teaching a false gospel. These false teachers are deliberately teaching a false gospel. These false teachers continually teach a false gospel. These false teachers are habitually teaching a false gospel. These false teachers will not change and do not relent. When the door is open, they move to shut it. When someone is close to entering, they slam the door close. When someone sees the light on the other side of the door, they slam it shut and keep the light out. This portion of Scripture makes it clear that false teachers are those who do not enter the kingdom by holding to and teaching a false gospel that will damn men's souls and damns their own souls.

Before we move on to Matthew 23:15, it may be helpful to see how the false teachers shut up the kingdom of heaven during John the Baptist's and Jesus' ministries. To help understand this, the solid bullet points are instances where the false teachers openly rejected either the person or work of Jesus or the subjective response of repentance and faith. The open circle bullet points are instances where, although the false teachers didn't openly reject the person or work of Jesus, they would have had knowledge of what Jesus had said and done as news about Him was spreading everywhere and, thus, they would have known of the event. Additionally, when putting this timeline of events together, a *Harmony of the Gospels* (8) was used to illustrate the constant, intentional, deliberate, and personal rejection of the person and work of Jesus as well as the refusal to repent and believe.

- The Subjective Response—Pharisees rejected the need for repentance (Matthew 3:1–9, John 7:30)
- The Work of Jesus—Pharisees rejected Jesus' healing of the invalid at the Pool of Bethesda (John 5:1–45)

- The Work of Jesus—Pharisees would have had knowledge of Jesus' miracle of turning water to wine which demonstrated Jesus' power and authority to create out of nothing which was evidence of His deity (John 2:1-11)
- The Work of Jesus—Pharisees would have had knowledge of Jesus' miracle of healing of the official's son which demonstrated Jesus' power to heal disease regardless of distance and save Gentiles which was evidence of Jesus' Messiahship and deity (John 4:46-54)
- The Work of Jesus—Pharisees would have had knowledge of Jesus' miracle of healing the demoniac on the Sabbath which demonstrated that Jesus had authority over demons and that Jesus' kingdom was superior to the kingdom of darkness which evidenced His deity and claim to be the Anointed One of God according to Isaiah (Luke 4:31-37)
- The Work of Jesus—Pharisees would have had knowledge of Jesus' miracle of Peter's mother-in-law being healed as well as many others which demonstrated his miracle power and that Jesus was the Anointed One of God, the Messiah, and Deliverer according to Isaiah and that He would proclaim good news of forgiveness and salvation (Luke 4:38-41)
- The Work of Jesus—Pharisees would have had knowledge of Jesus' miracle of healing the leper which proved Jesus was holy, innocent, undefiled, and separate from sinners in that He could touch and heal the worst of diseases in a defiled and ceremonially unclean leper, make the leper ceremonially clean, and yet He remained undefiled which was evidence of His deity (Luke 5:12-16
- The Work of Jesus—Pharisees would have had knowledge of Jesus' miracle of healing the paralytic which

was a demonstration that Jesus had authority to forgive sins which demonstrated His deity (Luke 5:17-26)

- The Person of Jesus—Pharisees rejected Jesus' claim to be equal with God which was a sign that Jesus was the Messiah, that He was sent from the Father, that He was compassionate, that He could give life, that He was God, and more (John 5:1-45)
- The Person of Jesus—Pharisees rejected Jesus' claim to be Lord of the Sabbath which was a demonstration that Jesus was compassionate, He could heal deformities, and that He was Lord of the Sabbath, or rather, Lord over the entire Levitical system which was evidence of His deity (Matthew 12:1-14)
- The Work of Jesus—Pharisees rejected Jesus' work of healing the man with the withered hand (Matthew 12:9–14)
    - The Work of Jesus—Pharisees would have had knowledge of Jesus' healing of the multitudes which was a fulfillment of Isaiah 42 which demonstrated that He was the servant of Yahweh by healing many which also exhibited His compassion and mercy which was evidence of His deity (Matthew 12:15-21)
    - The Work of Jesus—Pharisees would have had knowledge of Jesus' healing of the centurion's servant which proved Jesus was willing to reach out and save Gentiles, but not only Gentiles, but a Gentile of the Roman army which oppressed Israel. This also demonstrated Jesus could heal disease regardless of distance and was evidence of His deity (Matthew 8:5-13)
    - The Work of Jesus—Pharisees would have had knowledge of Jesus raising a widow's son from the dead demonstrated Jesus' authority to give life and resurrect the dead, but also showed forth His compassion for widows and the helpless which was evidence of His deity (Luke 7:11-17)

- The Work of Jesus—Pharisees rejected Jesus's work of casting out a demon of a blind and mute man demonstrated that Jesus' kingdom was separate, distinct, different, more powerful, and greater than Satan's kingdom. It also exhibited His deity and omniscience by reading the Pharisee's thoughts (Matthew 12:22-28)
- The Person of Jesus—Pharisees rejected Jesus' title of Son of David and called Him Beelzebul (Matthew 12:22–28)
- The Person of Jesus—Pharisees rejected Jesus' claims thus far to deity and demanded a sign (Matthew 12:38–42)
- The Work of Jesus—Pharisees rejected Jesus' works and miracles thus far and demanded a different sign (Matthew 12:38–42)
    - The Work of Jesus—Pharisees may have had knowledge of Jesus' miracle of calming the storm which demonstrated Jesus' control over nature which was evidence of His deity (Matthew 8:23-27)
    - The Work of Jesus—Pharisees would have had knowledge of Jesus' miracle of restoring two demon-possessed men in the Gadarenes which was a sign that Jesus had authority over demons and to spiritually heal and save a defiled, Gentile, demon-possessed man which was evidence of His deity (Matthew 8:28-34)
    - The Work of Jesus—Pharisees would have had knowledge of Jesus' miracle of raising Jairus' daughter from the dead and healing the woman with the hemorrhage which demonstrated Jesus' authority to give life and resurrect the dead. It also showed Jesus as the compassionate Savior by healing and saving a woman who was continually ceremonially unclean and ostracized from the Jewish community according to Leviticus 15 which evidenced His deity (Matthew 9:18-26)
- The Work of Jesus—Pharisees rejected Jesus' works of healing the blind man and the mute which demonstrated

the Messiah's power over demons as well as the authority to restore sight and sound which was evidence of His deity (Matthew 9:27-34)

  - The Work of Jesus—Pharisees would have had knowledge of Jesus' miracle of feeding of the five thousand which demonstrated Jesus' compassion and power to heal as well as His creative power and authority. This miracle would also demonstrate and enforce that He was the Bread of Life and the spiritual provision from Heaven which was evidence of His deity (Matthew 14:13-21)
  - The Work of Jesus—Pharisees would have had knowledge of Jesus' miracle of healing the sick of Gennesaret (Matthew 14:34–36)
  - The Person of Jesus—Pharisees would have had knowledge of Jesus' claim to be the Bread of Life which was a claim to deity (John 6:25–69)
- The Work of Jesus—Pharisees rejected Jesus' teaching on the law versus the Pharisees' tradition and that which defiles (Matthew 15:1–14)
  - The Work of Jesus—Pharisees would have had knowledge of Jesus' miracle of healing the Syrophoenician which demonstrated Jesus' compassion to save a Caananite woman who would have been despised by the Jews. It also exhibited His authority and power to cast out demons regardless of distance which was evidence of His deity (Matthew 15:21-28)
  - The Work of Jesus—Pharisees would have had knowledge of Jesus' miracle of healing those on the mountainside by the Sea of Galilee (Matthew 15:29–31)
  - The Work of Jesus—Pharisees would have had knowledge of Jesus' miracle of feeding the four thousand (Matthew 15:32–39)

- The Work of Jesus—Pharisees rejected Jesus' signs that had been performed and needed more evidence (Matthew 16:1–4)
- The Person of Jesus—Pharisees rejected Jesus' claims to deity and demanded more signs (Matthew 16:1–4)
  - The Work of Jesus—Pharisees would have had knowledge of Jesus' healing of the boy with the impure spirit (Matthew 17:14–21)
- The Person of Jesus—Pharisees rejected Jesus' claims to deity of being the Living Water (John 7:11–52)
- The Person of Jesus—Pharisees rejected Jesus' claims to deity of being the Light of the World (John 8:12–20)
- The Person of Jesus—Pharisees rejected Jesus' claims to deity of being I Am (John 8:21–58)
- The Person of Jesus—Pharisees rejected Jesus' divinity and called Him Beelzebul demonstrated that Jesus' kingdom was separate, distinct, different, more powerful, and greater than Satan's kingdom. It also exhibited His deity and omniscience by reading the Pharisees thoughts (Luke 11:14-23)
- The Work of Jesus—Pharisees rejected Jesus' work of driving out a demon who was mute (Luke 11:14–23)
  - The Work of Jesus—Pharisees would have had knowledge and rejected Jesus' miracle of healing the crippled woman on the Sabbath where Jesus exposed false religion and hypocrisy in a Synagogue (Luke 13:10-17)
- The Person of Jesus—Pharisees rejected Jesus' healing of the blind man and the blind man's claim that Jesus was from God (John 9:1–41)
- The Work of Jesus—Pharisees rejected the work of Jesus healing the blind man which demonstrated Jesus' creative power by creating eyes for the blind man which was evidence of His deity. Through this miracle, Jesus also showed forth the Pharisees' spiritual blindness (John 9:1-41)

- The Person of Jesus—Pharisees rejected Jesus' claim to deity by claiming to be the Gate (John 10:1–42)
- The Person of Jesus—Pharisees rejected Jesus' claim to deity by claiming to be the Good Shepherd (John 10:1–42)
- The Person of Jesus—Pharisees rejected Jesus' claim to be God's Son (John 10:30–42)
- The Work of Jesus—Pharisees rejected the many good works that Jesus was showing them (John 10:1–42)
- The Person of Jesus—Pharisees rejected Jesus' claim to deity by claiming to be the Resurrection and the Life (John 11:1–53)
- The Work of Jesus—Pharisees rejected Jesus' miracle of raising Lazarus from the dead which demonstrated Jesus' authority as the ultimate giver of life by giving life and resurrecting the dead which was evidence of His deity (John 11:1-53)
- The Subjective Response—Pharisees ultimately rejected the person and work of Christ and refused to repent and believe (Matthew 23:13–40)
- The Person and Work of Jesus – The Pharisees rejected Jesus' resurrection from the dead. Jesus' resurrection from the dead substantiated all of Jesus' teaching, preaching, miracles, and claims to deity (Matthew 28:11-15)

The false teachers consistently rejected Jesus' works. The false teachers consistently rejected Jesus' claims to deity. The false teachers consistently rejected the need to repent and put saving faith in Jesus. Additionally, not only did they reject the person of Christ, the work of Christ, and the subjective response to the person and work of Christ, but they also scared and intimated others into rejecting Christ as well (John 9:22, 12:42) and desired to kill Lazarus because many Jews were going away and believing in Jesus (John 12:9–11). These were hard and fast gate closers. Even today in Christianity, there are many false teaching gate closers and gospel perverters.

- The **Catholic** priest who consistently, deliberately, purposefully, and unrepentantly teaches that you are saved by faith and works is a false teaching gate closer and gospel perverter (Galatians 1:7)
- The **Lutheran** pastor who consistently, deliberately, purposefully, and unrepentantly teaches that you are born again and saved through water baptism is a false teaching gate closer and gospel perverter (Galatians 1:7)
- The **Eastern Orthodox** priest who consistently, deliberately, purposefully, and unrepentantly teaches that you are born again and saved through water baptism is a false teaching gate closer and gospel perverter (Galatians 1:7)
- The **Unitarian Universalist** teacher who consistently, deliberately, purposefully, and unrepentantly teaches that a loving God would not send sinful man to hell is a false teaching gate closer and gospel perverter (Galatians 1:7)
- The **Presbyterian, Baptist and Methodist** pastor who consistently, deliberately, purposefully, and unrepentantly teaches that homosexuality is not a sin is a false teaching gate closer and gospel perverter (Galatians 1:7)

Matthew 23:15—Woe to you, scribes and Pharisees, hypocrites! For you travel across sea and land to make a single proselyte, and when he becomes a proselyte, you make him twice as much a child of hell as yourselves.

The Israelites were not only to be God's chosen people, but they were to go out and reach people in the world. Psalm 18:49 captures this evangelistic zeal where the psalmist says, "For this I will praise you, O LORD, among the nations, and sing to your name." Israel was always meant to be evangelistic in their zeal to reach the nations for the LORD. Jonah had this very mission to go and preach to Nineveh. When Jesus came, He was the long-awaited Son of David, the Christ, the Son of the Living God and He was to be accepted and embraced as their Lord, Savior, God, and King. However, the Pharisees ended up doing just the opposite and steering people away from Christ and turning them to Pharisaic Judaism. When they did this, Jesus said they made their converts double sons of hell.

The word *hell* comes from the original word *Gehenna*. This place had to do with a valley that was near Jerusalem called the Valley of Hinnom. In Old Testament time pagans would burn their children alive. It says in 2 Chronicles 28:3, "and he made offerings in the Valley of the Son of Hinnom and burned his sons as an offering, according to the abominations of the nations whom the LORD drove out before the people of Israel." King Josiah would declare this place unclean and defiled in 2 Kings 23:10, where it says, "And he defiled Topheth, which is in the Valley of the Son of Hinnom, that no one might burn his son or his daughter as an offering to Molech." This place eventually became a place where garbage and refuse would be brought and where there was a continual burning of the garbage. So, this place came to be known as a cursed place with constant burning and fire that was fit only for the waste of humanity. This is where false teachers bring their followers. False teachers make their converts double sons of hell just as they are. The Pharisees ended up making their followers double sons of a place of God's full wrath and blackest darkness, filled with furious and concentrated fire everywhere, where there is weeping and anger against God for the unrepentant Christ-rejecting and Christ-neglecting sinners where they will spend all eternity paying for every sin they've ever committed with no hope of escape, and only the expectation of excruciating torments to their body, soul, and spirit and an undying conscience that will haunt them day and night, forever and ever, with no reprieve. What a tragic result for those who follow these false teachers into hell!

Jesus would go on in Matthew 23:16–22 and denounce the religious teachers for their false religious system that allowed for lying. They had devised a system where they would take oaths but not uphold the oath based on what they took their oath upon. For example, an oath meant something if they swore by gold in the temple, but not if they swore by the temple (Matthew 23:16). The religious leaders should have known that all oaths taken should be treated as if taking the oath toward God (Matthew 23:22, Numbers 30:2).

Jesus also denounced the false teachers for majoring in minor points of the law and neglecting the more important matters of the law (Matthew 23:23–24). The false teachers focused on the externals of the law, but willfully resisted the spiritual meaning of the law which was exposed in the Lord's Sermon on the Mount where Jesus exposited the attitudes of people in the Kingdom (Matthew 5:3–12), Jesus exposed the spiritual meaning of the law such as the true requirements of not murdering (Matthew 5:21–26) and not committing adultery (Matthew 5:27:30) and more.

Jesus denounced the false teachers for being blind guides. The Pharisees would go to extreme lengths to keep from defiling themselves, by straining out a gnat which was the smallest unclean animal (Leviticus 11:23). However, by rejecting the important matters of the law and rejecting Jesus, they were swallowing a camel or the largest unclean animal (Leviticus 11:4) and were defiling themselves to the largest extent that was possible by leading others away from Christ which showed their utter blindness.

Jesus denounced the false teachers for focusing on external issues rather than focusing on the internal issues of the heart that would have been exposed by a true understanding of the law (Matthew 23:25–26). Though the Pharisees had an outward appearance of morality, Jesus knew that their hearts were still full of wickedness. Jesus denounced them again in Matthew 23:27–28, where He said they were like whitewashed tombs which had an appearance of looking clean and undefiled, but inside they were unclean and full of dead men's bones. Jesus essentially proclaimed that to come under the teaching of the false religious leaders was tantamount to being defiled and unclean by touching a grave.

Finally, Jesus denounces the false religious teachers for their self-righteousness. He proclaims that the false religious leaders honored their ancestors and prophets but were going to kill the greatest Prophet, the Messiah, the Son of God (Matthew 23:29–32). All this culminates in their condemnation, where Jesus says, "You serpents, you brood of vipers, how are you to escape being sentenced to hell?" We learned in the second chapter that false teachers are those who teach a false gospel which leads to a false religious system, and they are damned by God and they damn other men's souls.

So, we see that false teachers not only do not enter the kingdom of heaven, they continually keep people who are trying to enter out of the kingdom of God, and they damn these people even more by making them a double son of hell by converting them to a false religion. It becomes painfully clear why Jesus pronounces such a devastating woe upon these false teachers. To stand before God and be accountable to explain diverting people away from the kingdom of God is a horrifying picture. To give an account because a false gospel was preached would be terrifying. Let us take away an understanding of how Jesus characterized false teachers, their damning gospels and compare it to the definition that has been developed.

- Definition: **A *false teacher* is one who holds to, unrepentantly, and persistently teaches and preaches a false gospel that damns men's souls by attacking, twisting,**

misinterpreting, adding to, or leaving out the essential components of the gospel or essential components of the bad news of sin, death, and hell.

- False teachers are cursed. (Matthew 23:13)
- False teachers claim to be religious and spiritual leaders that offer salvation. (Matthew 23:13)
- False teachers keep people out of the kingdom of heaven through a false gospel. (Matthew 23:13)
- False teachers do not enter the kingdom of heaven. (Matthew 23:13)
- False teachers consistently, deliberately, purposefully, and willfully keep people out of the kingdom because of their false gospel. There is no repentance over their false gospels. (Matthew 23:13)
- False teachers damn men's souls when they convert them over to their false religion or false gospel. (Matthew 23:15)
- False teachers and their converts are double sons of hell. (Matthew 23:15)

Chapter 4: False Gospels through Misinterpretation of Scripture

Luke 11:52—Woe to you lawyers! For you have taken away the key of knowledge. You did not enter yourselves, and you hindered those who were entering.

Thus far in the book, we've learned several things about false teachers. We've learned that a false teacher is closely tied to one who teaches a false gospel (Galatians 1:8–9, Matthew 23:13–15). We've learned that false teachers are accursed by God (Galatians 1:8–9, Matthew 23:15). We've learned that false teachers put a curse on those who embrace their false gospel (Galatians 3:10, Matthew 23:13–15). We've learned that false teachers teach a false gospel that severs people from Christ (Galatians 5:4, Matthew 23:13–15). We've learned that false teachers teach a false gospel purposefully, deliberately, continually, and habitually (Galatians 1:8–9, Matthew 23:13–15). We've learned of the dangers of tolerating a false gospel (Galatians 2:21, 5:9). We've learned that false teachers make their disciples full-fledged pagans (Galatians 5:12, Matthew 23:15). Let's keep these important points in mind as we understand how false teachers can develop false gospels through misinterpretation of Scripture.

In Luke 11:37–52, Jesus pronounces condemnation on the false teachers in His Judean and Perean ministry. Jesus issues six woes to the Pharisees with many of the woes being of similar nature to His sermon in Matthew 23. Jesus condemns them for their external morality rather than focusing on the internal issues of the heart that would have been exposed by a true understanding of the law (Luke 11:39–41). Jesus condemns them for majoring in minor points of the law and neglecting the more important matters of the law and not comprehending the spiritual meaning of the law (Luke 11:42). Jesus condemns them for their spiritual pride, self-righteousness, hypocritical attitude, and love for the honor and praise of men (Luke 11:43, John 12:43). Jesus condemned them because their teaching defiled others like that of touching an unmarked grave (Luke 11:44). Jesus condemned them for loading a false religious system on the backs of their disciples which could not save men and for their complete lack of care, concern, and love for Israel's people (Luke 11:46). Jesus condemns the false religious leaders for honoring their ancestors and prophets but being no different than their ancestors who stoned and killed the prophets as the Pharisees and Sadducees were rejecting Christ (Luke 11:47–51). This ultimately leads to Jesus' condemnation of the false religious leaders for keeping people out of the kingdom of God through misinterpretation of Scripture.

Luke 11:52—Woe to you lawyers! For you have taken away the key of knowledge. You did not enter yourselves, and you hindered those who were entering.

Medicine in the past century has taken huge leaps and bounds. With today's technology, we're able to screen for diseases which allows us to treat a condition and provide preventive care as well as reactive care. We regularly depend on such screening devices such as blood tests, X-rays, CT scans, MRIs, and more to help monitor or diagnose medical conditions. However, although these screening tools are available, let's imagine a scenario where a misinterpretation of one of these tools could lead to devastating results. Imagine a patient came in with signs of vision loss, headaches, loss of balance, weakness, personality or behavior changes, but was also a methamphetamine abuser. The patient had complained of these symptoms for about two months and the doctor ordered a urine analysis to be performed as well as an X-ray. The doctor first received the urine analysis results which came back positive for methamphetamines. The doctor quickly glanced over the X-ray and found nothing. The patient returned six months later with the same symptoms and the doctor ordered the same tests. However, this time, the doctor could see that there was a tumor that had formed and diagnosed the patient with stage IV brain tumor cancer. When the doctor went back to review the X-ray that was taken six months earlier, he noticed there was a small gray area and also noted that it was in the exact same spot where the patient's cancer now was. The doctor had made a fatal error of misinterpreting the first X-ray which led to an untreated tumor that was now fatal.

Jesus announces condemnation on the lawyers for this very error. The word *lawyer* is translated from *nomikos*, which is a lawyer or a scribe. Most sources consider the lawyers to be scribes who specialized in the jurisprudence of the law of Moses. They were to be the ones who would be experts in the law to such an extent that they could properly interpret the law as well as understand the philosophy or "spirit" of the law. Jesus confronted the false religious leaders of His day several times over their misinterpretations and inability to perform their duty. In John 5:39, Jesus scolded them for their lack of scriptural clarity, where He says, "You search the Scriptures because you think that in them you have eternal life; and it is they that bear witness about me, yet you refuse to come to me that you may have life." In Matthew 16:1–3, Jesus rebuked the religious leaders for their inability to see what was right in from of them, where it says, "And the Pharisees and Sadducees came, and to test him they asked him to show them a sign from heaven. He answered them, 'When it is evening, you say, "It will be fair weather, for the sky is red." And in the morning, "It will be stormy today, for the sky is red and threatening." You know how to interpret the appearance of the sky, but you cannot interpret the signs of the times.'" Additionally, in Mark 7:9, Jesus rebukes the false teachers for elevating their man made traditions and not elevating God's Word where He says, "You have a fine way of rejecting the commandment of God in order to establish your tradition!" This severe misinterpretation of Scripture led to them not being able to identify the Messiah and also created a false religious system that kept people out of the kingdom of God.

As we learned earlier, the word *woe* has been translated from the original word *ouai* and this word can be said as "alas!" or "woe" uttered in grief or denunciation. It is an onomatopoeic word (an imitation of the sound) which serves as an interjection expression a cry of intense distress, displeasure, or horror. The reason Jesus announces this denunciation on them is because they have taken away the key of knowledge. The word *airó* has been translated as "taken away." *Airó* has more of a forceful meaning as it can mean "to take away from another what is his" or "to take by force." When *airó* is used in other verses, it carries this very meaning of taking something away by force. This isn't someone taking something from someone as if it's a gift. No, the word carries with it the meaning of ripping something out of another's hand by force.

The other phrase to dissect is *what is the key of knowledge? Knowledge* should be understood as Scripture and *key* should be understood as correct interpretation. The deadly error that the lawyers are being condemned for is incorrect interpretation or misinterpretation of Scripture. Paul gives this command to Timothy in 2 Timothy 2:15, where he says, "Do your best to present yourself to God as one approved, a worker who has no need to be ashamed, rightly handling the word of truth." The phrase *rightly handling* is translated from *orthotomeó*. *Temnō* means "to cut" and *orthós* means "straight." Thus, *orthotomeó* means to "cut straight," "rightly divide," or "correctly handle." Paul is telling Timothy to do exactly what the lawyers did not do, which was to rightly handle and interpret Scripture. When Paul is telling Timothy this, it's as if Paul is telling Timothy, "Timothy, do your very best to have a correct Christology. Timothy, do your best to have a correct soteriology. Timothy, do your best to have a correct systematic theology. Timothy, do your best to have a correct hamartiology. Timothy, do your best to have a correct eschatology. Timothy, do your best to have a correct ecclesiology. Timothy, do your best to have a correct pneumatology. Timothy, do your best to have a correct anthropology. Timothy, do your best to have a correct bibliology." Thus, proper interpretation of Scripture is critical.

Jesus condemns the lawyers for this very thing. The lawyers hindered people by having a wrong understanding of the Messiah. The lawyers hindered the people by having a wrong understanding of how man was saved and polluted the way of salvation with their works–righteousness system. The lawyers hindered the people by having wrong Scriptural interpretations of the Bible, which is evidenced by the oral tradition of the Pharisees captured in the Talmud. There's something else to highlight as it relates to misinterpreting Scripture. In 1 Corinthians 2:14, it says, "The natural person does not accept the things of the Spirit of God, for they are folly to him, and he is not able to understand them because they are spiritually discerned." Since we know that all Scripture is inspired by God (2 Timothy 3:16) and that all Scripture was written by man as man was inspired by the Holy Spirit (2 Peter 1:21), we see here that unless the Spirit of God enables a man to understand the very words that were inspired by the Holy Spirit, man cannot understand God's Word. Thus, misinterpretation of God's Word to such an extent that it produces a false gospel is evidence of the absence of the Holy Spirit in the one misinterpreting the Scripture.

Notice that taking away the key of knowledge is not a small misinterpretation of Scripture. No, this is a misinterpretation that keeps false teachers outside the kingdom of heaven where Jesus says, "You did not enter yourselves." As we've learned earlier, those that preach a false gospel are accursed and outside the kingdom of God (Galatians 1:8, Matthew 23:13–15). We've also learned that there are smaller matters in the law and larger matters (Matthew 23:23) and this misinterpretation is a large matter that inevitably produces a false gospel and curses those who teach it as they are "outside the kingdom of God."

Let's also notice that this is a misinterpretation of Scripture that hinders others who are entering. The word *hinders* is translated from *kóluó*. *Kóluó* means "to prevent," "to hinder," "to cut off, cut short," or "to prevent or forbid." Only a false gospel produces such an effect of damning men's souls (Galatians 3:10). This misinterpretation is a monumental catastrophe that prevents people from entering the kingdom of heaven. Let's also notice the phrase "you hindered those who were entering." This was not a passive action. This was not a spontaneous action. No, this was purposeful, deliberate, and fixed taking away of the key of knowledge. This was a purposeful, deliberate, and fixed misinterpretation that put a curse on people (Galatians 3:10), severed people from Christ (Galatians 5:4), and made people full-fledged pagans (Galatians 5:12). These people were trying to enter the kingdom. These people were coming close to the kingdom of heaven and seeking it (Matthew 7:7). These people were seeking first the kingdom of God (Matthew 6:33, Luke 12:31). These people were agonizing to enter through the narrow door (Luke 13:24). These people had come to the Gate (John 10:7, 9). These people were seeking to enter through the narrow gate (Matthew 7:13–14). These people had come right up to Jesus who is the Gate, the narrow door, the narrow gate, entrance into the kingdom of heaven, and the only way to the Father (John 14:6); and, the lawyers, just like the Pharisees, slammed the door shut right in people's faces through misinterpretation of Scripture.

Modern Christianity

We can clearly see how lawyers and Pharisees misinterpreted Scripture during Jesus' ministry, but damning misinterpretation is still present today. For demonstration purposes, it may be helpful to see how incorrect misinterpretation around soteriology, or salvation, could easily lead to a false gospel. I will present some verses that could be easily misinterpreted and lead to a false understanding of how one is saved.

- Yet she will be saved through childbearing—if they continue in faith and love and holiness, with self-control. (1 Timothy 2:15)
    - Is Paul meaning to suggest that women can be saved through childbearing? Is he meaning to say that women are saved through childbearing but must also have faith, love, holiness, and self-control? Is this passage a salvation verse?
- Therefore, my beloved, as you have always obeyed, so now, not only as in my presence but much more in my absence, work out your salvation with fear and trembling. (Philippians 2:12)
    - Is Paul meaning to suggest that we work for our salvation? Is he meaning to suggest that we work out the salvation we already possess? Is he meaning to suggest that we work out our salvation with the help of God? Is he meaning to suggest that we work for our salvation with the help of God?
- Whoever believes and is baptized will be saved, but whoever does not believe will be condemned. (Mark 16:16)

  - Is Jesus meaning to say that we must believe and be baptized to be saved? Is Jesus meaning to say that one can be saved through baptism? Is Jesus saying we could be saved through either believing or baptism?
- And Peter said to them, "Repent and be baptized every one of you in the name of Jesus Christ for the forgiveness of your sins, and you will receive the gift of the Holy Spirit." (Acts 2:38)
  - Is Peter meaning to say that we must repent and be baptized to be forgiven? Is Peter meaning to say that forgiveness comes from being baptized only, repenting only, or by both repentance and baptism?
- for, "Everyone who calls on the name of the Lord will be saved" (Romans 10:13)
  - Is salvation just a matter of calling on the name of the Lord? If someone simply says, "Lord save me" but is unwilling to repent, deny themselves, submit to Jesus as Lord, God, and Savior and trust Him alone, are they saved by saying, "Lord save me"?
- You see that a person is justified by works and not by faith alone. (James 2:24)
  - Are we saved by our works and not by faith alone? Can people be saved by other's works and faith?
- For we hold that one is justified by faith apart from works of the law (Romans 3:28)
  - Are we now saved only by faith apart from works of the law? How are we to understand Romans 3:28 in light of James 2:24?

As you can, if we were to take these verses and misinterpret them and take them out of context without a clear understanding of the subjective response of salvation to the objective person and work of Christ, we could fatally misinterpret salvation. In fact, a *soteriology*, or understanding of salvation, could be misconstrued to be that for one to be saved they could be saved by any and all of the following: saved through childbearing, saved through working out our salvation, saved through believing "mental assent," saved through being baptized, saved through repentance, saved through calling on the name of the Lord, saved through faith, saved through faith along with works. As you can see, this is why we labored to understand what true repentance and saving faith looked like as we are not saved by our works. We are not saved through baptism. We are not saved through childbearing. We are saved through faith, which God grants to us and which is never separate or apart from repentance, which is also granted by God.

How devastating is it to misinterpret a verse and, thus, attack, twist, misinterpret, add to, or leave out the essential components of the gospel or essential components of the bad news of sin, death, and hell? Let's take a look at the implications of misinterpreting verses regarding salvation and the subjective response to the objective person and work of Jesus. Can a misinterpretation of Scripture have an eternal impact?

Catholic Church

- 1.2 billion members
    - False Gospel of Baptismal Regeneration—Error in the Subjective Response to the Objective Person and Work of Jesus
        - Misinterpretation of Titus 3:5, Galatians 3:27, John 3:5, and more
            - Result—Members believe themselves to be saved because they underwent the sacrament of baptism
            - Result—The Catholic Church cannot warn the congregation that they may not be born again
    - False Gospel of Faith Plus Works—Error in the Subjective Response to the Objective Person and Work of Jesus

        - Misinterpretation of James 2:14–26
            - Result—Members believe that their good works and faith in Jesus merit salvation

Eastern Orthodox Church

- 220 million members
    - False Gospel of Baptismal Regeneration—Error in the Subjective Response to the Objective Person and Work of Jesus
        - Misinterpretation of Galatians 3:27 and John 3:5
            - Result—Members believe themselves to be saved because they underwent the sacrament of baptism
            - Result—The Eastern Orthodox Church cannot warn the congregation that they may not be born again
    - False Gospel of Faith Plus Works—Error in the Subjective Response to the Objective Person and Work of Jesus
        - Misinterpretation of James 2:14–26
            - Result—Members believe that their good works and faith in Jesus merit salvation

Lutheran Church

- 81 million members
    - False Gospel of Baptismal Regeneration—Error in the Subjective Response to the Objective Person and Work of Jesus
        - Misinterpretation of John 3:5, Romans 6:3–4, Galatians 3:26–27, Ephesians 5:26, Titus 3:5, Acts 2:38, 22:16
            - Result—Members believe themselves to be saved because they underwent the sacrament of baptism
            - Result—The Lutheran Church cannot warn the congregation that they may not be born again

Anglican Church

- 110 million members
  - False Gospel of Baptismal Regeneration—Error in the Subjective Response to the Objective Person and Work of Jesus
    - Misinterpretation of Galatians 3:26–27, Colossians 2:11–13
      - Result—Members believe themselves to be saved because they underwent the sacrament of baptism
      - Result—The Anglican Church cannot warn the congregation that they may not be born again

As you can see, in examining just four churches, we can see that within these four churches, there are 1.6 billion people who are taught that they were born again or regenerated when they were baptized and there are 1.4 billion people who are taught that one is saved through faith and works rather than God giving new birth which enables man to repent and put their faith in Christ alone. These are churches that profess to preach Christ crucified and claim to teach how to be reconciled to Christ. However, you also see that a misinterpretation of verses can lead to devastating results where someone believes they are saved through a means or response other than repentance and faith in Christ.

As we close this chapter, we can understand the following with regard to false teachers:

- Definition: **A *false teacher* is one who holds to, unrepentantly, and persistently teaches and preaches a false gospel that damns men's souls by attacking, twisting, misinterpreting, adding to, or leaving out the essential**

components of the gospel or essential components of the bad news of sin, death, and hell.

- A false teacher can take away the key of knowledge or, rather, misinterpret Scripture which leads to a false gospel. (Luke 11:52)
- The misinterpretation is not a small error, but rather a significant misinterpretation that keeps people out of the kingdom of heaven. (Luke 11:52)
- Misinterpretation of God's Word to such an extent that it produces a false gospel is evidence of the absence of the Holy Spirit in the one teaching. (1 Corinthians 2:14, 1 Timothy 3:16, 2 Peter 1:21)
- The misinterpretation of God's Word is significant enough to keep those who teach it out of the kingdom of God and, thus, those who teach it are cursed. (Galatians 1:8–9, Luke 11:52)
- The misinterpretation of God's Word is significant enough to keep those who embrace it out of the kingdom of God and, thus, those who embrace it are cursed. (Galatians 3:10, Luke 11:52)
- Luke implies that this was a purposeful, deliberate, and fixed action of taking away the key of knowledge or misinterpreting Scripture which continually led people astray. (Luke 11:52)
- We see the importance of how Scripture is an essential component of the gospel as Scripture contains the gospel and a misinterpretation of an essential component of the gospel can lead to a false gospel. (Luke 11:52)

Chapter 5: Destructive Heresies

2 Peter 2:1—But false prophets also arose among the people, just as there will be false teachers among you, who will secretly bring in destructive heresies, even denying the Master who bought them, bringing upon themselves swift destruction.

The Second Book of Peter was written for the purpose of exposing, thwarting, and defeating the proliferation and invasion of false teachers into the church. Peter wrote this letter with the intention to provide instructions and explanations on how to protect his listeners against false teachers and their lies. Although Peter does not identify the specific destructive heresies, he does give a general characterization and calls out that they have destructive heresies, deny Christ, and twist Scripture. Of particular importance is Peter's emphasis on knowledge. Peter links knowledge of God and of the Lord Jesus Christ to receiving grace and peace (2 Peter 1:2). Peter links knowledge of God to being able to live a godly life (2 Peter 1:3). Peter links knowledge of the Lord Jesus Christ to prevent living an idle and unfruitful life (2 Peter 1:8). Peter links knowledge of the Lord Jesus Christ and living a godly life to assurance of salvation (2 Peter 1:10–11). Peter talks about knowledge of the Lord's coming (2 Peter 1:16). Peter links lack of knowledge with blaspheming (2 Peter 2:12). Peter talks about the damning results of apostasy where a false teacher has full knowledge of the Lord Jesus Christ, but turned from the knowledge of Jesus Christ (2 Peter 2:21). Peter links growing in the knowledge of the Lord and Savior Jesus Christ to not being led astray by false teachers (2 Peter 3:17–18). The following is a good outline of this epistle (4).

I. Salutation (1:1–2)
II. Know Your Salvation (1:3–11)
    a. Sustained by God's Power (1:3–4)
    a. Confirmed by Christian Graces (1:5–7)
    a. Honored by Abundant Reward (1:8–11)
III. Know Your Scriptures (1:12–21)
    a. Certified by Apostolic Witness (1:12–18)
    a. Inspired by the Holy Spirit (1:19–21)
IV. Know Your Adversaries (2:1–22)
    a. Deceptive in Their Infiltration (2:1–3)
    a. Doomed by Their Iniquity (2:4–10)
    a. Disdainful in Their Impurity (2:11–17)
    a. Devastating in Their Impact (2:18–22)
V. Know Your Prophecy (3:1–18)
    a. The Sureness of the Day of the Lord (3:1–10)
    a. The Sanctification of God's People (3:11–18)

As we transition into Peter's portrait of false teachers, we can see that Peter has spent time ensuring that everyone know their salvation which would come from knowing the gospel (2 Peter 1:3–11). Peter will then remind his people to remember, recall, and retain the truth (2 Peter 1:12–15). Peter then confirms the truths of the gospel are not man-made but from God (2 Peter 1:16). He defends his apostleship by being an eyewitness account which would affirm the transfiguration of Jesus (2 Peter 1:16). He confirms the Lord's second coming (2 Peter 1:16). He confirms Jesus being the Son of God by hearing the Father's affirmation of the Son (2 Peter 1:17). He confirms hearing the voice of the Father (2 Peter 1:18). He confirms the importance of Scripture, more specifically, the Old Testament which confirms prophecies that were foretold (2 Peter 1:19). He confirms that Scripture is all inspired by God and not from man (2 Peter

1:20), and that all Scripture was written by man as they were inspired by the Holy Spirit (2 Peter 1:21). This transitions us into his teaching on false teachers.

It is probably good to stop and reflect at this point as we followed a similar approach to Peter. As you remember, we sought to understand the gospel, but realized that the good news could only be understood by first understanding the bad news. Once we understood the bad news, we set out to understand the gospel and the essential components of the gospel. We developed some definitions of the bad news as well as the good news which are as follows:

- The bad news is that man has sinned, which is breaking God's law by either not doing what His law demands or doing what His law prohibits by any thought, word, deed, or intent. God's disposition toward sin is one of hatred, anger, abhorrence, defilement, wickedness, evil, hostility, and is warfare against Him. Man is incapable of curing his problem with sin. Man cannot propitiate the righteous anger of God, redeem himself, earn forgiveness, or be made right with God on his own merits. God's attributes such as being eternal, loving, just, good, faithful, omniscient, and immutable demand that God must punish sin. The punishment of sin is hell, which is a place of God's full wrath and a place of blackest darkness, filled with furious and concentrated fire everywhere, weeping and anger against God where the unrepentant Christ-rejecting and Christ-neglecting sinners will spend all eternity paying for every sin they've ever committed with no hope of escape, and only the expectation of excruciating torments to their body, soul, and spirit and an undying conscience that will haunt them day and night, forever and ever, with no reprieve.

- The good news or the gospel is the good news of salvation that God has authored and owns. God had promised this plan of salvation through His prophets and Holy Scripture and has fully revealed the good news of salvation through Scripture which is the authoritative, inspired inerrant, and infallible Word of God. The good news concerns the person and work of Jesus Christ. The person of Jesus is He is the Christ, the Creator of the universe, the promised Jewish Messiah, the only begotten Son of the Living God, which makes Him God and equal with God the Father and God the Holy Spirit. Jesus was born of a virgin and conceived by the Holy Spirit and became a man and is, thus, truly God and truly man and can represent God to man and man to God. The work of Jesus is that Jesus lived a sinless life and fulfilled all righteousness found in the law and prophets and declared Himself to be the Christ, the only begotten Son of the Living God through His teaching which was attested to by His miracles and the Holy Spirit. Jesus offered himself as a sinless, spotless, and blameless sacrifice for sin to propitiate the righteous anger of God by taking all the sins of God's people on Himself and, thus, the full wrath of God that was due to man. His sacrifice propitiated the righteous anger of God and reconciled and brought peace from man to God and God to man. His substitutionary sacrifice and death also redeemed sinful man to Holy God by forgiving man's sin and imputing His righteousness to man, so man could stand before God with the righteousness of Jesus Christ in judgment. Jesus was resurrected from the dead on the third day by His own power, by God the Father, and by God the Holy Spirit which affirmed His person, His teachings, and salvific work for sinners. He ascended to the right hand of the Father and is empowered with all authority to bring about the plan of salvation for all His people by causing

> them to be born again and justified by His grace. He will also return to bring all of His own to heaven with Him to be glorified while also judging and condemning Satan, demons, and sinful man. The benefits of Christ's person and work are available to those who repent and put saving faith in Christ. *Repentance* is a gift from God where the sinner understands his sin against God (intellect), has godly sorrow and mourns over his sin against God (emotions and affections), and turns away from his sin and toward God for righteousness (will or volition). *Saving faith* is a gift from God where a sinner has knowledge of Jesus' person and work where a sinner will respond to Christ's person and work by denying themselves, picking up their cross, submitting and committing their life to Jesus, and trusting in Him only for salvation.

Only after we understood the gospel could we begin to understand false teachers. We needed to understand the essential components of the bad news: sin, death, and hell. We needed to understand the **essential components of the gospel: authored by God, found in Scripture, objective person of Jesus, objective work of Jesus, and the subjective response to the objective person and work of Jesus which is faith and repentance in Jesus**. The point being is that false teachers cannot be identified aside from knowing the gospel. Peter knows this and was desiring that his people would continue on in the truth of what they had learned. One of the reasons this book is written in this order where the gospel is explained first is for this very reason. Apart from a scriptural understanding of the gospel, it would be impossible to detect error. As we transition into 2 Peter 2, let's keep this in mind as we seek to better understand what makes a false teacher.

2 Peter 2:1—But false prophets also arose among the people, just as there will be false teachers among you, who will secretly bring in destructive heresies, even denying the Master who bought them, bringing upon themselves swift destruction.

The first point to emphasize is that false teachers will be among Christians. This is not speaking of false religions outside of Christianity. No, this is speaking of false teachers being amongst believers. Peter knew of the history of false prophets rising up among the Israelites. There were certainly many instances where the people of Israel were led astray by false teachers or false prophets such as Korah, Dathan, and Abiram opposing Aaron and Moses (Numbers 16:1–49), the prophets of Baal on Mount Carmel (1 Kings 18), the false prophets who prophesied good news to King Ahab (1 Kings 21), the false prophets during Jeremiah's time prophesying peace when there was no peace (Jeremiah 6:13–17, 23:9–32), the false prophets of Isaiah's time prophesying peace when there was no peace (Isaiah 44:24–26), the false prophets during Ezekiel's time prophesying peace when there was no peace (Ezekiel 13:1–16), and many more instances. In fact, Peter would have known the same truths as Paul that false teachers could spring up from inside the church (Acts 20:29–30), from outside the church (Acts 20:29), that they would teach different objective truths about the person of Jesus (2 Corinthians 11:4), that they would teach different objective truths about the work of Jesus (2 Corinthians 11:4), that they would have different and deceptive spirits (2 Corinthians 11:4), that they would be deceitful and would disguise themselves as apostles of Christ (2 Corinthians 11:13), that Satan was in false religion and disguised himself as an angel of light (2 Corinthians 11:14), that those who serve Satan would disguise themselves as servants of righteousness (2 Corinthians 11:15), and that they would have smooth and flattering speech (Romans 16:18). Peter knew the same thing. In fact, as we learned earlier, Peter needed to be corrected by Paul in Galatians when Peter's actions with the Judaizers were causing people to be led astray.

The lexicon describes a *pseudoprophétés* or a false prophet as "one who in God's name teaches what is false" or "someone pretending to speak the word of the Lord (prophesy) but in fact is a phony (imposter), acting as a wolf in sheep's cloth." The lexicon describes a *pseudodidaskalos* or a false teacher as "a teacher of false things" or "a spurious teacher (i.e., propagator of erroneous Christian doctrine)." Let's remember our definition of a *false teacher* as we'll see that this definition will line up with Peter's definition: **A *false teacher* is one who holds to, unrepentantly, and persistently teaches and preaches a false gospel that damns men's souls by attacking, twisting, misinterpreting, adding to, or leaving out the essential components of the gospel or essential components of the bad news of sin, death, and hell.**

The second point to notice is that the false teachers will secretly introduce their destructive heresies. The phrase *secretly bring in* comes from *pareisagó*, which is a compound word of *pará*, which means "*from* close beside," and *eiságō*, which means "introduce." Properly, it means to "introduce from close beside (i.e., enter by stealth)." This secretly introduced heresy could be a simple misinterpretation (Luke 11:52), man-made rule or oral tradition (Mark 7:9), a twisting of Scripture (2 Peter 3:16), or adding to or taking away from Scripture (Revelation 22:18–19). There is often just enough truth in the lie to pass as something that may be truth. Peter is warning the believers that this is not going to be obvious. This is going to be very subtle. This is going to be hard to detect. This is going to require knowledge of the truth and careful examination. Just as the Bereans were commended for comparing Paul's message with Scripture (Acts 17:10–12), it is also required of believers to pay attention to the message and what is being taught because Peter is stating that the heresies are going to enter stealthily. Jude adds a little bit to this where, in Jude 4, he says something similar, "For certain people have crept in unnoticed who long ago were designated for this condemnation, ungodly people, who pervert the grace of our God into sensuality and deny our only Master and Lord, Jesus Christ." So, putting both Peter and Jude's verses together we see that false teachers enter stealthily and introduce their heresies stealthily as well.

The third point to note is that the heresies that they introduce are destructive heresies. *Destruction* is *apóleia* and it means "destruction, causing someone or something to be completely severed." It does not mean annihilation but rather speaks of the complete loss of well-being. This word *apóleia* is often used to describe destruction which is eternal destruction or eternal misery.

Heresies comes from *hairesis* and means a self-chosen opinion, a religious or philosophical sect, discord, or contention. This stresses a personal aspect of choice. The word *hairesis* evolved to mean a self-willed opinion. A self-willed opinion stands in opposition to the submission to the power of truth, and leads to division and the formation of sects. Paul helps us understand the extent of this self-chosen opinion or religious sect where he says in Titus 3:10–11, "As for a person who stirs up division, after warning him once and then twice, have nothing more to do with him, knowing that such a person is warped and sinful; he is self-condemned." The phrase *who stirs up division* comes from *hairetikos,* which carries the same meaning as *hairesis.* Therefore, it should be noted that these heresies aren't minor. No, these heresies are eternally destructive to those who hear them and are eternally destructive to those who teach them.

Fourth, these teachers have no submission to the Lord. There is a difficult phrase to dissect in this verse which is *even denying the master who bought them,* so it will be important to understand these words and put them together to help understand what Peter is saying. *Denying* is translated from *arneomai,* which means "to deny, refuse" or "contract, refuse to affirm or to confess."

Arneomai is used when Peter denied the Lord, such as in Mark 14:68. *Arneomai* is used Luke 12:8–9 where Jesus says, "And I tell you, everyone who acknowledges me before men, the Son of Man also will acknowledge before the angels of God, but the one who denies me before men will be denied before the angels of God." The second word to understand is *agorazó* and it properly means "to make purchases in the marketplace" or "acquire by purchasing." The third word to understand is *Master*, which is *despotés. Despotés* means "a lord" or "master." *Despotés* carries with it the unrestricted power and absolute domination, confessing no limitations or restraints. Still, even after understanding these words, this phrase can be hard to dissect, but upon careful inspection, we'll see what Peter is trying to say.

When Peter is saying that they are "even denying the master who bought them," he is saying that although they claim to be Christ's, they deny Him by their teaching or manner of life. They contradict and deny the Lord by their actions and teaching. One of Jesus' most compassionate invitations to accept Him as Lord and Savior comes in Matthew 11:28–30, where He says, "Come to me, all who labor and are heavy laden, and I will give you rest. Take my yoke upon you, and learn from me, for I am gentle and lowly in heart, and you will find rest for your souls. For my yoke is easy, and my burden is light." Notice in Matthew 11:29, Jesus says, "Take my yoke upon you, and learn from me." This is a picture of submission. Farmers back in the ancient world knew the frustration of trying to plow a field or transport a cart with a stiff-necked animal. An animal that refused to bow his head in submission to the yoke was useless to perform any real work. When someone accepts Jesus as their Lord and Savior, there is a bowing of the head and a submission to Christ's yoke. When Jesus stops, you stop. When Jesus goes, you go. When Jesus commands you to pick up the pace, you will pick up the pace. When Jesus commands that you turn to the left, you'll turn to the left. This is not perfect obedience, but Peter is saying that there is no submission with these false teachers. As we learned just above, these false teachers have self-willed opinions and religious sects which goes hand in hand with no submission to the Lord. Jude helps clarify this a little more where he says in Jude 4, "For certain people have crept in unnoticed who long ago were designated for this condemnation, ungodly people, who pervert the grace of our God into sensuality and deny our only Master and Lord, Jesus Christ." Jude gives the same picture of these false teachers who enter the church stealthily but deny the Lord and Master, Jesus Christ. This is to say that they claim allegiance to Christ, but by their teaching and actions, they deny Him. Paul likewise gives the same idea where he says in Titus 1:16, "They profess to know God, but by their actions they deny Him. They are detestable, disobedient, and unfit for any good work." Therefore, we can understand that Peter is saying these false teachers claim allegiance to Christ but deny Him through their teaching and lives. Let's also note that this verse doesn't suggest that these false teachers are Christians. We'll see this as we transition to the fifth point which is that they bring destruction upon themselves.

Fifth, let's notice that they will be destroyed. Peter says, "bringing upon themselves swift destruction." Not only do these false teachers introduce destructive heresies which damn their hearers, they bring destruction upon themselves. *Tachinos* is translated to "swift" and carries with it the idea of something or an event being swift, quick, or impending. Jude gives this same picture in Jude 23 where he says, "Save others by snatching them out of the fire; to others show mercy with fear, hating even the garment stained by the flesh." This carries the idea that these false teachers are right on the precipice of entering eternal punishment and need to be rescued. However, it is also a dangerous task to reach your hand in the fire to help pull them out as they are deceitful and misleading. They are like unmarked graves and they can defile you by their teaching (Luke 11:44). As we've understood throughout the book, false teachers teach a false gospel that ultimately curses and damns them. Peter fully agrees that such a teaching that produces a false gospel is a teaching that will damn the one who teaches it.

2 Peter 2:2—And will follow their sensuality, and because of them the way of truth will be blasphemed

As we've been discussing, it is quite clear that false teachers will teach false doctrines that will damn men's souls. Up until this point, we haven't necessarily discussed a false teacher's actions or walk of life. However, Peter's statement in verse 2 explains that a teacher's walk of life can also be an indication of whether or not they are a false teacher. Paul said this very thing to Timothy where he says in 1 Timothy 4:16, "Keep a close watch on yourself and on the teaching. Persist in this, for by so doing you will save both yourself and your hearers." Paul's exhortation was that Timothy carefully watch over his walk of life as well as his doctrine for the sake of Timothy's life as well as those around him. The wickedness that is produced out of a false teacher is not the product of sound doctrine, but of "destructive heresies."

First, let's notice that teaching destructive heresies can lead to following sensuality. *Sensuality* has been translated from *aselgeia,* which means "licentiousness," "wantonness," or "outrageous conduct, conduct shocking to public decency." Paul gives a picture of what these false teachers may look like in 2 Timothy 3:1–7, where he says, "But understand this, that in the last days there will come times of difficulty. For people will be lovers of self, lovers of money, proud, arrogant, abusive, disobedient to their parents, ungrateful, unholy, heartless, unappeasable, slanderous, without self-control, brutal, not loving good, treacherous, reckless, swollen with conceit, lovers of pleasure rather than lovers of God, having the appearance of godliness, but denying its power. Avoid such people. For among them are those who creep into households and capture weak women, burdened with sins and led astray by various passion, always learning and never able to arrive at a knowledge of the truth." Paul gives another picture of false teachers in 1 Timothy 6:3–5, 9–10, "If anyone teaches a different doctrine and does not agree with the sound words of our Lord Jesus Christ and the teaching that accords with godliness, he is puffed up with conceit and understands nothing. He has an unhealthy craving for controversy and for quarrels about words, which produce envy, dissension, slander, evil suspicions, and constant friction among people who are depraved in mind and deprived of the truth, imagining that godliness is a means of gain. But those who desire to be rich fall into temptation, into a snare, into many senseless and harmful desires that plunge people into ruin and destruction. For the love of money is a root of all kinds of evils. It is through this craving that some have wandered away from the faith and pierced themselves with many pangs." In 2 Timothy 2:16, Paul says of false teachers, "Avoid godless chatter, because those who indulge in it will become more and more ungodly." Paul says of false teachers in Titus 1:10, "For there are many who are insubordinate, empty talkers and deceivers, especially those of the circumcision party. They must be silenced since they are upsetting whole families by teaching for shameful gain what they ought not to teach." Therefore, we can understand the outward behavior and internal motives of a false teacher could encompass the following from the following passages as well as from the rest of 2 Peter and Jude:

- Lovers of self—someone preoccupied with their own selfish desires (2 Timothy 3:2)
- Lovers of money—someone in love with personal gain of money (2 Timothy 3:2)
- Boastful—an empty pretender, bragger (2 Timothy 3:2, Jude 16)
- Proud—arrogant, going beyond what God directs (2 Timothy 3:2)

- Abusive to parents—slanderous and evil-speaking toward parents (2 Timothy 3:2)
- Disobedient—unwilling to be persuaded by God (2 Timothy 3:2)
- Ungrateful—without God's grace which results in unthankfulness (2 Timothy 3:2)
- Unholy—having utter disregard of what is sacred (2 Timothy 3:2)
- Unloving—devoid of natural affection (2 Timothy 3:3)
- Unappeasable—unable to be pleased or satisfied (2 Timothy 3:3)
- Slanderous—falsely accusing (2 Timothy 3:3)
- Without self-control—powerless, inclined to excess, lacking self-restraint (2 Timothy 3:3)
- Brutal—not tame; savage, fierce (2 Timothy 3:3)
- Not loving good—someone who is hostile to the things of God (2 Timothy 3:3)
- Treacherous—betraying or being a traitor (2 Timothy 3:4)
- Reckless—impulsive, rash, reckless, headstrong brought on by unbridled passion (2 Timothy 3:4)
- Swollen with conceit—having a cloudy mindset or moral blindness resulting from poor judgment which brings further loss of spiritual perception (2 Timothy 3:4)
- Lovers of pleasure—loving the bodily or natural senses of pleasure (2 Timothy 3:4)
- Not lovers of God—not a lover of God or the things of God (2 Timothy 3:4)
- Having a form of godliness but denying its power—outward moralism but not true believers and no inward reality of the power of the Holy Spirit or partakers in God's divine nature (2 Timothy 3:5)
- Creep into houses and capture weak women—taking advantage of the weak and vulnerable (2 Timothy 3:6)

- Learning but never able to come to a knowledge of the truth—learners but do not possess saving knowledge (2 Timothy 3:7)
- Teaches a different doctrine that doesn't agree with Christ's teaching (1 Timothy 6:3)
- Is inclined toward meaningless debates and questions and idle speculations (1 Timothy 6:4)
- Argue over words—argue over terminology and minor doctrinal subjects (1 Timothy 6:4)
- They have a corrupted mind—unregenerate mind that does not have in mind the things of God (1 Timothy 6:5)
- They are deprived of the truth—do not have the truth of God's word and more specifically, the gospel (1 Timothy 6:5)
- They engage in godless chatter—empty discussion or discussion of vain and useless matters (2 Timothy 2:16)
- Insubordinate—not subject to rule, not submissive to God and unwilling to come under Christ's Lordship, not submissive to God's plan with a defiant attitude (Titus 1:10)
- Empty talkers—an idle talker, one who utters empty senseless things (Titus 1:10)
- Deceivers—leading others into delusion or away from the truth (Titus 1:10)
- Indulge in defiling lust and passion (2 Peter 2:10)
- Blaspheming glorious ones—commanding or speaking blasphemously against demons and Satan which have more power over them (2 Peter 2:10, Jude 8)
- Bold—darers or very bold people who foolishly ignore what should make them afraid (2 Peter 2:10)
- Despising authority—unwilling to submit to authority, but especially to Christ's authority (2 Peter 2:10, Jude 8)
- Self-willed—seeking only to gratify themselves by being self-satisfied, arrogant, or stubborn (2 Peter 2:10)

- Irrational—without reason or contrary to reason but refers to irrational thinking from God's point of view or what is completely against divine reason (2 Peter 2:12, Jude 10)
- Creatures of instinct—natural, describing the behavior of an unregenerate person and lacking divine transformation (2 Peter 2:12)
- Blaspheme in matters in which they are ignorant—speaking irreverently and slanderously about divine truth and may also be willful ignorance (2 Peter 2:12, Jude 10)
- Revel in the daytime—living outright debauched, indulgent, and sinful lives in public and not hiding (2 Peter 2:13)
- Blots and blemishes—they are dirty, foul, diseased, and polluted (2 Peter 2:13)
- Eyes full of adultery—they view women as potential adulterers or as sexual objects (2 Peter 2:14)
- Hearts trained in greed—they can never have enough pride, power, preeminence, money, materials, and authority (2 Peter 2:14)
- Waterless springs, clouds, and mists—they appear to provide a spiritual need but provide nothing (2 Peter 2:17, Jude 12)
- Promise freedom, but are slaves—they appear to provide spiritual freedom and knowledge but provide nothing (2 Peter 2:19)
- Relying on dreams—they give undue preeminence to their personal dreams rather than give the preeminence which is only due to Scripture (Jude 8)
- Fruitless trees and twice dead—they appear to provide a spiritual need but provide nothing because they are spiritually dead (Jude 12)
- Murmurer—one who discontentedly complains (Jude 16)
- Discontent—complaining over allotted portion (Jude 16)

It's important to note that a false teacher may not have all these characteristics or traits. However, these traits are important in helping discern the outward fruit of a teacher's life to determine if they are a false teacher.

It's also important to note that in Paul's description he says they are "having an appearance of godliness, but denying its power." Jude says they have "crept in unnoticed" and "pervert the grace of our God into sensuality." Jesus says in Matthew 7:15, "Beware of false prophets, who come to you in sheep's clothing but inwardly are ravenous wolves." Jesus says in Matthew 23:27 that they may have outward morality, "Woe to you, scribes and Pharisees, hypocrites! For you are like whitewashed tombs, which outwardly appear beautiful, but within are full of dead people's bones and all uncleanness." Here, both Jesus and Paul note that they are going to be hard to spot and will have a form of godliness and be dressed like a shepherd or a teacher. Therefore, outward sensuality can be a strong indication of someone being a false teacher, but this may not always be the case as we've seen that outward morality is an effective means to hide a false teacher.

Second, we should see that false teachers who follow their sensuality will blaspheme the way of the truth. The word *blaspheme* comes from *blasphémeó*. *Blasphémeó* refers to speaking evil against or refusing to acknowledge good; hence, *blaspheming* reverses that which is good. Jesus warned of the sin of blasphemy of the Holy Spirit when He had driven out an impure spirit and the Pharisees accused Jesus of driving out the impure spirit by the power of Satan. What the Pharisees were doing was attributing the works of God to Satan. The Pharisees were speaking evil against Jesus's person and work where He had claimed He was the Lord of the Sabbath by healing a man with a shriveled hand (Matthew 12:8) and, now, after healing a demon-possessed man and people asking if He could be the Son of David, the Pharisees attributed His works to Satan (Matthew 12:22–33). Blaspheming the way of the truth can be understood from two different perspectives and both would be correct. The first way a false teacher could blaspheme the way of the truth by their sensuality is by giving the correct doctrine, but having their life disagree with the correct doctrine. For example, if a pastor who said that one must repent and put their faith in Jesus but was actively committing adultery with another woman would certainly be blaspheming the way of truth because, by his actions, he is claiming he belongs to God but his life vehemently opposes the truth. This could cause his listeners to dismiss the true doctrine by the hypocrisy of his life. Another way a false teacher could blaspheme the way of the truth is by teaching a false doctrine which accepts a sensuous lifestyle and, thus, blasphemes the gospel call to saving faith or blasphemes the believer's sanctified walk of life. In both cases, whether the false teacher gives true doctrine and lives sensuously or gives false doctrine and lives sensuously, this blasphemes the way of truth of how someone understands to come to Jesus in a saving way or how a believer is to live their sanctified Christian life.

2 Peter 2:3 – And in their greed they will exploit you with false words. Their condemnation from long ago is not idle, and their destruction is not asleep.

As we see above, there are many reasons why false teachers may continue in their false doctrine. This could be for love of money, job security, pride, love of prominence, comfort, keeping friends, and a host of other factors. In any case, it is God who knows the heart. In Proverbs 21:2, it says, "Every way of a man is right in his own eyes, but the LORD weighs the heart." We don't know what the reason is for false teachers and their motives, but we can be assured they have their own reasons for teaching their damning doctrines.

First, Peter notes that the false teachers will continue in their false doctrine because of greed. *Greed* has been translated from *pleonexia,* which means "covetousness" or, properly, "the desire for more things (lusting for a greater number of temporal things that go beyond what God determines is eternally best)." As mentioned above, it's impossible to know the true motive of a false teacher, but the text strongly suggests that the false teacher is unwilling to give up the damning doctrine for covetous reasons.

Second, we should see that they deceive through false words. The word *false* is actually *plastos* in the original language, which means "formed, molded," "shaped according to a mold," or "made-up, fabricated." It carries with it the idea of molding at will to suit one's vain imaginations. Once again, this is fake or molded theology. This is not God's Word. They may use words in the Bible and may use theology terminology, but this is not actually God's truth. As we noted above, these false teachers are self-willed and deny submission to the Lord through either their actions or teachings. The false words are just an outcome of their self-will and unsubmissive hearts and minds. False teachers may use the same terminology, but they have a different dictionary. False teachers may use the same words as true teachers, but the words have different meanings which are false.

Third, we see that they exploit their listeners through their false words. The word *exploit* comes from *emporeuomai,* which carries the idea of "a place for trading or doing business." Peter is saying here that they take advantage of their listeners for money. Peter would certainly be thinking of the outrageous televangelists who have huge mansions and private jets, but he also has in mind those who make their living off false teaching. For example, it's not necessarily that these false teachers are getting rich off their trade but, rather, they are able to get what they want through their profession. This certainly carries the heavy implication that false teachers do this for money. However, as we noted earlier, false teachers can certainly be covetous for money, but they can also be covetous for power, prestige, preeminence, comfort, friends, and more.

Fourth, we see that their condemnation is confirmed. As we learned earlier in Galatians, those who teach destructive heresies are those who preach a different or false gospel (Galatians 1:8–9). Those who teach the false gospel are accursed and headed for destruction (Galatians 1:8–9, Matthew 23:13–15). Although we haven't stressed this point in this chapter, it should be noted that these false teachers are those who hold to and persistently teach and preach a false gospel.

Fifth, we should see that they will not take correction. They will not submit to the Lord. They are self-willed. They are driven by their own desires. They will not repent. In fact, Peter says of them in 2 Peter 2:19–21, "For if, after they have escaped the defilements of the world through the knowledge of our Lord and Savior Jesus Christ, they are again entangled in them and overcome, the last state has become worse for them than the first. For it would have been better for them never to have known the way of righteousness than after knowing it to turn back from the holy commandment delivered to them. What the true proverb says has happened to them: `The dog returns to its vomit, and the sow, after washing herself, returns to wall in the mire.'" Peter is describing those false teachers who knew the truth, but then decided to turn back to false teaching. Those who knew the whole truth of the gospel but decided to return back to the vomit of a false gospel. These false teachers aren't just making a one-time choice. No, they have purposefully, deliberately, and decisively chosen to continue teaching a false gospel. Thus, we see that the definition we developed for a *false teacher* holds true to Peter's understanding of a false teacher as well: **A *false teacher* is one who holds to, unrepentantly, and persistently teaches and preaches a false gospel that damns men's souls by attacking, twisting, misinterpreting, adding to, or leaving out the essential components of the gospel or essential components of the bad news of sin, death, and hell.** Although there is much more that could be done to further explain a false teacher in 2 Peter

2:4–22, we certainly come away with an understanding of what Peter believed made a false teacher.

- False teachers can and will be amongst true believers. (2 Peter 2:1)
- False teachers secretly introduce destructive heresies. (2 Peter 2:1)
- False teachers will teach destructive heresies that are damning (i.e., false gospels). (2 Peter 2:1)
- False teachers claim allegiance to the Lord but by their actions and teachings, deny Him. (2 Peter 2:1)
- False teachers bring on swift destruction for themselves. (2 Peter 2:1)
- False teachers may lead a life of sensuality. (2 Peter 2:2)
- We must be careful to pay attention to the false teacher's life and doctrine as they will look like shepherds and true teachers. (Matthew 7:15–20, 23:27; 2 Timothy 3:1–7)
- False teachers will blaspheme the way of truth by their sensuality. (2 Peter 2:2)
- False teachers will take advantage of their listeners because of greed. (2 Peter 2:3)
- False teachers will take advantage of their listeners through false doctrine. (2 Peter 2:3)
- False teachers will be condemned for their destructive heresies. (2 Peter 2:3)
- False teachers are self-willed, not submissive, not repentant, and are deliberately choosing to preach and teach a false gospel. (2 Peter 2:1–3, 19–22)

Chapter 6: Scripture Twisters

2 Peter 3:15–16—And count the patience of our Lord as salvation, just as our beloved brother Paul also wrote to you according to the wisdom given him, as he does in all his letters when he speaks in them of these matters. There are some things in them that are hard to understand, which the ignorant and unstable twist to their own destruction, as they do the other Scriptures.

As we've progressed through this book, we've been able to see how an understanding of the gospel and the essential components of the gospel are necessary to identify false teachers. We've laid out a definition of *false teachers* at the beginning of chapter 2 to act as a guide and guardrails for us as we move through different portions of Scripture that address false teaching. Thus far, we've seen the definition has helped us not only define a false teacher, but not label someone a false teacher when the error doesn't lead to a false gospel and eternal destruction.

Since we've already laid the groundwork for the Second Book of Peter, we need only to do a brief introduction before we get into the text of interest. As we mentioned in the previous chapter, there is reason to believe that the false teachers had taught there was going to be no second coming of the Lord. Peter defends the Day of the Lord and the Second Coming in 2 Peter 3:1–13 and dovetails into sanctified living. As Peter is about to finish his letter, he makes mention of Paul where he says in 2 Peter 3:15, "And count the patience of our Lord as salvation, just as our beloved brother Paul also wrote to you according to the wisdom given him." This will be an important segue into verse 16.

2 Peter 3:16—as he does in all his letters when he speaks in them of these matters. There are some things in them that are hard to understand, which the ignorant and unstable twist to their own destruction, as they do the other Scriptures.

As we know, the apostle Paul had also written about the Second Coming in the First and Second Books of Thessalonians. When Peter mentions that Paul "speaks in them of these matters," it is likely in reference to the Second Coming as well. Peter will also state that Paul says things that are "hard to understand." The phrase *hard to understand* comes from *dusnoétos. Dusnoétos* is a compound word with *dys* meaning "difficult" and *noētos* meaning "understanding." *Dusnoétos* properly means "difficult to grasp; hard to mentally process, i.e., what is intellectually difficult to capture the true sense of." Peter was not saying that Paul was hard to understand, but rather, the truths contained within his epistles or writings were spiritually lofty and weighty. Peter was not throwing a slanderous accusation at Paul regarding his letters or teaching, but rather that the things of God can be hard for the human mind to comprehend. We can know this as Peter says in verse 15, "Paul wrote to you according to the wisdom given to him." Therefore, we can know that it was not Paul that was difficult to understand, but the lofty and high wisdom of God.

First, let's notice that Peter says the ignorant and unstable twist to their own destruction. *Ignorant* comes from the original word *amathés,* with *a* being a negative prefix and *manthanó* meaning "to learn." Properly, they are unlearned and, thus, ignorant. *Unstable* comes from *astériktos,* with *a* meaning "not" and *stērízō* meaning "confirm." Properly, this is one who was not established (unstable), describing someone who (literally) does not have a staff to lean on—hence, a person who cannot be relied on because they are *not steady* (do not remain fixed, i.e., unstable). These false teachers were unlearned and unstable. Let's think back to what we learned in the previous chapter. We learned that these false teachers were self-willed and stiff-necked. These false teachers claimed allegiance to Christ but, by their teaching and/or walk of life, denied Him. As you'll remember, in Matthew 11:29, Jesus said, "Take my yoke and learn from me." These teachers did not want to learn from Christ and did not want to submit. Thus, Peter's description of them makes perfect sense as they will not submit and will not learn, thus, they are unlearned and unstable.

Second, we should see that Peter understood Paul's writing. Although Peter says that Paul's writings are hard to understand, he does not say they are impossible to understand. No, Peter makes a very clear and fine distinction that he is not the one who doesn't understand, but rather, it is the unlearned and unstable who do not understand Paul's writings.

Third, we should see what happens when the unlearned and unstable come to hard-to-understand sayings of Paul. They twist Paul's words to their own destruction. The word *twist* comes from the original word *strebloó,* which means to "twist," "torture," or "pervert with language." *Streblē* refers to an instrument of torture and implies "to torture; put to the rack" (i.e., to twist or dislocate like limbs on a torture rack). Peter is saying that when these false teachers come to a hard-to-understand saying of Paul, they will inevitably torture or twist the Scripture and provide a false meaning. This certainly carries with it the idea of misinterpretation as in Luke 11:52 where Jesus says, "Woe to you, lawyers! For you have taken away the key of knowledge. You did not enter yourselves, and you hindered those who were entering." This is very similar to Satan twisting Scripture during Jesus' temptation. For example, Satan quotes Psalm 91:11–12, where it says, "For he will command his angels concerning you to guard you in all your ways. On their hands they will bear you up lest you strike your foot against a stone" and uses this verse to justify tempting God when this verse is used for trusting God. Another example is taking Matthew 7:1, where it says, "Judge not, that you be not judged." Here, Jesus is speaking of self-righteous, hypocritical judgments. This verse is often misquoted as an authoritative verse to never judge anyone's actions, lawlessness, or sin. However, Jesus commands in Matthew 7:6 that we do not give to dogs what is sacred and throw our pearls to swine. Therefore, Jesus does command that we be discerning and judge without self-righteousness, without hypocrisy, and without final judgment of others. Another example of twisting Scripture is using John 3:5 as a verse to justify baptismal regeneration where Jesus says, "Truly, truly, I say to you, unless one is born of water and the Spirit, he cannot enter the kingdom of God." In the John 3:5 example, pastors and priests who twist this verse to mean baptismal regeneration completely ignore that Nicodemus was a premier teacher of the Pharisees and was a legalist and ritualist and they also ignore how Jesus emphasizes the sovereign monergistic work of God in regeneration in John 3:3, 6, 7, and 8. These are examples of how Scripture can easily be twisted to suit one's own desires. The context in this verse is that the false teachers will twist a portion of Scripture that will ultimately lead to a false gospel and, thus, will damn them and damn those who believe it.

Fourth, we should note that this twisting of Paul's hard-to-understand sayings results in the false teacher's own destruction. As we have noted several times throughout the book, the definition of a *false teacher* is as follows: **A *false teacher* is one who holds to, unrepentantly, and persistently teaches and preaches a false gospel that damns men's souls by attacking, twisting, misinterpreting, adding to, or leaving out the essential components of the gospel or essential components of the bad news of sin, death, and hell.** If we would simply stick with the essential component of Jesus' work, we would see that part of Jesus' work is that He will also return to bring all His own to heaven with Him to be glorified while also judging and condemning Satan, demons, and sinful man. Thus, what would happen if Christ was not coming again to judge? Answer, if there is no judgment, there is no need to worry about sin and hell. This was an attack on the work of Christ which results in a false gospel that doesn't require repentance and faith in Jesus to escape the wrath to come (1 Thessalonians 1:10). As you can see, such a teaching would produce a false gospel that would ultimately damn those teaching as well as those embracing the teaching.

Fifth, let's note that Paul's letters are placed in the category of Scripture. Peter implies this when he says wisdom was given to Paul (2 Peter 3:15). Now, Peter says that the unlearned and unstable twist Paul's words as they do with other Scripture. Peter is essentially putting Paul's letters and teachings as equivalent to Scripture. This is an important passage which authenticates Paul's letters as Scripture.

Sixth, let's note that false teachers can distort and twist Scripture to such a degree that they create a false gospel which will inevitably distort and twist other Scripture. Peter makes this abundantly clear when he says, "The ignorant and unstable twist to their own destruction, as they do the other Scriptures." As we learned from Paul in Galatians 5:9, "A little leaven leavens the whole lump." When there is a false gospel, this will inevitably lead to more error. Let's just take the example that Peter was facing. If Christ was not coming again, why would He have come to die in the place of sinners in the first place? If Christ was not coming again, why would He have promised that He was going to prepare a place for His disciples (John 14:3)? If Christ was not coming again, what was the point of the Parable of the Ten Virgins (Matthew 25:1–13), the Parable of the Talents (Matthew 25:14–30), and the Sheep and the Goats (Matthew 25:31–46)? As you can see, just this simple lie will have impact on many other teachings of Scripture.

As we close this chapter, we see the danger in twisting and distorting Scripture to put a false and wrong meaning on the text of Scripture. As we mentioned earlier, man is sinful, fallen, and prone to error and any teacher will have some error or misunderstanding of God's Word. However, there is a clear distinction that someone who twists and distorts Scripture in such a way that produces a false gospel is a false teacher and headed for destruction.

- There will be Scripture that the unlearned and unstable will not understand. (2 Peter 3:16)
- Although hard to understand, Peter was able to understand Paul's hard to understand sayings. (2 Peter 3:16)
- The ignorant and unstable will twist Scripture that they don't understand. (2 Peter 3:16)
- When the ignorant and unstable twist Scripture that leads to their destruction, we can be sure that the Scripture they twisted and subsequent false teaching led to a false gospel. (2 Peter 3:16)
- Peter upholds Paul's writings as wisdom from God and counts it as Scripture. (2 Peter 3:15–16)
- Twisting Scripture that leads to a false gospel will lead to the twisting of other Scripture. (2 Peter 3:16)

Chapter 7: A Call to Discernment from Jesus, John, and Paul

2 Corinthians 10:4–5—For the weapons of our warfare are not of the flesh but have divine power to destroy strongholds. We destroy arguments and every lofty opinion raised against the knowledge of God, and take every thought captive to obey Christ.

The topic of false teaching is certainly not a very exciting theological topic to discuss and identifying false teachers can be even more uncomfortable and undesirable. When someone is thinking about their Christian life, they may be thinking about how to conform their prayer life to God's will, how to conform their marriage to God's will, how to use their time and energy to God's glory, how to raise their children according to God's will, how to fight sin, how to properly use their materials according to God's will, how to select a college that would conform to God's will, how to select a profession that would conform to God's will, and more. In addition to all these things that are important in the Christian life, we are also commanded to be spiritually discerning as it relates to identifying true and false teaching.

At this point in the book, we've identified what a false teacher is, which is: **A *false teacher* is one who holds to, unrepentantly, and persistently teaches and preaches a false gospel that damns men's souls by attacking, twisting, misinterpreting, adding to,**

or leaving out the essential components of the gospel or essential components of the bad news of sin, death, and hell. We've also clarified that an error in understanding and teaching Scripture does not make someone a false teacher as all men are prone to errors. We've also highlighted the importance of knowing the true gospel to be able to identify a false or counterfeit gospel.

As we move into the Bible's call for discernment on false teaching, we should understand that this is a demanding task the Lord is asking of us. We certainly know that this will not be easy, but we can be assured that it is eternally important and worthy of our diligence and attention. We'll start with Christ's call and warning to discern false teaching and false teachers in Matthew 7:15–20. We will review 1 John 4:1–4 and understand how John commands us to discern false teaching. Finally, we'll end in 2 Corinthians 10:3–5 where Paul will describe how he discerns and demolishes false teaching.

Jesus' Command to Discern False Teachers

Matthew 7:15–20 comes to us as the Lord is winding down the Sermon on the Mount. Jesus is telling His followers that there are going to be two gates and two paths and that the narrow gate and narrow path are the ones that will lead to life while the broad gate and broad road lead to destruction (Matthew 7:13–14). He will warn that there are going to be false prophets that will make it hard to find the narrow gate, enter the narrow gate, and walk the narrow path (Matthew 7:15–20). Jesus will warn that there will be false disciples that will make it hard to find the narrow gate, enter the narrow gate, and walk the narrow path (Matthew 7:21–23). Finally, Jesus will warn that there is danger in listening to His words but never acting on them. There is danger in listening and hearing but never finding the narrow gate, entering the narrow gate, and walking the narrow path.

Matthew 7:15—Beware of false prophets, who come to you in sheep's clothing but inwardly are ravenous wolves.

The first phrase that sticks out is *Beware of false prophets.* The word *beware* comes to us from the word *prosechó,* with *pros* meaning "toward" and *éxō* meaning "have." *Prosechó,* properly, means "to pay attention," beware and be cautious," "devote oneself to," "give heed," "to guard oneself," or "beware." As we defined earlier, a *false prophet* is "one who in God's name teaches what is false" or "someone pretending to speak the word of the Lord (prophesy) but in fact is a phony (imposter)." How did we learn that these false prophets will come in sheep's clothing? We learned they would come from inside the church (Acts 20:29–30), they could come from outside the church (Acts 20:29), they would teach false objective truths about the person of Jesus (2 Corinthians 11:4), they would teach false objective truths about the work of Jesus (2 Corinthians 11:4), they would have false and deceptive spirits (2 Corinthians 11:4), they would be deceitful and would disguise themselves as apostles of Christ (2 Corinthians 11:13),they would come as false christs (Matthew 24:24), they would be like Satan disguised as an angel of light (2 Corinthians 11:14), they would disguise themselves as servants of righteousness (2 Corinthians 11:15), they would use smooth and flattering speech (Romans 16:18), they would engage in godless chatter (2 Timothy 2:16), they would introduce destructive heresies (2 Peter 2:1), they would give false gospels (Galatians 1:8–9), they would misinterpret Scripture (Luke 11:52), they would twist Scripture to give false gospels (2 Peter 3:16), they would prey on the weak women (2 Timothy 3:6), and more. Therefore, the Lord tells us to beware of false teachers as they are deceptive, damning, and dangerous.

So, how did we learn that they were inwardly ravenous wolves? We learned that false teachers would propagate and teach false gospels that damn their souls and damn men's souls (Galatians

1:8–9, Matthew 23:13–15, Luke 11:52, 2 Peter 2:1, 3:16). We also learned more about who they are inwardly when we learned how they may live corrupt and immoral lives. We also learned that they have a form of godliness but deny its power, meaning they have outward moralism but are not true believers and do not have the internal and indwelling power of the Holy Spirit (2 Timothy 3:5). They are learning but never able to come to a knowledge of the truth, meaning they do not possess saving knowledge (2 Timothy 3:7). They have a corrupted mind, which means an unregenerate mind that does not have in mind the things of God (1 Timothy 6:5). They are deprived of the truth, which means they do not have the truth of God's word and, more specifically, the gospel (1 Timothy 6:5). They are insubordinate, meaning they are not subject to rule, not submissive to God, unwilling to come under Christ's Lordship, are not submissive to God's plan, and have a defiant attitude (Titus 1:10). They despise authority, meaning they are unwilling to submit to authority, especially, to Christ's authority (2 Peter 2:10, Jude 8). They are self-willed, meaning they seek only to gratify themselves by being self-satisfied, arrogant, or stubborn (2 Peter 2:10).

This is what Jesus is warning about. These false teachers and prophets will use Bible language. They will use Christ's name. They will hold a Bible. They will use Scripture. They will offer prayers. They will sing Christian songs. They will be in buildings that have crosses. They will come from Christian seminaries. This is what Jesus is warning against. The false teachers and false prophets will look the part of pastors, elders, deacons, priests, ministers, missionaries, televangelists, and more, but they will not all be true teachers and true prophets.

Matthew 7:16–18—You will recognize them by their fruits. Are grapes gathered from thornbushes, or figs from thistles? So, every healthy tree bears good fruit, but the diseased tree bears bad fruit. A healthy tree cannot bear bad fruit, nor can a diseased tree bear good fruit.

When Jesus is talking about fruits, He is talking about the fruit of their doctrine and the fruit of their life. Jesus is saying that you will need to pay attention to what the false teacher is teaching and discern if it lines up with God's Word (Acts 17:10–12). It's important to note that the fruit may not be an immoral life and a false doctrine. No, what will make this difficult is that the false teachers may have a moral life, but false doctrine (2 Timothy 3:6, Matthew 23:37). As we learned earlier, the Pharisees were known to be very moral and law-abiding people. However, they were outside God's kingdom. It may be easier to find a false teacher by their life, but it is much more difficult when the false prophet teaches truth, mixes in error, and lives a moral life. Thus, we will need to be knowledgeable in Scripture and the gospel (2 Peter 1:1–21). Additionally, it is not always in what the false teacher says explicitly, but also what the false teacher doesn't say. For example, a false teacher may preach the truth about the person and work of Jesus but may never talk about true repentance and, thus, the congregation is never called to repentance even if they are outwardly moral but know not Christ.

Jesus does make a promise that we will be able to recognize them by their fruits. *Recognize* comes to us from the original word *epiginóskó*. *Epiginóskó* is a compound word combining *epí*, which means "*on*, fitting" and *ginōskō*, which means "*know* through personal relationship." Properly, *epiginóskó* means experientially knowing through direct relationship. In other words, Jesus promises that we can know a false teacher through first-hand knowledge of what someone teaches and/or by their life. Just as apples won't grow from crabgrass and bananas won't grow from cornstalks, so a false teacher will produce bad fruit of false teaching/false gospel or an outwardly immoral lifestyle. Jesus promises we will experientially know a false teacher by their fruits.

- The voice of the Catholic priest consistently, deliberately, and purposefully claiming that you are saved by faith and works is the voice of a ravenous wolf that produces bad doctrinal fruit.
- The voice of the Lutheran pastor consistently, deliberately, and purposefully claiming that you are born again and saved through water baptism is the voice of a ravenous wolf that produces bad doctrinal fruit.
- The voice of the Eastern Orthodox priest consistently, deliberately, and purposefully claiming that you are saved through water baptism is the voice of a ravenous wolf that produces bad doctrinal fruit.
- The voice of a Mormon pastor consistently, deliberately, and purposefully claiming that Jesus is a spirit child like all of mankind is the voice of a ravenous wolf that produces bad doctrinal fruit.
- The voice of a Jehovah's Witness consistently, deliberately, and purposefully claiming that Jesus Christ was the archangel Michael before the physical world existed is a ravenous wolf that produces bad doctrinal fruit.
- The voice of the Christian Science leader that consistently, deliberately, and purposefully quotes Mary Baker Eddy's writings as equivalent to the authority of Scripture is the voice of a ravenous wolf that produces bad doctrinal fruit.
- The voice of the Unitarian Universalist leader consistently, deliberately, and purposefully stating that a loving God would not send sinful man to hell is the voice of a ravenous wolf that produces bad doctrinal fruit.
- The voice of the pastor that teaches the true way to be saved but is consistently, deliberately, and purposefully having an adulterous relationship is a ravenous wolf that produces bad moral fruit.

Likewise, good trees will bear good fruit. The good trees will proclaim the gospel. The good trees will tell the truth of God's Word. The good trees will have fruit of a moral life as well. If you were to look at a good tree closely and inspect it, you would undoubtedly find some bad or rotten fruit on it. However, you would be able to tell that the tree is a good tree and produces good fruit. So it is with a good tree. The good tree is not perfect (James 3:2, 1 John 1:8). The good tree will still make doctrinal errors. The good tree will have areas of sin and weakness in their life. However, it will be obvious because the good tree is producing good fruit of God's truth and walking in the light (1 John 1:7). It will be obvious because the good tree is a workman approved by God to rightly handle the Word of Truth (2 Timothy 2:15). It will be obvious because the good tree will watch over his flock because he is willing and eager to serve (1 Peter 5:1). It will be obvious because the good tree will preach the gospel (1 Corinthians 9:16). It will be obvious because the good tree will watch over his flock as one who will give an account (Hebrews 13:17). It will be obvious because the good tree will have a humble view of himself (1 Corinthians 4:1). It will be obvious because the good tree will act as a slave of Christ and will do what Christ did and say what Christ said (Romans 6:15–23). It will be obvious because the good tree will meet the Lord's requirements for being an elder (1 Timothy 3:1–12, Titus 1:5–9). If your pastor is a good tree, he is worthy of double honor (1 Timothy 5:17). Make sure to honor him.

Matthew 7:19–20—Every tree that does not bear good fruit is cut down and thrown into the fire. Thus, you will recognize them by their fruits.

As we learned earlier, one who preaches a false gospel is accursed by God and they end up cursing others. The only thing a false teacher has to look forward to is a place of God's full wrath and blackest darkness, filled with furious and concentrated fire everywhere, where there is weeping and anger against God for the unrepentant Christ-rejecting and Christ-neglecting sinners where they will spend all eternity paying for every sin they've ever committed with no hope of escape, and only the expectation of excruciating torments to their body, soul, and spirit and an undying conscience that will haunt them day and night, forever and ever, with no reprieve. Although we know that the end of a false teacher is horrific, we can thank God that we may know them by their fruits and can lovingly command and warn them to stop their false teaching when God calls us to do so.

John's Command to Discern False Teachers

1 John 4:1—Beloved, do not believe every spirit, but test the spirits to see whether they are from God, for many false prophets have gone out into the world.

John has the heart of a pastor as he warns his listeners of the danger of false prophets. You can see that he gives a very similar warning as Jesus did to beware of false prophets. Likewise, Paul warns that false doctrine will be spread from demons to men where he says in 1 Timothy 4:1, "Now the Spirit expressly says that in later times some will depart from the faith by devoting themselves to deceitful spirits and teachings of demons." John is very aware that there are going to be many deceiving doctrines and spirits that will invade the church. Therefore, he gives a warning to not believe every wind of doctrine.

As we've noted before, a noble thing that one can do is to measure what they're taught against Scripture. John certainly has this in mind when he tells his listeners to "test the spirits." The word *test* comes from the original word *dokimazo,* which means "put to the test," "prove," "examine," "distinguish by testing," "approve after testing," "to show something is acceptable or real," "to show something passes the necessary test." This word is used twenty-two times in the New Testament. This word was used for the examination of metals by fire where the fire would melt away the dross and one could see how pure the metal was. Additionally, this word was used in Greek literature as a technical expression referring to the action of an examining board putting its approval upon those who had successfully passed the examinations for the degree of Doctor of Medicine. David carries this same thought in Psalm 26:2, where he says, "Prove me, O LORD, and try me; test my heart and my mind." How does David test his heart and his mind? Only by comparing it to Scripture. What does God think of a works plus faith in Christ salvation? What does God think of baptism or circumcision saving? What does God think of purgatory? What does God think about extrabiblical dreams and visions? What does God the Father think about His Son? Does our salvation originate from God or man? John's answer is to put it to the test. Hold your question up against the Word of God. Hold someone's teaching up against the Word of God and let the Word expose the teaching as false or as true. Let the Word answer your question.

Let's also note that John notes that there are many false prophets that have gone out into the world. There are many false prophets, there are many false doctrines, and there are many false gospels that will be preached and taught. Therefore, John is commanding his listeners to test the spirits. His listeners will need to learn the Scripture, know the Scripture, apply the Scripture, and trust the Scripture. There is no other means to test the spirits other than God's Word as Jesus told the devil in Matthew 4:4 as He quotes from Deuteronomy 8:3, "It is written, 'Man shall not live by bread alone, but by every word that comes from the mouth of God.'"

1 John 4:2–3—By this you know the Spirit of God: every spirit that confesses that Jesus Christ has come in the flesh is from

God, and every spirit that does not confess Jesus is not from God. This is the spirit of the antichrist, which you heard was coming and now is in the world already."

John is helping his listeners develop a test to see if teachers are from God. I'm taking some liberty to restate his test. John is essentially saying this:

- Do the spirits say that Jesus is the Christ, the only begotten Son of the Living God, who is co-equal and co-eternal with the Father and was born of a virgin? They should say He came in the flesh (1 John 1:1). They should say that He is eternal (1 John 1:1). They should say He's the Son of God (1 John 1:3). They should say He is light (1 John 1:5, John 8:12). They should say He is the Christ (1 John 2:22–23).
- What do the spirits say about the work of Jesus? They should say that the Jesus is our advocate with the Father (1 John 2:1). They should say that Jesus is the propitiation for our sins (1 John 2:2). They should say that He is coming again (1 John 2:28, 3:2). They should say that those who are His children will be glorified with Him (1 John 3:2). They should know of Christ's sacrificial and substitutionary death (1 John 3:16). They should say that Jesus came to take away our sins (1 John 3:5).
- What do the spirits say about the subjective response to the objective person and work of Jesus? They should know it is to believe in the name of Jesus Christ (1 John 3:23). They should say that those who belong to Christ will walk in the same way He walked which means they have been converted to Christ and will deny themselves and lay down their life for Christ just as Christ laid down His life for His sheep (1 John 2:6).

- What do the spirits say about assurance of salvation? They should say those who walk in the light as He is in the light should have assurance (1 John 1:7). They should say that if we are confessing our sins we will be cleansed and forgiven and should have assurance of salvation (1 John 1:9). They should say if we are keeping His commands we should have assurance of salvation (1 John 2:3). They should say that those who walk as Jesus walked should have assurance of salvation (1 John 2:6). They should say that those who love their brother and sister should have assurance of salvation (1 John 2:10). They should say that those who do the will of God should have assurance of salvation (1 John 2:17). They should say that those who know the truth have assurance of salvation because this came from the Holy Spirit (1 John 2:20). They should say that those who acknowledge Christ or, rather, Christ's person, work, and teachings, should have assurance of salvation (1 John 2:23). They should say that all those whose hope is Christ will purify themselves and should have assurance of salvation (1 John 3:3). They should say that those who practice sin neither know God nor have seen Him (1 John 3:6). They should say that those born of God do not practice sin (1 John 3:9).

Of course, there are more tests that one can administer to test the spirits, but John has given his readers enough Scripture up to this point in just this epistle to test the spirits regarding the person of Christ, the work of Christ, the assurance of salvation, and the subjective response to the objective person and work of Jesus. Notice here that if someone comes and starts failing these tests, John is calling them the *antichrist*, or those who are against Christ. Let's remember that a false teacher is someone who holds to and continually preaches and teaches a false gospel that damns men's souls. John has given a very simple test by stating, "Every spirit that does not confess Jesus is not from God," which, as we learned, carries several tests. Continually testing doctrine against God's Word is the sure way to test the spirits.

1 John 4:4—Little children, you are from God and have overcome them, for he who is in you is greater than he who is in the world.

John stops here and pauses to provide comfort for his listeners. In John 2:20, he says, "But you have been anointed by the Holy One, and you all have knowledge. I write to you, not because you do not know the truth, but because you know it, and because no lie is of the truth." He goes on to say in 1 John 2:26–27, "I write these things to you about those who are trying to deceive you. But the anointing that you received from him abides in you, and you have no need that anyone should teach you. But as his anointing teaches you about everything, and is true, and is no lie just as it has taught you, abide in him." John is telling his listeners that their understanding and acceptance of the truth of Jesus and the truth of the gospel is evidence of being in fellowship with Christ. You can almost hear John saying this:

- Dear children, no one who is born of God embraces a false understanding of who Jesus is.
- Dear children, no one who is born of God embraces a false understanding of what Jesus did.
- Dear children, no one who is born of God embraces a false understanding of salvation.
- Dear children, the reason you accept a correct understanding of Jesus' person, work, salvation, and walk in the truth is because the Holy Spirit abides in you and you are born of God.

John is reassuring his listeners that they know the truth, they have God's Word, and they can test the spirits using what they know about the gospel to determine if a teacher is true or false because they have the Holy Spirit to teach them.

Paul's Command to Discern

2 Corinthians 10:3—For though we walk in the flesh, we are not waging war according to the flesh.

Paul was no stranger when dealing with false teachers. He had to address the Philippian church regarding the Judaizers. He had to address the Galatians regarding the Judaizers. He had to address the Colossian church regarding legalism and visions. He had to address the Thessalonians regarding the resurrection and the Second Coming. He had to provide Timothy with guidance on dealing with false teachers. Paul had concern for the daily pressure of the churches. As we transition into this text, we find that Paul is having his credibility being attacked by false apostles in the Corinthian church. It's within this attack that we see how Paul dealt with false teaching and false ideologies.

The false apostles had attacked Paul's credentials and his ministry. Paul was saddened that the attack against his credentials were so easily attacked and given credibility as Paul had given his life for the Corinthians. Paul was eager to preach the gospel to the Corinthians (1 Corinthians 1:17). Paul had shown that he was faithful to the ministry he had been given (1 Corinthians 4:2). Paul conducted his ministry with a clear conscience (1 Corinthians 4:4). Paul had shown that he did not go beyond Scripture either in his teaching or life (1 Corinthians 4:6). Paul had been a spiritual father to the Corinthians (1 Corinthians 4:15). Paul chose to offer his ministry free of charge so as not to hinder the gospel of Christ (1 Corinthians 9:1–18). Paul became amiable to everyone to win people for Christ (1 Corinthians 9:19–23). Paul lived a disciplined life and buffeted his body so he would not be disqualified to teach (1 Corinthians 9:24–27). Paul worked hard as an apostle (1 Corinthians 15:10). Paul did not peddle the gospel for profit (2 Corinthians 2:17). Paul had renounced secret and shameful ways and did not live in deception (2 Corinthians 4:2). Paul did not promote himself, but preached Christ (2 Corinthians 4:5). Paul considered himself a clay pot and dispensable (2 Corinthians 4:7). Paul showed that he lived by faith and not by sight (2 Corinthians 5:7). Paul put no stumbling block in anyone's way through his teaching or his life (2 Corinthians 6:3). Paul persevered in ministry despite hardship (2 Corinthians 6:4–10). Paul had performed signs and miracles as authentication of his apostleship (2 Corinthians 12:12). As we can see, Paul had carried out his ministry faithfully to the Corinthians. In Paul's absence, the false apostles had crept their way into the Corinthian church (2 Corinthians 11:1–15).

At the beginning of verse 3, Paul has a slight play on words where he says, "For though we walk in the flesh, we are not waging war according to the flesh." Paul was being accused of walking in the flesh and being deceitful (2 Corinthians 12:14–18). Paul affirms that he is in the flesh or human, but he explains that he will not wage war like the false teachers who are slanderous (2 Timothy 3:3), boastful (2 Timothy 3:2, Jude 16), proud (2 Timothy 3:2), and giving a different gospel (2 Corinthians 11:4). No, Paul is going to wage war with weapons that are not of the flesh. *Strateuó* means "to contend, fighting like a soldier in war." Paul is about to explain that the way he is going to fight back is not the way that false teachers fight back. He is not going to wage war as they do with human wisdom, eloquent speech, godless chatter, idle talk, myths, and so on. No, we will see how Paul is going to fight back.

2 Corinthians 10:4—For the weapons of our warfare are not of the flesh but have divine power to destroy strongholds.

Paul here announces that the weapons he uses for spiritual warfare are not of the flesh but have divine power to destroy strongholds. Paul doesn't war against false teachers the same way false teachers fight against Paul. In fact, Paul did not come to the Corinthians with eloquent speech or human wisdom, but with the testimony of God or the gospel (1 Corinthians 2:1). Paul knew that these fleshly weapons of warfare were of no power to save. He knew the gospel was the power of God to save (Romans 1:16). He knew the message of the cross was the power of God for those who were being saved (1 Corinthians 1:18). Paul knew that Christ was the power of God (1 Corinthians 1:24). Paul didn't want to fight with human wisdom, eloquent words, or the wisdom of the world. Paul fought the good fight of faith by preaching the Word. God's Word was Paul's weapon of warfare.

Paul knew that the Word of God was powerful to destroy strongholds. *Destroy* comes from *kathairesis,* which means "taking down," "razing," "destroying," or "demolition." K*athairesis* carries the idea of completely demolishing or destroying a building and demolishing it down to the very foundation. *Strongholds* come to us from *ochuróma. Ochuróma* is "a fortified, military stronghold," "a strong-walled fortress," "a heavily-fortified containment." The idea of a *stronghold* is a thick impenetrable military fort that is heavily guarded, heavily armed, with high walls. So, what are the strongholds? We will find out in verse 5.

2 Corinthians 10:5—We destroy arguments and every lofty opinion raised against the knowledge of God, and take every thought captive to obey Christ.

The strongholds are arguments. *Argument* comes from *logismos,* which is "reasoning," "thinking," "a conception," "device," "calculated arguments or thoughts," and emphasizes reaching a personal opinion. This is every human thought, worldly philosophy, world religion, and more. These strongholds are the political strongholds of communism, the political strongholds of Marxism, the philosophical strongholds of nihilism, the antireligious strongholds of atheism, the religious strongholds of Islam, the religious strongholds of Buddhism, the human wisdom of "love is love," the religious doctrinal stronghold of baptismal regeneration, the religious strongholds of Catholicism, the doctrinal stronghold of transubstantiation, the doctrinal stronghold of purgatory, the political stronghold of the Democratic Party, and much more. These are the strongholds. A *lofty opinion* comes from the original word *hupsóma* and carries the idea of "a high thing," "bulwark," or "rampart." This gives the idea that these are powerful and mighty strongholds that keep people captive. These ideologies, false religions, and philosophies are powerful spiritual strongholds.

Paul states that every argument, or *logismos,* and lofty opinion, or *hupsóma,* that is raised against the knowledge of God or God's Word is brought captive to Christ. *Captive* means to literally take as a prisoner. Imagine a prisoner being led in handcuffs and shackles by a prison guard armed with a shotgun. This is the exact imagery Paul is using. Paul is going to take every teaching, every thought, and every doctrine and submit it to Christ in this way. This is how Paul attacks false doctrine. The fortifications and strongholds that set themselves against the knowledge of God are high lofty structures that can only be brought down by Scripture. If you want to learn how to fight against transubstantiation, learn Scripture. If you want to confront a works-based salvation, study Scripture. If you want to fight against anti-Trinitarian doctrine, learn Scripture. As we discussed earlier, how do we fight against a false gospel? Answer, we must know the true gospel and Scripture.

Notice the phrase *to obey Christ*. *Obey* is from *hupakoé,* which literally means "submission to what is heard." Paul is literally saying, "I'm going to take this thought and submit it to Christ and see what He thinks. I'm going to take this ideology and will learn to think of it the way Christ thinks of it. I'm going to take this doctrine and will determine to mentally, emotionally, and volitionally perceive, feel, and act on it as Christ would." This is what Paul is saying. This is how Paul takes captive the thoughts and submits them to Christ.

As we close, we see that Paul wasn't passive when it came to false doctrines. Paul took every *logismos* and brought it under the submission of Christ. Paul used the Word of God to discern truth and error. Paul was able to spot a false gospel because he knew the true gospel. Likewise, Paul spotted false teachers by their teaching and life and called out a false gospel, false teachers, and false apostles. John has commanded us to test the spirits and to be wary of false prophets. Jesus has commanded us to beware of false teachers and false prophets and that we will be able to know them by the fruit of their life and the fruit of their teaching. The call to discern true teaching and false teaching is commanded by our Lord. The command to discern true teachers and false teachers is commanded by our Lord. Just as we are to flee sexual immorality (1 Corinthians 6:18), we are also required to discern true teaching and false teaching. Let us remember that this is a command from the Lord and not an option. Though it will take much work in learning Scripture, we see that our eternal destiny and the eternal destiny of others are what are at stake.

Chapter 8: How to Deal with a False Teacher

There is going to be an immense amount of tension as we try to understand how to deal with a false teacher. There is no doubt that it will take much deliberation, much study of Scripture, and much prayer and guidance from the Lord if you are one who must deal with a false teacher. Further, having a close friend, family member, colleague, pastor, or the like will only add to the difficulty in navigating through this complex issue. Additionally, the context will also drive many of your decisions. The approach may be different for a pastor, deacon, church member, friend, or family member. Confrontation is never pleasant or something to be sought where it's not warranted. However, the striking balance it takes to follow the Lord in dealing with a false teacher comes with much complexity.

The commands on how to deal with a false teacher can range from "beware of them" to "do not give him a greeting." Every scenario will take discernment. For example, the person reading this book could have come out from a very spiritually abusive false teacher and the best command for that person may be to "do not give him a greeting" as in 2 John 9–11. On the other hand, there could be a situation where a false teacher may not even be aware that they have been teaching a false gospel, such as baptismal regeneration, and the best course of action may be 1 Timothy 1:3–5 and command them not to teach the false gospel but do so out of love from a pure heart, a good conscience, and sincere faith. Quite simply, this last chapter is not going to be a step-by-step guide, although it may feel like it, but rather a systematic way of thinking about dealing with false teachers.

It is important to distinguish between a false teacher and those under the false teacher. The Bible clearly teaches that we are to love our enemies (Matthew 5:43–48). However, the Bible also makes a distinction that false teachers who lead people astray hold more responsibility and, thus, will be judged with greater strictness (James 3:1) as more people are affected (1 Timothy 4:16) and teachers are to be a model (1 Timothy 4:12). Therefore, there should be a clear distinction between a false teacher and those in false religious systems but are not false teachers. **False teachers are to be treated differently from those in false systems**.

It is also important to note that we are not to go deliberately out of our way to find false teachers and try to debate them or argue with them. As we'll see down below, if there is any bit of self-righteousness, self-purpose, hypocrisy, or the like when dealing with false teachers, and not a pure heart and good conscience, then we are in no position to address or deal with a false teacher.

Before we start, it would be helpful to go over the bad news of sin, death, and hell as well as the gospel to help ground us.

- The bad news is that man has sinned, which is breaking God's law by either not doing what His law demands or doing what His law prohibits by any thought, word, deed, or intent. God's disposition toward sin is one of hatred, anger, abhorrence, defilement, wickedness, evil, hostility, and is warfare against Him. Man is incapable of curing his problem with sin. Man cannot propitiate the righteous anger of God, redeem himself, earn forgiveness, or be made right with God on his own merits. God's attributes, such as being eternal, loving, just, good, faithful, omniscient, and immutable, demand that God must punish sin. The punishment of sin is hell which is hell is a place of God's full wrath and blackest darkness, filled with furious and concentrated fire everywhere, where there is weeping and anger against God for the unrepentant Christ-rejecting and Christ-neglecting sinners where they will spend all eternity paying for every sin they've ever committed with no hope of escape, and only the expectation of excruciating torments to their body, soul, and spirit, and an undying conscience that will haunt them day and night, forever and ever, with no reprieve.

- The good news or the gospel is the good news of salvation that God has authored and owns. God had promised this plan of salvation through His prophets and Holy Scripture and has fully revealed the good news of salvation through Scripture which is the authoritative, inspired inerrant, and infallible Word of God. The good news concerns the person and work of Jesus Christ. The person of Jesus is He is the Christ, the Creator of the universe, the promised Jewish Messiah, the promised Jewish Messiah, the only begotten Son of the Living God, which makes Him God and equal with God the Father and God the Holy Spirit. Jesus was born of a virgin and conceived by the Holy Spirit and became a man and is, thus, truly God and truly man and can represent God to man and man to God. The work of Jesus is that Jesus lived a sinless life and fulfilled all righteousness found in the law and prophets and declared Himself to be the Christ, the only begotten Son of the Living God through His teaching which was attested to by His miracles and the Holy Spirit. Jesus offered Himself as a sinless, spotless, and blameless sacrifice for sin to propitiate the righteous anger of God by taking all the sins of God's people on Himself and, thus, the full wrath of God that was due to man in hell. His sacrifice propitiated the righteous anger of God and reconciled and brought peace from man to God and God to man. His substitutionary sacrifice and

> death also redeemed sinful man to Holy God by forgiving man's sin and imputing His righteousness to man, so man could stand before God with the righteousness of Jesus Christ in judgment. Jesus was resurrected from the dead on the third day by His own power, by God the Father, and God the Holy Spirit, which affirmed His person, His teachings, and salvific work for sinners. He ascended to the right hand of the Father and is empowered with all authority to bring about the plan of salvation for all His people by causing them to be born again and justified by His grace. He will also return to bring all of His own to heaven with Him to be glorified while also judging and condemning Satan, demons, and sinful man. The benefits of Christ's person and work are available to those who repent and put saving faith in Christ. *Repentance* is a gift from God where the sinner understands his sin against God (intellect), has Godly sorrow and mourns over his sin against God (emotions and affections), and turns away from his sin and toward God for righteousness (will or volition). *Saving faith* is a gift from God where a sinner has knowledge of Jesus' person and work where a sinner will respond to Christ's person and work by denying themselves, picking up their cross, submitting and committing their life to Jesus, and trusting in Him only for salvation.

Additionally, we have developed a definition of a *false teacher* which is: **A *false teacher* is one who holds to, unrepentantly, and persistently teaches and preaches a false gospel that damns men's souls by attacking, twisting, misinterpreting, adding to, or leaving out the essential components of the gospel or essential components of the bad news of sin, death, and hell.** As we noted earlier, we do not want to elevate a doctrine and make it a gospel issue when it's not. For example, Scripture simply does not allow us to call someone a false teacher because they hold a different view on women's head coverings, type of worship service chosen, format of a worship service, and the like. Therefore, one must discern that what is being taught is serious enough to be considered a false gospel and not elevate doctrinal matters that do not rise to the level of being a false gospel.

Know the Gospel and Know Your Salvation

As we discussed in the Second Book of Peter, Peter wanted his listeners to know their salvation (1:3–11) to know their Scriptures (1:12–21) and, thus, know their adversaries (2:1–22). Peter knows that unless one knows the gospel and is saved, they are very vulnerable to be swept away by other false doctrines. In this very same way, we are called to know the gospel and know our salvation. If you recall earlier in the book, we discussed the implications of what to do once we know the gospel which were as follows:

We should understand the gospel is the power of God to save mankind (Romans 1:16). We should believe the gospel (Mark 1:15). We should give our lives for the gospel of God (Mark 8:35). We should seek to understand the gospel clearly (Acts 18:26). We should live our lives in a manner worthy of the gospel (Philippians 1:27). We should fear preaching a wrong or false gospel (Galatians 1:8–9). We should fear preaching the gospel from wrong motives (Philippians 1:15). We should not be ashamed of the gospel (Romans 1:16). We should be eager to preach the gospel (Romans 1:15). We should proclaim the gospel without fear (Philippians 1:14). We should defend the gospel (Philippians 1:16, Jude 3). We should understand the gospel is not ours (Romans 1:1). We should understand that God guarantees the success of His gospel for His Name's sake (Romans 1:5).

Knowing the gospel helps one discern a false gospel with more ease. For example, it is a sad, painful, and unfortunate thing to watch a Lutheran and a Catholic argue over justification by faith alone when the Lutheran and the Catholic both believe a false gospel of baptismal regeneration, or, rather, being born again and saved through baptism. The Lutheran has not taken the log out of his own eye (Matthew 7:3–5) to see that he, just like the Catholic, teaches and preaches a false gospel as well. Although the Lutheran really believes one is justified by faith when speaking to the Catholic, the Lutheran doesn't realize that he has a false gospel that is propagated within his own church. Thus, knowing the gospel and knowing your salvation is the first and necessary step if one is ever to deal with a false teacher.

Watch, Beware, and Test for False Teachers

Matthew 7:15—**Beware** of false prophets, who come to you in sheep's clothing but inwardly are ravenous wolves.

Matthew 16:6, 12—Jesus said to them, "**Watch and beware** of the leaven of the Pharisees and Sadducees." Then they understood that he did not tell them to beware of the leaven of bread, but of the teaching of the Pharisees and Sadducees.

Luke 12:1—In the meantime, when so many thousands of the people had gathered together that they were trampling one another, he began to say to his disciples first, "**Beware** of the leaven of the Pharisees, which is hypocrisy."

Mark 8:15—And he cautioned them, saying, "**Watch out; beware** of the leaven of the Pharisees and the leaven of Herod."

1 John 4:1—Beloved, do not believe every spirit, but **test the spirits** to see whether they are from God, for many false prophets have gone out into the world.

2 Peter 3:17—You therefore, beloved, knowing this beforehand, **take care** that you are not carried away with the error of lawless people and lose your own stability.

Philippians 3:2 – **Look out** for the dogs, **look out** for the evildoers, **look out** for those who mutilate the flesh.

As we mentioned in the previous chapter, it is important that we pay attention to what we are taught and test it against Scripture and to beware, watch out, and test the spirits for false teachers. Sometimes, the false teaching or false teacher will be made obvious immediately. However, when it is not obvious, it necessitates that one continues to listen, discern, and compare the teaching against Scripture. It is a dangerous thing to rush in and claim someone is a false teacher without testing the spirits and examining their doctrine.

As one point of clarification, it is a very dangerous thing to poke and prod every word, phrase, and sentence of a teacher with a spirit of being a Pharisee and being overly critical. In Luke 11:53–54, it says of the Pharisees after Jesus had just finished denouncing them, “As he went away from there, the scribes and the Pharisees began to press him hard and to provoke him to speak about many things, lying in wait for him, to catch him in something he might say.” We won't examine this verse word by word, but the idea is that they were relentlessly pressing Jesus with questions to see if He would slip up. In verse 54, it says they were trying to “catch him.” The word *catch* comes from *thēreuó,* which means “to hunt” or “entrap.” The idea is that they were hunting Jesus as if He were an animal and just waiting to pounce on Him with just one little slipup. As we mentioned earlier, we can be sure that there will be error in everyone's teaching. However, the line that turns a teacher into a false teacher is where a false gospel is consistently taught. Although there is careful discernment that takes place, there is also abundant grace that must be given as well when a false gospel is not being taught. Additionally, we are supposed to be a joy to those who are watching over us and not a burden as it says in Hebrews 13:17, “Obey your leaders and submit to them, for they are keeping watch over your souls, as those who will have to give an account. Let them do this with joy and not with groaning, for that would be of no advantage to you.” Thus, when there are doctrinal differences not related to the gospel, it is of utmost importance to be submissive to the leaders with utmost humility and not erroneously give them the title of a false teacher.

Identify the Type of False Teacher: Show Mercy and/or Mercy Mixed with Fear

Jude 22–23—And have mercy on those who doubt; save others by snatching them out of the fire; to others show mercy with fear, hating even the garment stained by the flesh.

In Jude's letter, he will warn of false teachers and will do so in a manner that is like Peter. Of one important note is that Jude gives two verses at the beginning and the end of the epistle that confirm the security of the believer where he says in Jude 1, "Jude, a servant of Jesus Christ and brother of James, to those who are called, beloved in God the Father and kept for Jesus Christ." Here, Jude is confirming that those who are effectually called by God the Father and kept for Jesus Christ can have security of their salvation even amid false teaching and false teachers. Likewise, as he closes his letter, he says in Jude 24–25, "Now to him who is able to keep you from stumbling and to present you blameless before the presence of his glory with great joy, to the only God, our Savior, through Jesus Christ our Lord, be glory, majesty, dominion, and authority, before all time and now and forever. Amen." Jude ends on a doxology of praise that, although the believer will come against many attacks of false teaching and false teachers, God the Father and the Lord Jesus Christ will keep the believer from falling away and present him blameless before His presence. Therefore, the believer should have this same confidence that the Lord will preserve them.

One point of interest is that Jude is very much talking about affections and attitudes of one dealing with a false teacher. Jude notes that there are the doubters who should be treated with mercy. Jude also distinguishes that there are the full-fledged and committed false teachers that should be treated with mercy and fear and hatred toward the false teaching. Thus, we see Jude has categorized the false teachers in three potential groups of confused, convinced and committed (9). When considering dealing with false teachers, it's important to see the spectrum and attitudes and affections we should have toward those who are false teachers. Not every false teacher is approached the same way.

Confused—Jude gives a warning regarding apostates. In Jude 22–23, it is difficult to ascertain whether he is talking about those in false religion or the teachers who propagate and teach the false gospels. However, it is most likely the false teachers as the letter is written against false teachers. In any case, he says in verse 22, "And have mercy on those who doubt." This could be understood as one category of a false teacher. Although they have been teaching and preaching a false gospel for a long time, there may be some doubt that they have regarding their doctrine. In this case, Jude tells us to have mercy on them. We see this as Jesus dealt with Nicodemus who was a Pharisee who sat on the Sanhedrin and was the premiere teacher of Judaism (John 3:1–21). It is likely that Nicodemus had questions about his own salvation and Jesus was willing to meet with him and discuss salvation. In this very same way, Jude tells us that there is mercy to be shown to those who doubt.

Convinced—Jude also defines another group by saying in Jude 23, "Save others by snatching them out of the fire." Once again, it is difficult to ascertain if this is regarding false teachers or false disciples, but the letter would suggest that it would be false teachers. This appears to be those that have been convinced that what they believe and teach is true. They're not doubting or confused, and they are convinced that they have the right teaching. Thus, Jude describes the operation as "snatching them from the fire." The word *snatching* comes from *harpazó,* which means to "seize," "snatch," "obtain by robbery," or "seize by force suddenly and decisively." When somebody is in a false religious system and is convinced they're right, you won't turn your back on them. You don't push them away. You don't shun them. However, you don't embrace them in true fellowship either. They are still damning false teachers. However, you confront the error, you are blunt, there are severe warnings, promise of judgment, devastation, and hell. This is how one can think of those who are convinced they're right but are truly in error. In John 12:42–43, it says, "Nevertheless many, even of the rulers, believed in Him, but because of the Pharisees they were not confessing Him, so that they would not be excommunicated from the Synagogue; for they loved the approval of people rather than the approval of God." This is to say that there may be some false teachers convinced that their religious system is correct, but are also recognizing the truth. Discernment is needed to understand how to address them as snatching them out of the fire.

Committed—Jude defines the final group and says of this group, "To others show mercy with fear, hating even the garment stained by the flesh." These are people that know the system and know their false gospel. They're more than convinced, they are committed and are very deceptive, sneaky, and misleading. There was a *chitón,* which was an undergarment, and there was *himation,* which was a cloak or robe. Jude uses the word *chitón,* which is like saying "hating the undergarment that's been stained by the flesh." Getting close to false religion is dangerous. In Jewish terms, this would have been like saying, "If you get too close to this false religion or false gospel, you will ceremonially defile yourself so make sure you have a healthy dose of fear as well as mercy." False gospels damn the men that teach it and damn the listeners who embrace it. Notice here that it says to hate the false gospel or system, but this gives no directive to hate the false teacher. We are commanded to think about these individuals with mercy and fear, but also hate the false gospel they propagate. Therefore, Jude is telling them to be careful around these types of false teachers. This is not to suggest that we necessarily go and address the false teacher, but this certainly calls someone to give heed to the dangers of addressing a committed false teacher.

Command Them to Stop Teaching False Doctrine

1 Timothy 1:3–5—As I urged you when I was going to Macedonia, remain at Ephesus so that you may charge certain persons not to teach any different doctrine, nor to devote themselves to myths and endless genealogies, which promote speculations rather than the stewardship from God that is by faith. The aim of our charge is love that issues from a pure heart and a good conscience and a sincere faith.

As we mentioned in Jude, the scenario and type of false teacher can very much drive how one will deal with a false teacher. We should notice how Paul instructs Timothy who must deal with false teachers in Ephesus. Once it has been discerned that someone is teaching a false gospel, then one must discern how to best approach the false teacher. Paul tells Timothy, "Charge certain persons not to teach any different doctrine, nor to devote themselves to myths and endless genealogies, which promote speculations rather than stewardship from God that is by faith." The word *charge* comes from *paraggelló,* which means "command," "charge," "entreat solemnly," or, properly, "to charge, give a command that is fully authorized because it has gone through all the proper and necessary channels." Here, we see that we are authorized to command them to stop teaching their false teaching with the full weight and authority of God.

Additionally, we see the effect of false teachers when they speak of myths and empty talk. The effect is that it produces speculations, or *zétésis,* which is "debate, controversy," or, properly, "a meaningless question to investigate a specific practice." As we noted above, more people are affected (1 Timothy 4:16) and teachers are to be a model (1 Timothy 4:12). When false teachers go on about myths and empty talk, this can cause unhealthy debate and controversy and have church members or other Christians focused on things that are not central to the Christian faith.

In addition to this command, we also see that the end goal is out of love. We are not commanding them to stop teaching because we want to win an argument. We are not commanding them to stop teaching because we're in a debate. We are not commanding them to stop teaching out of any self-righteous reason. No, the end goal is out of love for the person teaching and his hearers. Let's also note that we are to do this out of a pure heart and a good conscience with sincere faith. A pure heart should be understood as one that is devoted to God. The heart intellectually knows God's will, affectionately loves God's will, and volitionally will do God's will. A *pure heart* is a heart that seeks to do the will of God with no corrupt or selfish desires. A *good conscience* is one that has evaluated what is good and what is wrong. *Sincere faith* is one that is not hypocritical, but has examined one's self to look for hypocrisy and wrong motives to eliminate any hypocrisy or wrong motives. For example, is it proper to point out someone's error in front of a group of people in a condescending and intimidating manner? What if the person you're addressing is an elder? Should you not respect your elders? Is this truly loving your neighbor as yourself (Matthew 22:39)? Do you consider meeting with the individual privately one-on-one or perhaps with another witness and letting them know why you're meeting (Matthew 18:15–20)? God's Word commands that the end goal of charging someone to stop false teaching be out of love and without hypocrisy. One should first examine themselves (1 Timothy 1:3–5), know your salvation (2 Corinthians 13:5), know the gospel clearly (Acts 18:26), and know the type of false teacher (Jude 22–23).

Titus 1:10–11—For there are many who are insubordinate, empty talkers and deceivers, especially those of the circumcision party. They must be silenced, since they are upsetting whole families by teaching for shameful gain what they ought not to teach.

Here we have a likewise command. In Titus 1:9, Paul tells Titus about the qualifications of an elder, "He must hold firm to the trustworthy word as taught, so that he may be able to give instruction in sound doctrine and also to rebuke those who contradict it." When Paul is telling Titus to rebuke those who contradict sound doctrine, he is saying that the teacher must be able to provide compelling scriptural evidence to expose the false teaching. In Titus 1:11, Paul is telling them that they must be *silenced,* which literally means to "muzzle" or "stop the mouth." Paul is telling Titus that they must be restrained. They must be forbidden to talk. In a practical way, this could be done by preventing the false teacher from teaching to any extent that you're able (i.e., revoking teaching permission in a church). Another way this could be done would be how Paul did this in 2 Corinthians 10:5, "We destroy arguments and every lofty opinion raised against the knowledge of God, and take every thought captive to obey Christ." Additionally, Paul says in Titus 2:1, "But as for you, teach what accords with sound doctrine." Simply put, give people God's Word and flood them with the truth. Another way is through holy living as Paul says in Titus 2:7, "Show yourself in all respects to be a model of good works, and in your teaching show integrity, dignity, and sound speech that cannot be condemned, so that an opponent may be put to shame, having nothing evil to say."

Titus 3:9–11—But avoid foolish controversies and genealogies and arguments and quarrels about the law, because these are unprofitable and useless. Warn a divisive person once, and then warn them a second time. After that, have nothing to do with them. You may be sure that such people are warped and sinful, they are self-condemned.

At the end of Paul's letter to Titus, Paul gives final instructions regarding false teachers. *Avoid* can be better understood as "shunning." Paul is telling Titus to shun foolish controversies and things of the law that aren't profitable. These types of controversies can often lead to petty arguments and unnecessary tension and strife. Paul says the same thing to Timothy in 1 Timothy 4:7, where he says, "Have nothing to do with irreverent, silly myths. Rather train yourself for godliness." Paul reiterates this in his second epistle to Timothy where he says in 2 Timothy 2:16–17, "But avoid irreverent babble, for it will lead people into more and more ungodliness, and their talk will spread like gangrene. Among them are Hymenaeus and Philetus, who have swerved from the truth, saying that the resurrection has already happened. They are upsetting the faith of some." Paul is wanting Titus to avoid worthless arguments as these set a bad example as a pastor (1 Timothy 3:3). If the congregation sees the pastor endlessly engaged in arguments, this sets a bad example to the flock and can promote an argumentative and debating culture. Therefore, it is profitable not to engage in many debates and, especially, not in front of the flock. One should be discerning that the confrontation of a false teacher does not turn into empty debates that weaken other brothers and sisters in Christ.

The church discipline, as we know, is supposed to be in love and gentleness and meant to be restorative and redemptive by causing godly repentance (2 Timothy 2:24–25). It is also to protect the church as false teaching can spread like gangrene (2 Timothy 2:17) and can also permeate throughout the church and impact the church as well as other doctrines (Galatians 5:9). However, notice that when proper church discipline has been followed and the false teacher is unrepentant, they are to be shunned as they are self-condemned. As we learned earlier, false teachers are those who hold to and teach and preach a false gospel that damns men's souls and are, thus, accursed (Galatians 1:8–9). When all attempts to restore and redeem are not possible, and godly repentance is not seen with a false teacher, Paul's end charge is shun them as they are self-condemned. Why are they self-condemned? Those that teach a false gospel are accursed by God (Galatians 1:8–9, Matthew 23:13–15).

Teach Them If Possible but Mixed with Fear

2 Timothy 2:23–25—Have nothing to do with foolish, ignorant controversies; you know that they breed quarrels. And the Lord's servant must not be quarrelsome but kind to everyone, able to teach, patiently enduring evil, correct his opponents with gentleness. God may perhaps grant them repentance leading to a knowledge of the truth, and they may come to their senses and escape from the snare of the devil, after being captured by him to do his will.

As we mentioned above, if a false teacher is willing to be taught sound doctrine from a true teacher, there is direction from Paul to Timothy that it must be done with patience and gentleness. This instruction is all dependent on the individual who is teaching the false teacher as well as the type of false teacher that was mentioned in Jude 22–23. *Gentleness* comes from *épios,* which means "gentle" or "mild," and refers to calming words that bring God's order to a situation. It describes the believer acting evenhandedly, avoiding unnecessary harshness or excess by speaking into a situation that God reveals. The true teacher must have the ability of enduring or bearing up, especially when harmed and treated unjustly, in addition to correcting and disciplining those who oppose him. This passage indicates that this type of scenario is where a true teacher is able to teach a false teacher. This passage does not seem to indicate that laity or church members would go to this extent as this individual should be a teacher and possess the qualities and characteristics of an elder to be able to deal with false teachers. Additionally, for those who confront false teachers and there is an opportunity to gently instruct them, it is to be done in such as manner as in Titus 2:7, "Show yourself in all respects to be a model of good works, and in your teaching show integrity, dignity, and sound speech that cannot be condemned, so that an opponent may be put to shame, having nothing evil to say." Scripture does not suggest here that a church member go and instruct a false teacher. Rather, this appears to be the responsibility of a qualified pastor or elder.

Avoid and Shun

It is quite stunning to see that the Bible calls for the shunning of false teachers in some instances. However, we see this command come from Paul, Jesus, and the apostle John. Therefore, we can know that this command came with purpose to protect the truth and protect the flock.

Matthew 15:14—Let them alone; they are blind guides. And if the blind lead the blind, both will fall into a pit.

Jesus gave the command to beware and look out for false teachers (Matthew 7:15–20), beware of the teaching of false teachers (Matthew 16:6, 12), beware of the hypocrisy of false teachers (Luke 12:1), and beware of the permeating effect of false teachers (Mark 8:15). Jesus would confront the false teachers and show them their error as well as allow them to follow and be taught and witness His miracles. However, there came a point where He began to give them incremental judgment. For example, Jesus taught in parables because of the people's unwillingness to receive Jesus' kingdom and messiahship (Matthew 13:10–15). As you see in the next page, there was sufficient evidence to acknowledge that Jesus' claims about Himself and the kingdom were true up to Matthew 13:10–15. However, as part of their judgment, he began speaking to them in parables.

- The Subjective Response—Pharisees rejected the need for repentance (Matthew 3:1–9)
- The Work of Jesus—Pharisees rejected Jesus' healing of the invalid at the Pool of Bethesda (John 5:1–45)
    - The Work of Jesus—Pharisees would have had knowledge of Jesus' miracle of turning water to wine (John 2:1–11)
    - The Work of Jesus—Pharisees would have had knowledge of Jesus' miracle of healing of the official's son (John 4:46–54)
    - The Work of Jesus—Pharisees would have had knowledge of Jesus' miracle of healing the demoniac on the Sabbath (Luke 4:31–37)
    - The Work of Jesus—Pharisees would have had knowledge of Jesus' miracle of Peter's mother-in-law being healed as well as many others (Luke 4:38–41)
    - The Work of Jesus—Pharisees would have had knowledge of Jesus' miracle of healing the leper (Luke 5:12–16)
    - The Work of Jesus—Pharisees would have had knowledge of Jesus' miracle of healing the paralytic (Luke 5:17–26)
- The Person of Jesus—Pharisees rejected Jesus' claim to be equal with God (John 5:1–45)
- The Person of Jesus—Pharisees rejected Jesus' claim to be Lord of the Sabbath (Matthew 12:1–14)
- The Work of Jesus—Pharisees rejected Jesus' work of healing the man with the withered hand (Matthew 12:9–14)
    - The Work of Jesus—Pharisees would have had knowledge of Jesus' healing of the multitudes (Matthew 12:15–21)

   - The Work of Jesus—Pharisees would have had knowledge of Jesus' healing of the centurion's servant (Matthew 8:5–13)
   - The Work of Jesus—Pharisees would have had knowledge of Jesus raising a widow's son from the dead (Luke 7:11–17)
- The Work of Jesus—Pharisees rejected Jesus's work of casting out a demon of a blind and mute man (Matthew 12:22–28)
- The Person of Jesus—Pharisees rejected Jesus' title of Son of David and called Him Beelzebul (Matthew 12:22–28)
- The Person of Jesus—Pharisees rejected Jesus' claims thus far to deity and demanded a sign (Matthew 12:38–42)
- The Work of Jesus—Pharisees rejected Jesus' works and miracles thus far and demanded a different sign (Matthew 12:38–42)
   - The Work of Jesus—Pharisees may have had knowledge of Jesus' miracle of calming the storm (Matthew 8:23–27)
   - The Work of Jesus—Pharisees would have had knowledge of Jesus' miracle of restoring two demon possessed men in the Gadarenes (Matthew 8:28–34)
   - The Work of Jesus—Pharisees would have had knowledge of Jesus' miracle of raising Jairus' daughter from the dead and healing the woman with the hemorrhage (Matthew 9:18–26)
- The Work of Jesus—Pharisees rejected Jesus' works of healing the blind man and the mute (Matthew 9:27–34)
   - The Work of Jesus—Pharisees would have had knowledge of Jesus' miracle of feeding of the five thousand (Matthew 14:13–21)
   - The Work of Jesus—Pharisees would have had knowledge of Jesus' miracle of healing the sick of Gennesaret (Matthew 14:34–36)

  - ○ The Person of Jesus—Pharisees would have had knowledge of Jesus' claim to be the Bread of Life which was a claim to deity (John 6:25–69)
- The Work of Jesus—Pharisees rejected Jesus' teaching on the law versus the Pharisees' tradition and that which defiles (Matthew 15:1–14)

In Matthew 15:14, Jesus had once again attacked the Pharisees for their adherence to human tradition rather than to the Word of God. Jesus attacks one of their traditions and calls them hypocrites (Matthew 15:3–8). The Pharisees were offended by Jesus' statements (15:12) and then Jesus gave His disciples an incredibly difficult command. He told them to "leave," or *aphiēmi,* them. *Aphiēmi* means to "send away," "let go," "let alone," "let be," "disregard," "to leave." This was a form of wrath and judgment on the false teachers. God can reveal his wrath indirectly through natural consequences (Galatians 6:6–7) and directly through His personal intervention such as the Flood (Genesis 6–8). God's wrath can include His eternal wrath, which is hell; eschatological wrath, which is the final Day of the Lord; cataclysmic wrath, such as the Flood; consequential wrath, or the principle of sowing and reaping; and, the wrath of abandonment, which is removing restraint and letting people go to their sins. This is what the Lord was doing with the Pharisees. They had been given God's Word, they were given John the Baptist, they were given the Lord, they were given teaching from the Lord, and they were given signs to accompany the teachings. At this point, Jesus gave them the wrath of abandonment and gave the religious false teachers over to their false system. Jesus gave His disciples the command to leave the Jewish religious leaders and let them be.

As we noted above, this is not the default position that one necessarily takes against a false teacher. However, when there is a stubborn, recalcitrant, and prideful heart, this type of treatment may be what the Lord is calling for. This may be the inevitable treatment when a false teacher refuses to repent and continues in their false gospel. This is when mercy has been exhausted, the command to stop teaching has been ignored, when gentle teaching has been disregarded, and there is only stubbornness and a dog returning to his vomit and a pig returning to the mire (2 Peter 2:22). Although it seems harsh and unloving, this is the last step in dealing with a false teacher.

2 John 9–11—Everyone who goes on ahead and does not abide in the teaching of Christ, does not have God. Whoever abides in the teaching has both the Father and the Son. If anyone comes to you and does not bring this teaching, do not receive him into your house or give him any greeting, for whoever greets him takes part in his wicked works.

John gives a very hard but similar statement regarding leaving or shunning false teachers. John's letter is written to a lady who has most likely been doing her best to exercise Christian hospitality to traveling teachers but has inadvertently or unwisely given hospitality and aid to false teachers. It is also possible that John may have feared that false teachers would attempt to take advantage of her kindness. John warns his readers of showing such hospitality to such deceivers. Although his exhortation may appear on the surface to be harsh or unloving, the damning false gospels that false teachers propagate warrant and justify these actions, especially as it threatens the very foundations of faith.

Not only are Christians to adhere to the fundamentals of the faith, but the gracious hospitality that is commanded of them (Romans 12:13) must be discriminating. The basis of hospitality must be common love of or interest in the truth, and Christians must share their love within the confines of that truth (4). They are not called to universal acceptance of anyone who claims to be a believer but is really a false teacher. Love must be discerning. Hospitality and kindness must be focused on those who are adhering to the fundamentals of the faith and gospel. Otherwise, Christians may actually aid those who are destroying the basic truths of the faith and the gospel. Sound doctrine and the gospel must serve as the test of fellowship (4).

Truth must always guide the exercise of love (Ephesians 4:15). Love and truth are inseparable in Christianity. Love must stand the test of truth. The main lesson of the Second Book of John is that truth determines the bounds of love, and, as a consequence, of unity. Therefore, truth must exist before love can unite, for truth generates love (1 Peter 1:22). When the truth is compromised, true Christian love and unity are destroyed. Only a shallow sentimentalism exists where the truth is not the foundation of unity.

We won't review the entire epistle but we see the word *love* being used five times, the word *truth* being used five times, and the word *walk* being used three times in the first six verses. The word *walk* is talking about one's manner of life or their walk of life. As you see, truth, love, and obedience are closely tied together.

In verse 8, John says, "Watch yourselves, so that you may not lose what we have worked for, but may win a full reward." John isn't speaking of losing her salvation as he has called her "the elect lady" in verse 1. However, John is talking about the rewards that a believer will receive (Revelation 22:12). We are promised in Scripture that those who are saved will be rewarded for their faithful service to the Lord (Matthew 10:41, 25:40). However, this is serving as a strong warning that those who show hospitality to a false teacher will have their reward diminished by aiding or abetting a false teacher. Once again, this is not talking about losing salvation where John makes it abundantly clear that those who are elect and saved by God will never be eternally lost (John 6:37–40, 10:27–29, 17:2, 6). However, we should really stop and meditate on what John is saying. Our actions here on earth echo throughout all eternity. The decision to aid and abet a false teacher is so against the Lord's command that there is a warning that rewards may be diminished. When pondering on whether to aid or abet a false teacher, one should consider the eternal repercussions to the false teacher, to those sitting under the false teacher, and what it demonstrates to others if you support a false teacher. This is the heart of what John is getting at.

In verse 9, he says, "Everyone who goes on ahead and does not abide in the teaching of Christ, does not have God. Whoever abides in the teaching has both the Father and the Son." What is the teaching of Christ? Is this to say that if we have different eschatological views that someone doesn't have the Father and the Son? Is this to say that if we don't understand or have wrong interpretations of a difficult verse, such as in Mark 9:49, where Jesus says, "For everyone will be salted with fire," that someone is a false teacher? The answer is a resounding no. However, we do know that those that teach a false gospel are accursed by God (Galatians 1:8–9, Matthew 23:13–15). Therefore, we know that those who teach a false gospel "does not have God" and have "gone ahead and does not abide in the teaching of Christ." Additionally, those who teach a false gospel have neither the Father nor the Son. Once again, John says that false teachers are those who do not abide in the teaching of Christ and do not have God. *Abide* comes from the word *menó,* which means "to remain, abide, stay, or wait." This is not random or a one-time event. No, this is someone who has demonstrated that they purposefully, constantly, and deliberately go beyond the teaching of Christ or give a false gospel. Once again, this lines up with our definition of a *false teacher* where they persistently and unrepentantly hold to a false gospel that damns men's souls and damns their own souls.

In verse 10, he says, "If anyone comes to you and does not bring this teaching, do not receive him into your house or give him any greeting." This is a shocking statement by John. As Paul said in his letter to the Corinthians, he was upset with how easily they went along with some who preached a different Jesus and a different gospel (2 Corinthians 11:4). John does not want this to happen. John is telling the lady not to receive them into her house and not even give them a *chairó,* or a Christian greeting or rejoicing. It's important to note that during this time period, it was dangerous for people to stay at inns. Therefore, it was preferred and safer to stay in the home of a Christian. However, the principle remains the same today in that those who preach a false gospel are not to be aided or abetted in any way. Additionally, they are not to be greeted as a Christian. Before someone goes to this extreme, it is important to thoroughly understand whether someone is a false teacher. It is a tremendous mistake to apply this command erroneously to someone who really is a true teacher. The utmost diligence in studying Scripture, discernment and prayer should be exercised when this command is to be obeyed. However, once it's been determined that someone is a false teacher and the false teacher has been commanded to stop teaching and preaching the false gospel and remains unrepentant, it is a tremendous mistake to ignore this command as well. Let's also note that John ties not receiving a false teacher into one's home or not giving false teachers a greeting as part of a Christian's obedience to knowing the truth and love for God.

In verse 11, he says, "For whoever greets him takes part in his wicked works." This is another shocking statement. If anyone even gives a false teacher a greeting or a Christian greeting, he partakes in the wickedness. *Partakes* comes from *koinóneó,* which means to "fellowship" or "participate in." This is what makes aiding or abetting a false teacher so shocking. If we know someone is a false teacher and give them a greeting, it is equivalent to fellowshipping in the false teacher's wicked works. As we remember earlier, Peter was reprimanded by Paul for this very thing where Peter's actions affirmed the Judaizer's teaching and caused others to be led astray. It's a very serious thing to even greet a false teacher when you know the false teacher is giving a false gospel that damns men's souls and act as though it's a trivial matter. John is warning that such behavior of even giving a Christian greeting is not allowed to be given to those who preach and teach a false gospel. Once again, this is not the default position one should take. It's a horrible thing to give this treatment to someone who is a true teacher. However, on the other side, it's a tremendous mistake to not give this treatment once it's been determined someone is a false teacher. In fact, it is acting in defiance and disobedience to God when one aids and abets a false teacher.

Romans 16:17—I appeal to you brothers, to watch out for those who cause divisions and create obstacles contrary to the doctrine that you have been taught; avoid them. For such persons do not serve our Lord Christ, but their own appetites, and by smooth talk and flattery they deceive the hearts of the naïve.

Paul gives a similar warning to what Jesus gave. Paul is warning the Romans that those who cause divisions and create obstacles contrary to the doctrine that one has been taught should be avoided. As Paul will say, these are people who do not serve the Lord Christ, which would indicate that they would be serving Satan. He says they also deceive the hearts of the naïve. Therefore, we can surmise they were false teachers as they didn't serve the Lord and they deceive others. What made them even more dangerous was that they used smooth talk or *chréstologia,* which means "a kind address," "gentle word," or "useful word," and flattery or *eulogia,* which means "praise," "blessing," or "a good word." The reason they are so deceptive is because they speak kindly and with much flattery. So, not only do they teach deceptive and damning doctrines taught by demons (1 Timothy 4:1), but they also use flattery and speak kindly. Therefore, Paul is telling them to "turn away" or *ekklinó,* which means "to deviate, to turn away" or to exclude or fully avoid by deliberate decisive rejection. As we see in this example, the reason for the shunning and deliberate rejection of these false teachers has to do with their deceptive false teaching as well as their deceptive behavior.

Paul also says of these false teachers that they serve their "own appetites." The word *appetite* comes from *koilia,* which means "belly" or "abdomen," but is a general term covering any organ in the abdomen. Metaphorically, *koilia* can also mean "the inner man" and is used in this way in John 7:38, "The one who believes in me, as the Scripture said, 'From his innermost being will flow rivers of living water.'" As we noted above, false teachers will certainly be self-willed, unsubmissive, and false teach for their own covetous reasons. Therefore, Paul has given the command to shun these false teachers.

2 Timothy 3:5—having the appearance of godliness, but denying its power. Avoid such people.

Paul here gives a similar command when dealing with false teachers as he did in Romans 16:17. These false teachers had a form of godliness or, rather, moralism. As Jesus said of the Pharisees, "Woe to you scribes, and Pharisees, hypocrites! For you are like whitewashed tombs, which outwardly appear beautiful, but within are full of dead people's bones and all uncleanness." In other words, they had a form of godliness and moralism, but had damning doctrine and a false gospel. This made them especially dangerous as the false religion looked good but had no power to save. Paul's final analysis, avoid such people.

As we close this section around the shunning of a false teacher, we can see how such an action can be warranted and is commanded by the Lord Jesus Christ, the apostle John, and Paul. However, this action should not be taken without knowing our salvation, knowing the gospel, discerning that our motives and intentions are pure, discerning the doctrine that is being taught and comparing against Scripture, knowing the type of false teacher, warning the false teacher, and taking all efforts to restore, redeem, and bring about repentance to the false teacher. Additionally, in some instances, shunning may be needed in the instance where there has been severe spiritual abuse and someone is not able to stand against the false teacher. As noted above, it will take much discernment to understand the best approach when dealing with a false teacher.

Lastly, we should note that when we strive for the gospel and obedience to Christ and seek to deal with false teachers according to God's Word, this serves as a sign to false teachers and unbelievers on where they stand spiritually. In Philippians 1:27-29, Paul says this regarding living one's life for the gospel and the implications to those who oppose the gospel, "Only let your manner of life be worthy of the gospel of Christ, so that whether I come and see you or am absent, I may hear of you that you are standing firm in one spirit, with one mind striving side by side for the faith of the gospel, and not frightened in anything by your opponents. This is a clear sign to them of their destruction, but of your salvation, and that from God. For it has been granted to you that for the sake of Christ you should not only believe in him but also suffer for his sake." When a believer lives his life for the gospel, stands firm for the gospel, and strives or contends for the gospel, this serves as assurance of the believer's salvation. Conversely, when the believer stands firm for the gospel of Christ, lives his life in a manner worthy of the gospel, and strives for the sake of the gospel, this serves as a sign to all those who oppose the gospel or give a false gospel, that they will be eternally destroyed. Paul notes that not only have true believers been granted or graced to believe in Christ, but they've also been granted or graced to suffer for His sake and the gospel. In the original language, "echaristhe" or "charizomai" has been translated to "granted". Charizomai comes from xaris and means "showing grace", "to extend favor", or "show favor". God has granted or graced His people to suffer for His name and the gospel. Suffering for the sake of Christ and His gospel produces joy because we know this produces perseverance, character, and hope (James 1:2-3, Romans 5:3-5). Suffering for the sake of Christ and His gospel strengthens and matures faith (James 1:4). Suffering for the sake of Christ and His gospel proves the genuineness of one's faith (1 Peter 1:6-7). Suffering for the sake of Christ and His gospel help us focus on the coming glory that will be revealed to us (Romans 8:18). Suffering for the sake of Christ and His gospel assures us that we are blessed and are a part of God's kingdom (Matthew 5:10, 1 Peter 4:12-14). Suffering for the sake of Christ and His gospel allows us to rejoice and look forward to heaven and being with Christ (Matthew 5:11-12). Suffering for the sake of Christ and His gospel produces comfort, hope in Christ, and drives us to prayer (2 Corinthians 1:3-11). Suffering for the sake of Christ and His gospel grows us in sanctification and Christlikeness (Philippians 3:10, 1 Peter 5:10). So, although we know that there will be conflict with false teachers, we can and must know that God will cause this suffering to work for the good of His people and use it as a sign of destruction for false teachers and unbelievers.

Pray for Them

In Matthew 5:44 Jesus commands us to do the following, "But I say to you, love your enemies and pray for those who persecute you". Pray for God to save false teachers. The Lord is the only one who is mighty to save and transfer false teachers from the kingdom of darkness to the kingdom of light (Colossians 1:13). Additionally false teachers are storing up wrath for themselves (Romans 2:5), they will receive a greater condemnation (Mark 12:40, 2 Peter 2:20-21), and they will be beaten with more blows (Luke 12:47-48). The end of a false teacher is hell, but the Bible clearly indicates that their punishment in hell will be more severe. If we could even imagine what hell will be like for a false teacher, it would not be out of line to say that their hell will be hotter and their physical, mental, and spiritual torments will be greater than those who simply neglected or rejected Christ. The end of a false teacher is absolutely dreadful and disastrous. Therefore, pray for their delivery.

Do Not Throw Your Pearls to Swine

In Matthew 7:6, Jesus says this regarding being discerning on when to stop sharing His Word where He says, "Do not give dogs what is holy, and do not throw your pearls before pigs, lest they trample them underfoot and turn to attack you." There comes a time when we are commanded to stop sharing God's Word and truth with false teachers and others. The reception we may receive where someone tramples underfoot pearls or what is sacred is where someone continually receives the Word with apathy, indifference, neglect, or a stoic behavior. The reception we may receive where someone turns and attacks is when the Word is shared and there is a verbal, emotional, or physical attack. In both scenarios where the Word is consistently being treated with either apathy or contempt, we are commanded to discern when to stop sharing what is sacred. In this instance of a false teacher, this may lead to avoidance and shunning. In the instance of someone who is not a false teacher, this does not necessarily lead to avoidance and shunning, but will lead one to discuss other topics and not God's Word unless the individual is willing to discuss the Word. Remember that you are not the one being neglected and rejected, it is God who is being neglected and rejected. We must also remember that a false teacher's natural response will be one of deceit and they will refute, ignore, deny, or shun the truth. In John 3:20, Jesus gives this statement about how those who are in darkness, which includes false teachers, will react to the truth, "For everyone who does wicked things hates the light and does not come to the light, lest his works should be exposed." The word "exposed" comes from elegcho which means "to reprove, rebuke, discipline", to expose or show to be guilty", or "to convince with solid, compelling evidence and prove wrong". False teachers will be deceitful and will likely refute, ignore, deny, or shun the truth because they will not come under the scrutiny of God's authoritative, infallible, inerrant, and inspired Word and be shown to be in error. They will hate God's Word when His Word shows them their error. They will likely be proud – arrogant and going beyond what God directs (2 Timothy 3:2), unholy – having utter disregard of what is sacred (2 Timothy 3:2), not loving good – being hostile to the things of God (2 Timothy 3:3), deceiving – leading others into delusion or away from the truth and being misleading (Titus 1:10), bold – being darers or very bold who foolishly ignore what should make them afraid (2 Peter 2:10), self-willed – seeking only to gratify themselves by being arrogant or stubborn (2 Peter 2:10), despising authority – unwilling to submit to authority, but especially to Christ's authority (2 Peter 2:10, Jude 8), insubordinate – not subject to rule or submissive to God with a defiant attitude against Christ's Lordship (Titus 1:10), and more. **The history of the Bible shows the history of false teachers ignoring God's warnings**. Therefore, pray for them, don't avenge yourself but leave room for God's wrath (Romans 12:18-19).

The Implications of Continually, Purposefully, and Deliberately Following a False Teacher

John 10:4–5—When he has brought out all his own, he goes before them, and the sheep follow him, for they know his voice. A stranger they will not follow, but they will flee from him, for they do not know the voice of strangers.

Lastly, we see a striking statement that Jesus makes in John 10 about a shepherd and sheep. Jesus had just finished healing a blind man in John 9 and the blind man was taken to the Pharisees. The Pharisees falsely accused Jesus of breaking the Sabbath by healing the blind man even though there's no law to prohibit doing good (John 9:16). The Pharisees were intimidating to such a degree that the blind man's parents would not testify truthfully for fear of being excommunicated from the Synagogue (John 9:22). The Pharisees called Jesus a sinner (John 9:24) and, eventually, the discussion disintegrated between the blind man and the Pharisees. The blind man who has been healed returns to Jesus and believes in Him while the Pharisees remain in unbelief (John 9:35–41).

This is the backdrop for the Good Shepherd. Jesus will compare Himself to the Pharisees and compare them to thieves and robbers while stating that He looks after and cares for the sheep as the Good Shepherd. In John 10:4, He says, "When he has brought out all his own, he goes before them, and the sheep follow him, for they know his voice." The puritans used to say you could tell a sheep in two ways: the foot and the ear. Jesus is confirming this very thing. Jesus is saying that His sheep follow Him because they know His voice. He says the same thing of the Gentile sheep that He will bring them out and they will listen to His voice and follow Him (John 10:16).

However, in John 10:5, Jesus says, "A stranger they will not follow, but they will flee from him, for they do not know the voice of strangers." Jesus is saying that His sheep will know His voice and will follow Him. However, He also says that His sheep will not follow a stranger or a false teacher. This is quite a distinguishing mark of a disciple or sheep of Christ. It's not to say that the sheep are perfect. It's not to say that the sheep are sinless. It's not to say that the sheep follow perfectly. However, it is to say that they do hear His voice and follow Him. It's not to say that sheep could hear a false gospel and not be confused or give it attention as what happened with the Galatians.

However, Jesus says that not only will His sheep follow Him, but they will also not follow a false teacher and they will flee from false teachers. The word for *flee* is *pheugó,* which means "flee," "escape," "shun." Let's note that fleeing is not jogging. Fleeing is not walking quickly. *Fleeing* is running as if running away from something to save your life. This is how Jesus' sheep will act. They will see eternal danger with a false teacher or false shepherd and run for their life. It is quite true that there are true believers that sit under false teachers and in false religious "Christian" systems. Not everyone in false religious "Christian" systems is lost. However, let's seriously pay attention to what Jesus is saying here, because those that continue to listen to a stranger or a false shepherd or false teacher and are not listening to Jesus and following Him, are in a dangerous spiritual state that requires much self-examination on whether they be in the faith (2 Corinthians 13:5). Those true Christians who are in false religious systems are commanded to follow Christ and not false teachers.

Conclusion

The topic of false teachers is a difficult topic to discuss. It requires knowing the gospel, knowing your salvation, discerning truth, studying Scripture, much prayer, and much guidance from the Lord. My hope in writing this book is that those who read it can further their understanding of the gospel, understand what makes someone a false teacher, and be protected from false gospels. My hope is that this book is meant to glorify God, defend His gospel, and build up His church. To Him be glory in the church and in Christ Jesus throughout all generations, for ever and ever! Amen.

Notes

(1) Lawson, Steve. "What is the Gospel?" Shepherd's Conference, 6 March 2020, Grace Community Church, California, Sun Valley. General Session 10.
(2) See W.E. Nunnally, "Gamaliel," in Eerdmans Dictionary of the Bible, ed. D.N. Freedman. Grand Rapids: Eerdmans, 2000, pp. 481-482.
(3) Lawson, Steve. "The Forgotten Doctrine: Whatever Happened to Preaching on Hell?". Expositor, 31. 2020.
(4) The Macarthur Study Bible New International Version, 2013.
(5) Macarthur, John. "The Supreme Confession", 26 Aug 1982, Grace Community Church, California, Sun Valley.
(6) Lawson, Steve. "It Will Cost You Everything". Resolved Conference, 18 February 2007. Long Beach, California.
(7) Foxe, J., & Berry, W. G. (1900). Foxe's Book of Martyrs. London: The Religious Trace Society.
(8) Thomas, R. L., & Gundry, S. N. (1988). The NIV Harmony of the Gospels: With explanations and essays, using the text of The New International Version: a revised edition of the John Broadus and A.T. Robertson Harmony of the Gospels. San Francisco: Harper & Row.
(9) Macarthur, John. "Survival Strategy for Apostate Times, Part 3" Sermon, 8 Aug 2004, Grace Community Church, California, Sun Valley.

www.ingramcontent.com/pod-product-compliance
Lightning Source LLC
LaVergne TN
LVHW050624100826
845148LV00011B/1721

* 9 7 8 1 6 3 3 5 7 2 6 2 1 *